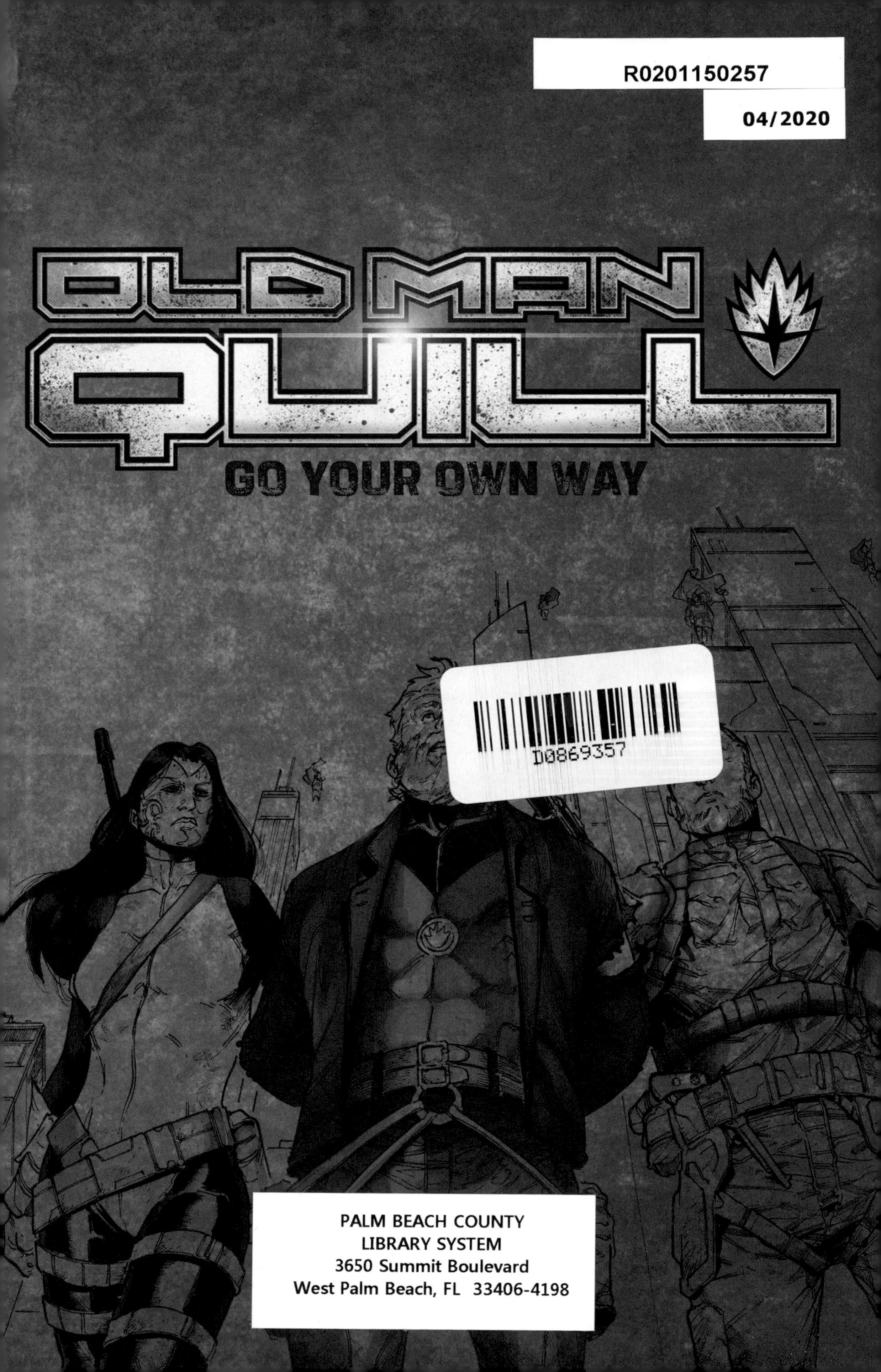
OLD MAN QUILL
GO YOUR OWN WAY

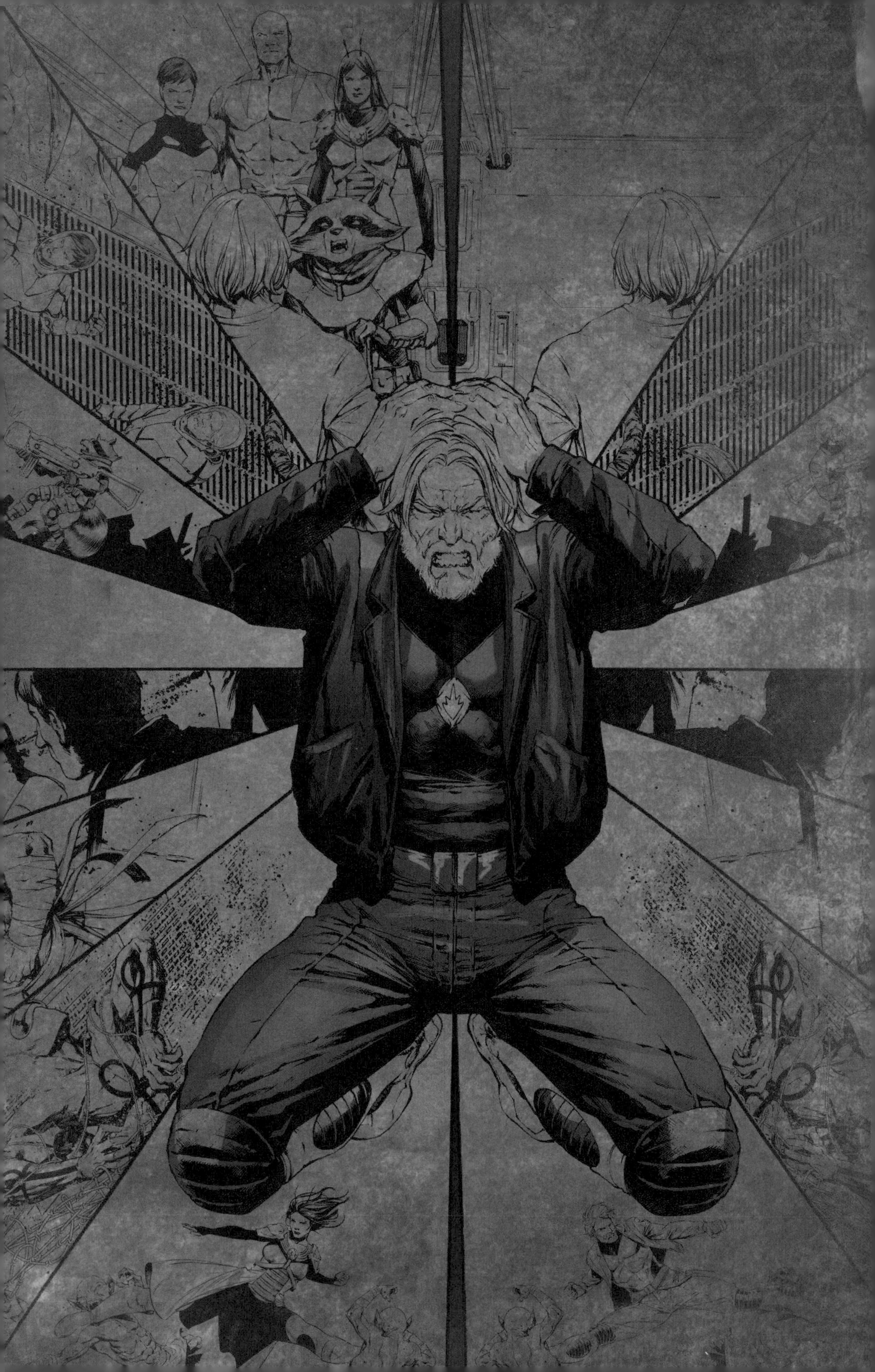

OLD MAN QUILL
GO YOUR OWN WAY

WRITER **ETHAN SACKS**

ARTISTS **ROBERT GILL** (#7, #9-12) &
IBRAIM ROBERSON (#8)

COLOR ARTISTS **ANDRES MOSSA** (#7, #12) &
RACHELLE ROSENBERG (#8-11)

LETTERER **VC's JOE CARAMAGNA**

COVER ART **JOHN TYLER CHRISTOPHER**

ASSISTANT EDITOR **MARTIN BIRO**

EDITOR **MARK BASSO**

NOTE: THE EVENTS OF THIS STORY TAKE PLACE AFTER
OLD MAN HAWKEYE AND THE ORIGINAL *OLD MAN LOGAN*.

COLLECTION EDITOR **JENNIFER GRÜNWALD**
ASSISTANT MANAGING EDITOR **MAIA LOY**
ASSISTANT EDITOR **CAITLIN O'CONNELL**
EDITOR, SPECIAL PROJECTS **MARK D. BEAZLEY**

VP PRODUCTION & SPECIAL PROJECTS **JEFF YOUNGQUIST**
BOOK DESIGNERS **SALENA MAHINA & STACIE ZUCKER**
SVP PRINT, SALES & MARKETING **DAVID GABRIEL**
EDITOR IN CHIEF **C.B. CEBULSKI**

OLD MAN QUILL VOL. 2: GO YOUR OWN WAY. Contains material originally published in magazine form as OLD MAN QUILL (2019) #7-12. First printing 2019. ISBN 978-1-302-91670-1. Published by MARVEL WORLDWIDE, INC., a subsidiary of MARVEL ENTERTAINMENT, LLC. OFFICE OF PUBLICATION: 1290 Avenue of the Americas, New York, NY 10104. © 2019 MARVEL. No similarity between any of the names, characters, persons, and/or institutions in this magazine with those of any living or dead person or institution is intended, and any such similarity which may exist is purely coincidental. Printed in Canada. KEVIN FEIGE, Chief Creative Officer; DAN BUCKLEY, President, Marvel Entertainment; JOHN NEE, Publisher; JOE QUESADA, EVP & Creative Director; TOM BREVOORT, SVP of Publishing; DAVID BOGART, Associate Publisher & SVP of Talent Affairs; Publishing & Partnership; DAVID GABRIEL, VP of Print & Digital Publishing; JEFF YOUNGQUIST, VP of Production & Special Projects; DAN CARR, Executive Director of Publishing Technology; ALEX MORALES, Director of Publishing Operations; DAN EDINGTON, Managing Editor; SUSAN CRESPI, Production Manager; STAN LEE, Chairman Emeritus. For information regarding advertising in Marvel Comics or on Marvel.com, please contact Vit DeBellis, Custom Solutions & Integrated Advertising Manager, at vdebellis@marvel.com. For Marvel subscription inquiries, please call 888-511-5480. Manufactured between 11/13/2019 and 1/14/2020 by SOLISCO PRINTERS, SCOTT, QC, CANADA.

10 9 8 7 6 5 4 3 2 1

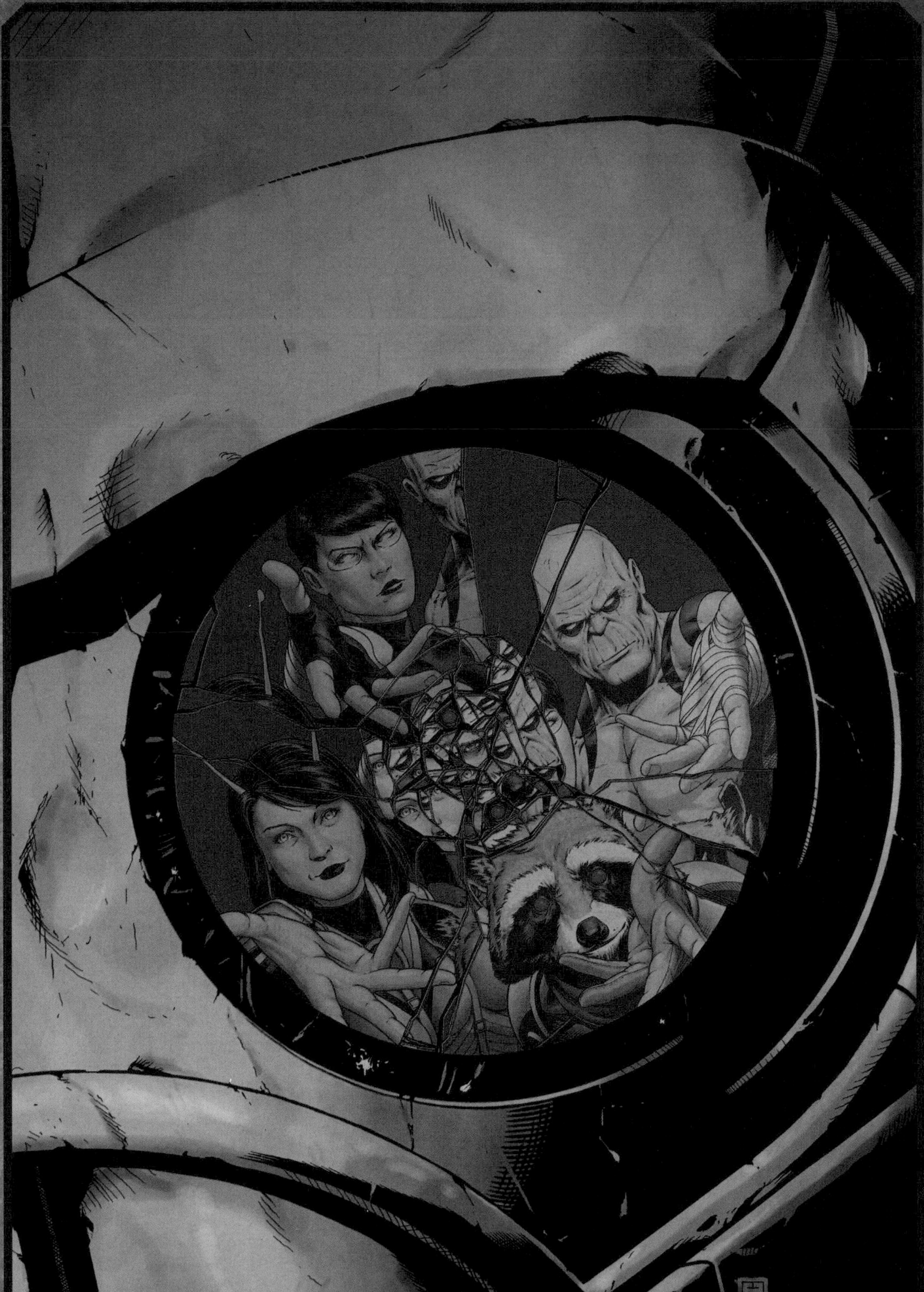

7

"WAY DOWN IN THE HOLE"

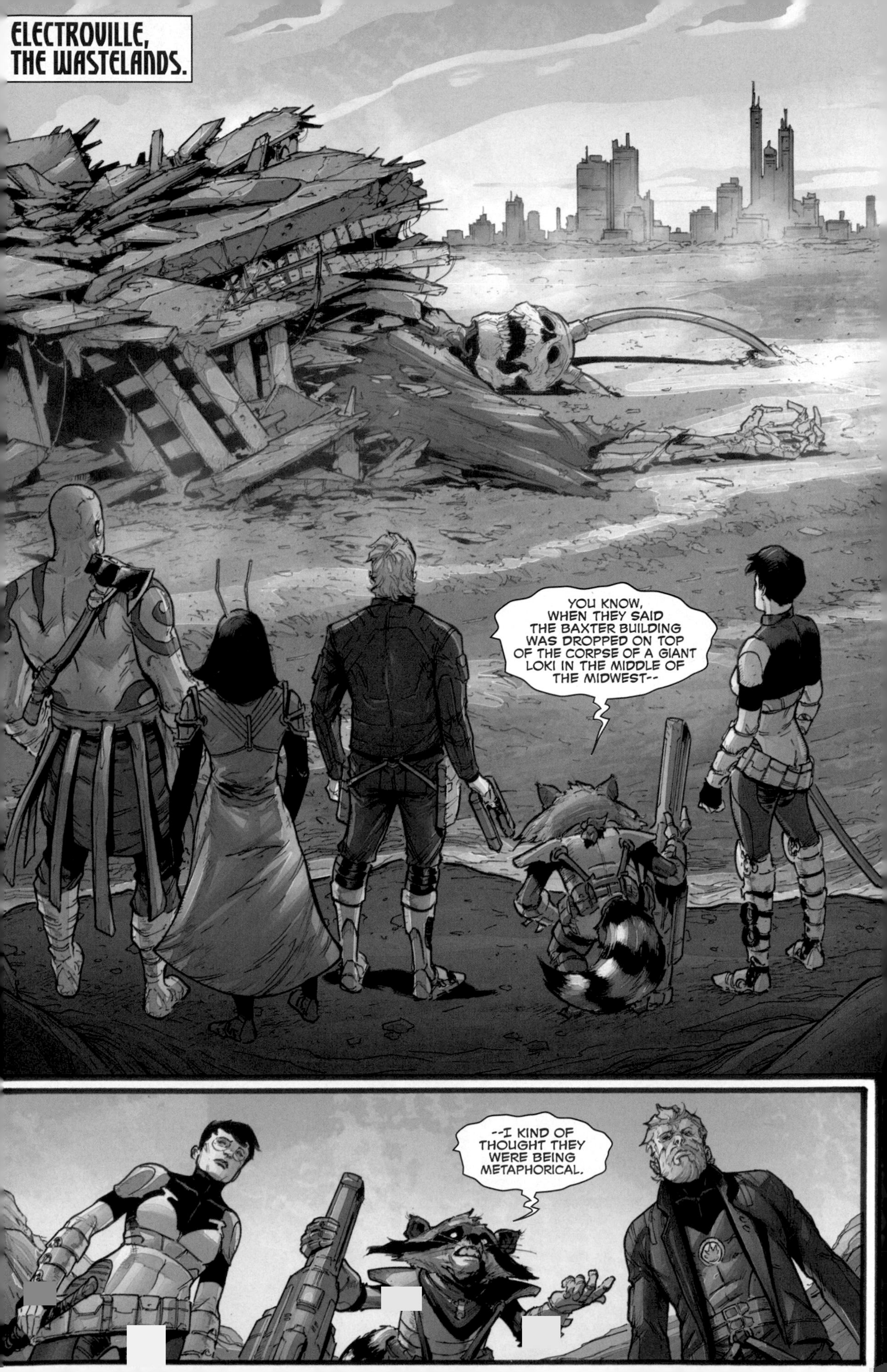
ELECTROVILLE, THE WASTELANDS.
YOU KNOW, WHEN THEY SAID THE BAXTER BUILDING WAS DROPPED ON TOP OF THE CORPSE OF A GIANT LOKI IN THE MIDDLE OF THE MIDWEST--
--I KIND OF THOUGHT THEY WERE BEING METAPHORICAL.

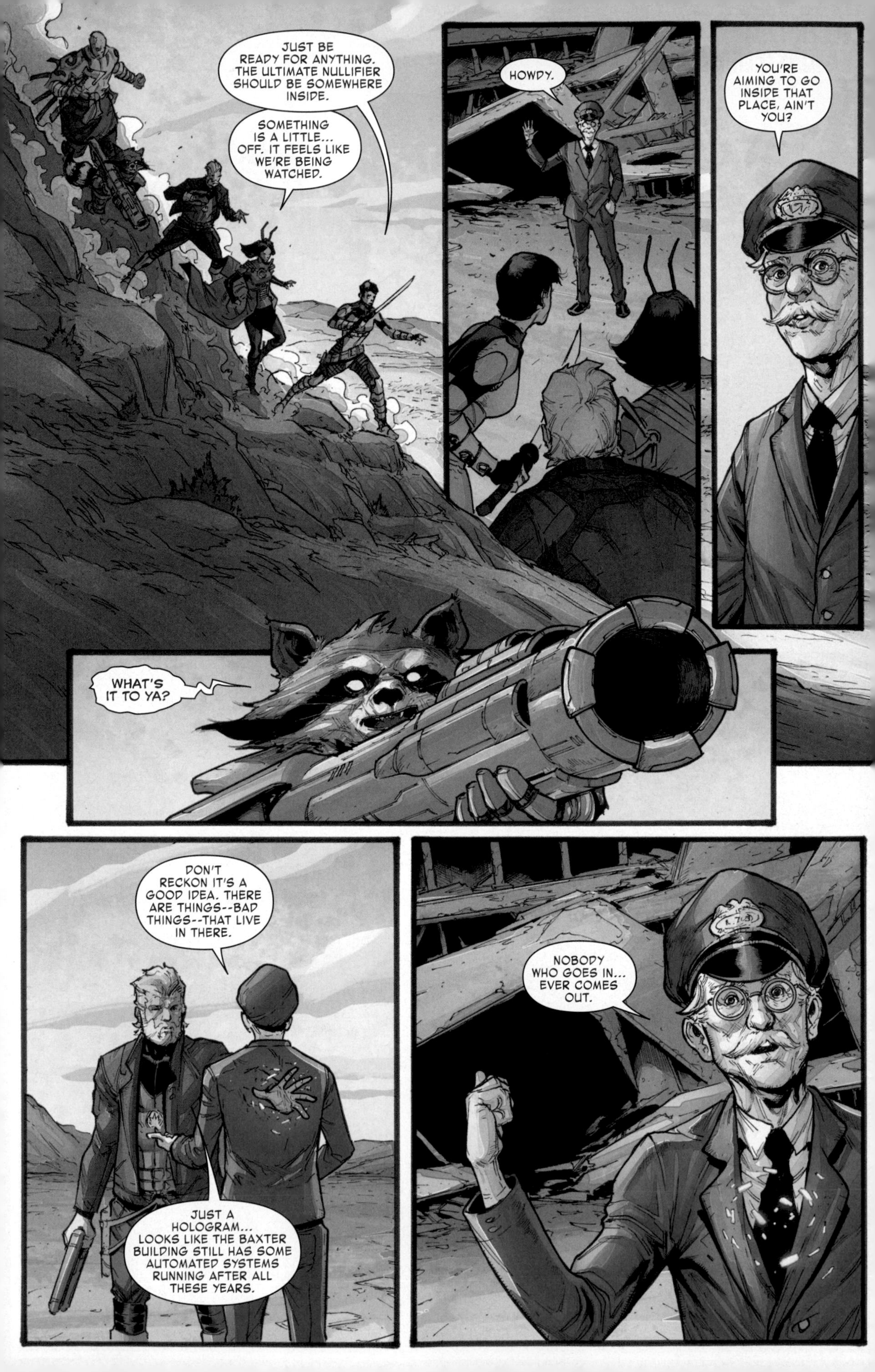
JUST BE READY FOR ANYTHING. THE ULTIMATE NULLIFIER SHOULD BE SOMEWHERE INSIDE.
SOMETHING IS A LITTLE... OFF. IT FEELS LIKE WE'RE BEING WATCHED.
HOWDY.
YOU'RE AIMING TO GO INSIDE THAT PLACE, AIN'T YOU?
WHAT'S IT TO YA?
DON'T RECKON IT'S A GOOD IDEA. THERE ARE THINGS--BAD THINGS--THAT LIVE IN THERE.
JUST A HOLOGRAM... LOOKS LIKE THE BAXTER BUILDING STILL HAS SOME AUTOMATED SYSTEMS RUNNING AFTER ALL THESE YEARS.
NOBODY WHO GOES IN... EVER COMES OUT.

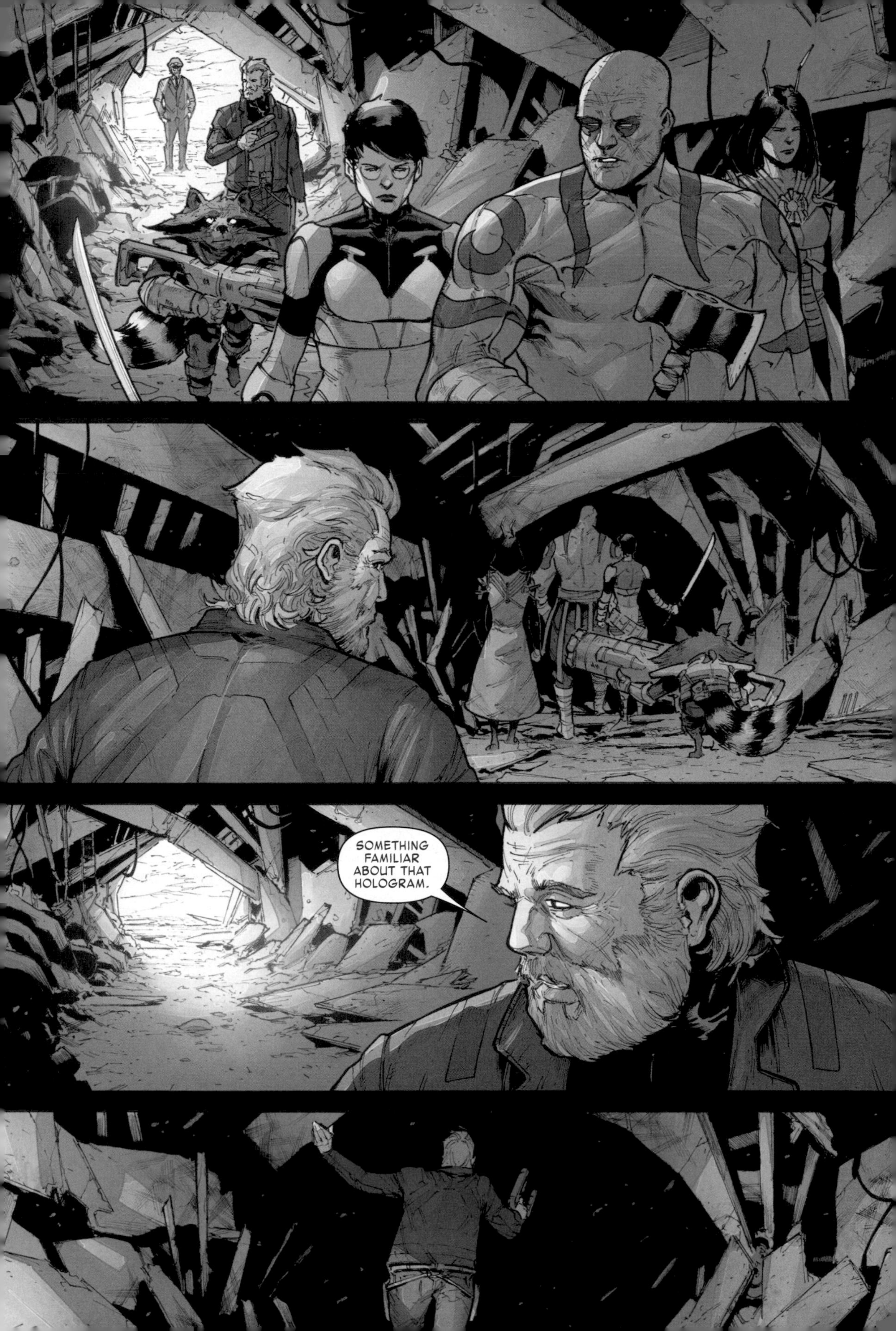
SOMETHING FAMILIAR ABOUT THAT HOLOGRAM.

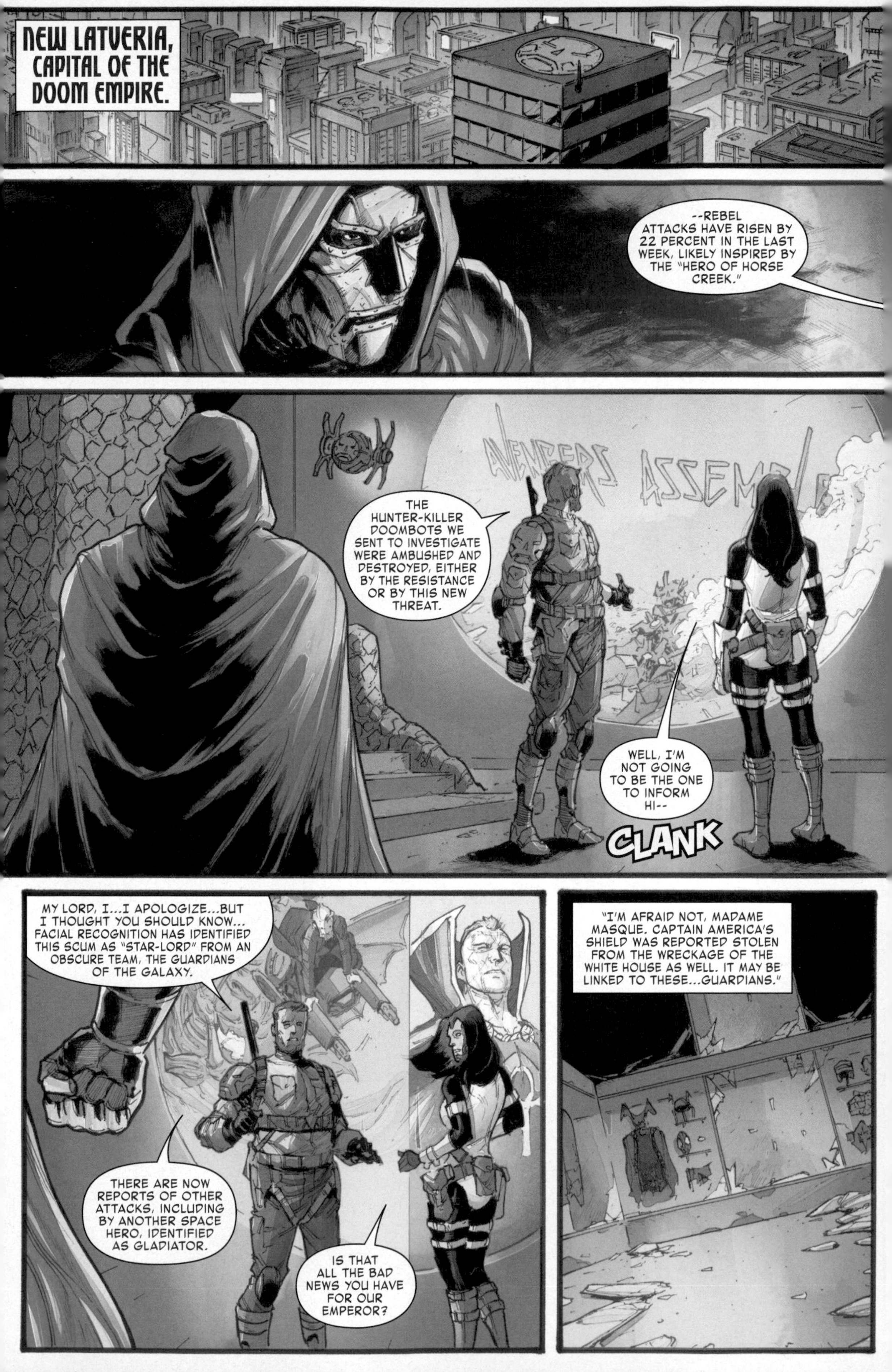
NEW LATVERIA, CAPITAL OF THE DOOM EMPIRE.
--REBEL ATTACKS HAVE RISEN BY 22 PERCENT IN THE LAST WEEK, LIKELY INSPIRED BY THE "HERO OF HORSE CREEK."
THE HUNTER-KILLER DOOMBOTS WE SENT TO INVESTIGATE WERE AMBUSHED AND DESTROYED, EITHER BY THE RESISTANCE OR BY THIS NEW THREAT.
WELL, I'M NOT GOING TO BE THE ONE TO INFORM HI--
CLANK
MY LORD, I...I APOLOGIZE...BUT I THOUGHT YOU SHOULD KNOW... FACIAL RECOGNITION HAS IDENTIFIED THIS SCUM AS "STAR-LORD" FROM AN OBSCURE TEAM, THE GUARDIANS OF THE GALAXY.
THERE ARE NOW REPORTS OF OTHER ATTACKS, INCLUDING BY ANOTHER SPACE HERO, IDENTIFIED AS GLADIATOR.
IS THAT ALL THE BAD NEWS YOU HAVE FOR OUR EMPEROR?
"I'M AFRAID NOT, MADAME MASQUE. CAPTAIN AMERICA'S SHIELD WAS REPORTED STOLEN FROM THE WRECKAGE OF THE WHITE HOUSE AS WELL. IT MAY BE LINKED TO THESE...GUARDIANS."

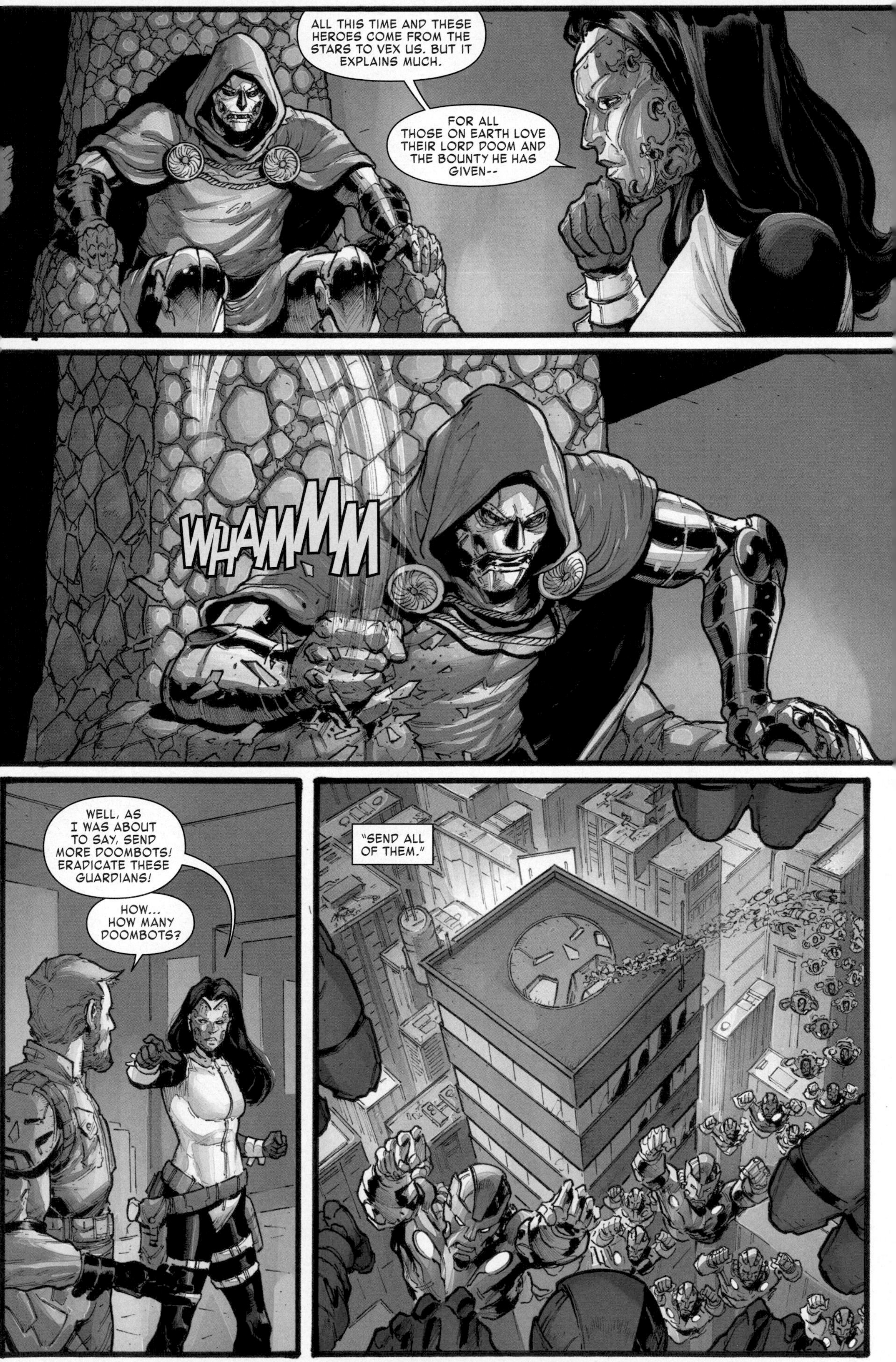
ALL THIS TIME AND THESE HEROES COME FROM THE STARS TO VEX US. BUT IT EXPLAINS MUCH.
FOR ALL THOSE ON EARTH LOVE THEIR LORD DOOM AND THE BOUNTY HE HAS GIVEN--
WHAMMMM
WELL, AS I WAS ABOUT TO SAY, SEND MORE DOOMBOTS! ERADICATE THESE GUARDIANS!
HOW... HOW MANY DOOMBOTS?
"SEND ALL OF THEM."

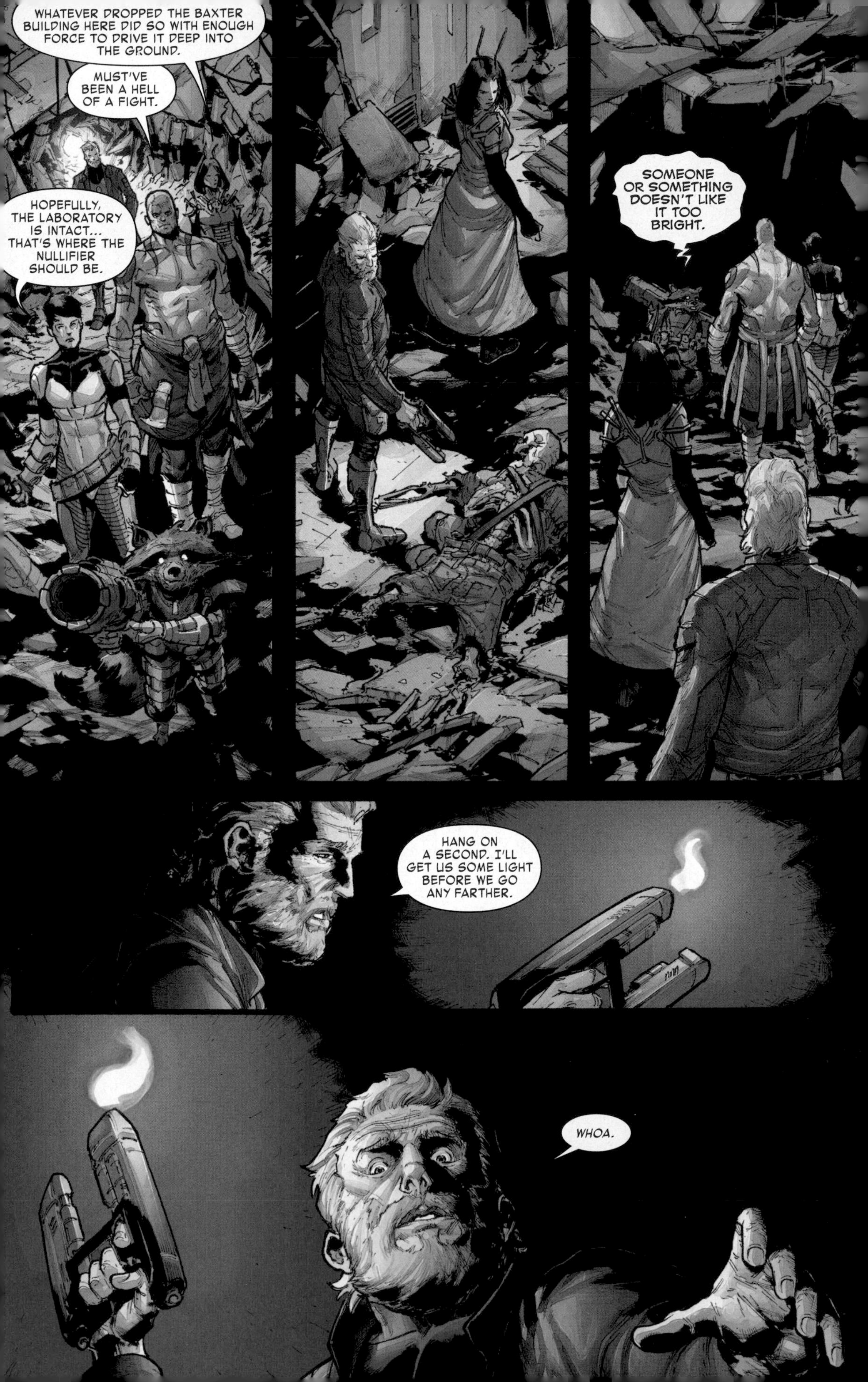
WHATEVER DROPPED THE BAXTER BUILDING HERE DID SO WITH ENOUGH FORCE TO DRIVE IT DEEP INTO THE GROUND.
MUST'VE BEEN A HELL OF A FIGHT.
HOPEFULLY, THE LABORATORY IS INTACT... THAT'S WHERE THE NULLIFIER SHOULD BE.
SOMEONE OR SOMETHING DOESN'T LIKE IT TOO BRIGHT.
HANG ON A SECOND. I'LL GET US SOME LIGHT BEFORE WE GO ANY FARTHER.
WHOA.

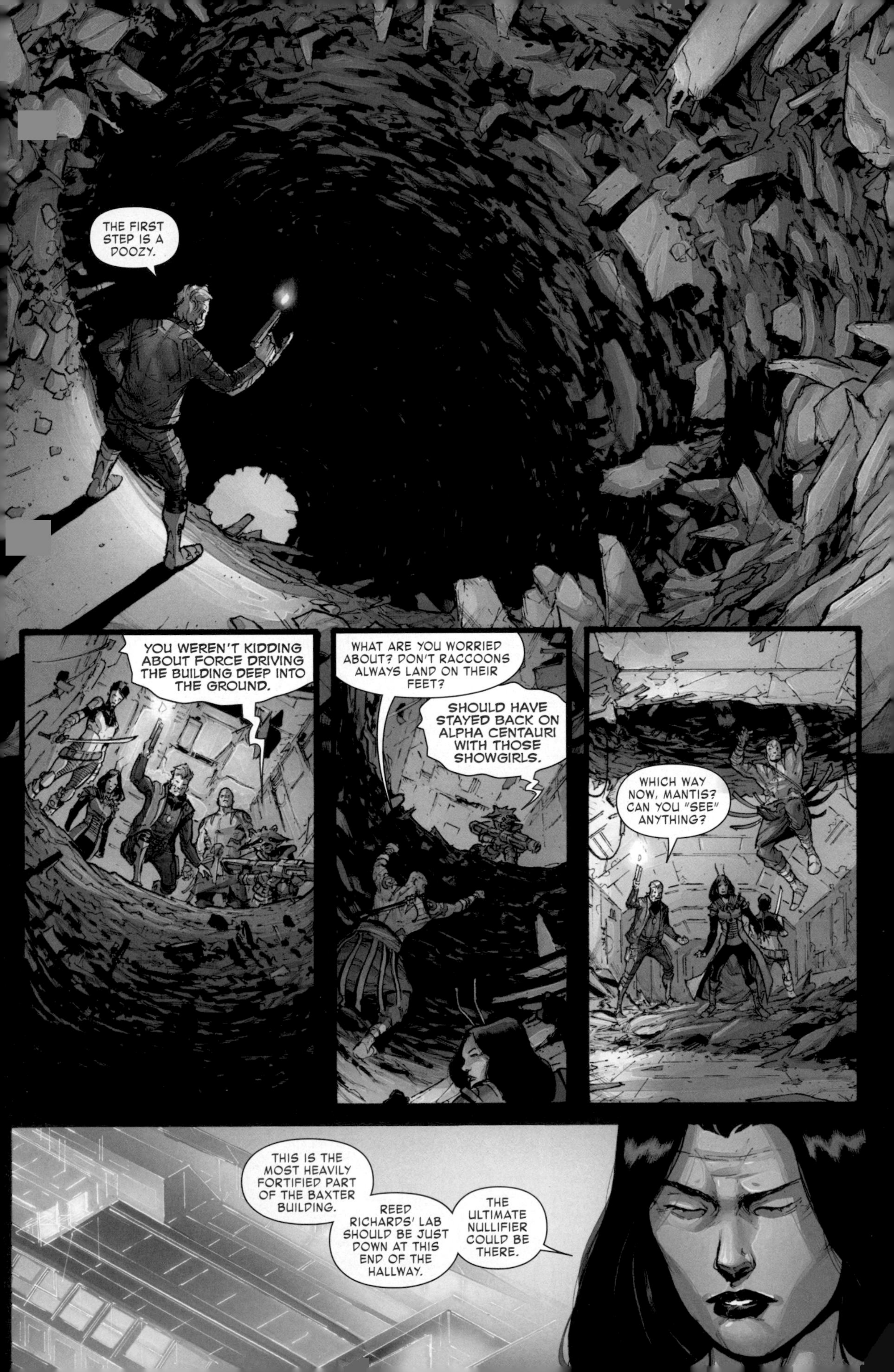
THE FIRST STEP IS A DOOZY.
YOU WEREN'T KIDDING ABOUT FORCE DRIVING THE BUILDING DEEP INTO THE GROUND.
WHAT ARE YOU WORRIED ABOUT? DON'T RACCOONS ALWAYS LAND ON THEIR FEET?
SHOULD HAVE STAYED BACK ON ALPHA CENTAURI WITH THOSE SHOWGIRLS.
WHICH WAY NOW, MANTIS? CAN YOU "SEE" ANYTHING?
THIS IS THE MOST HEAVILY FORTIFIED PART OF THE BAXTER BUILDING.
REED RICHARDS' LAB SHOULD BE JUST DOWN AT THIS END OF THE HALLWAY.
THE ULTIMATE NULLIFIER COULD BE THERE.

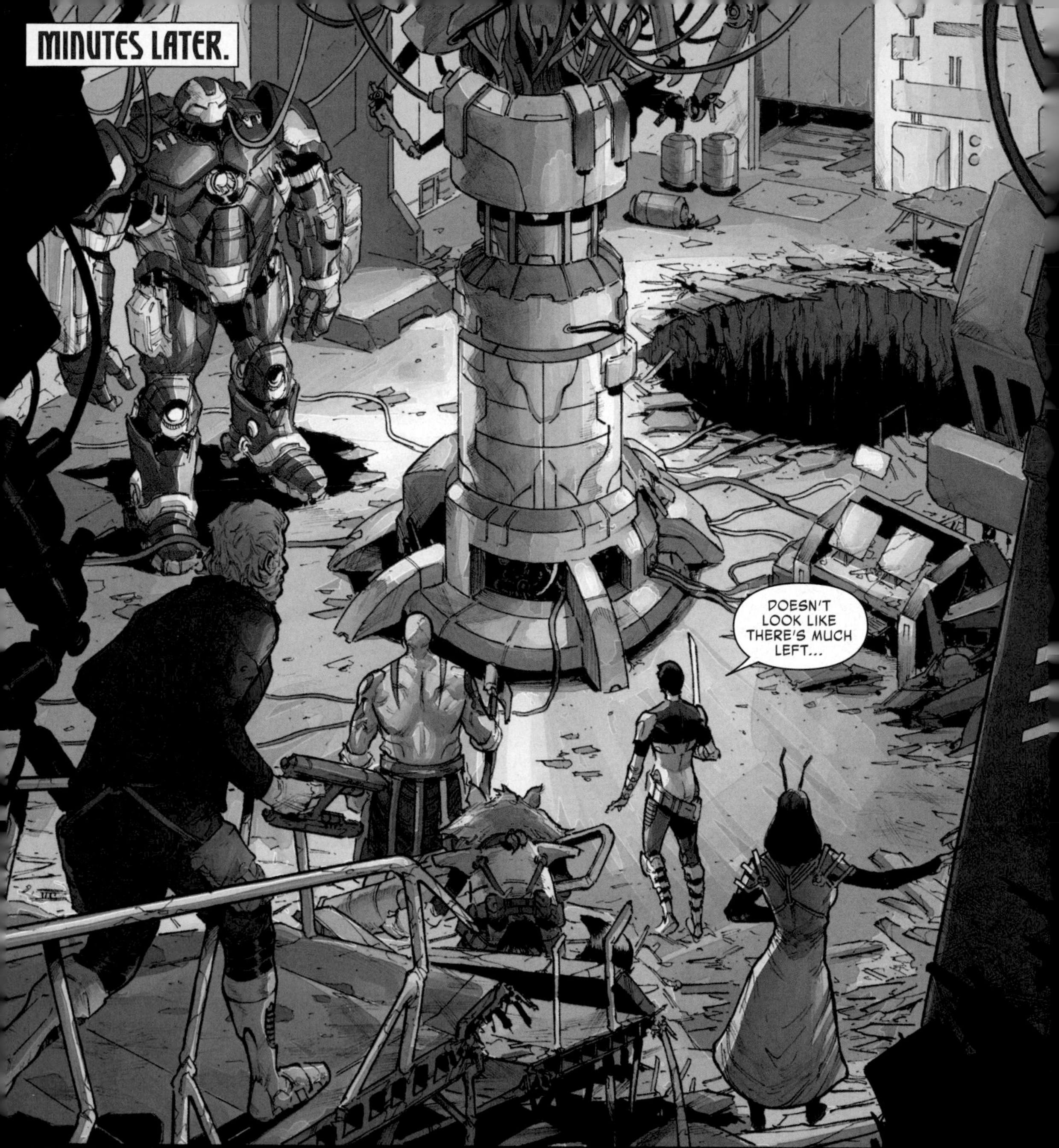
MINUTES LATER.
DOESN'T LOOK LIKE THERE'S MUCH LEFT...

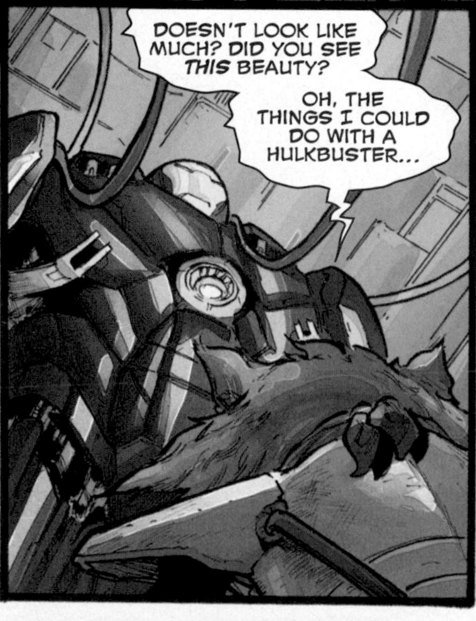
DOESN'T LOOK LIKE MUCH? DID YOU SEE *THIS* BEAUTY?
OH, THE THINGS I COULD DO WITH A HULKBUSTER...

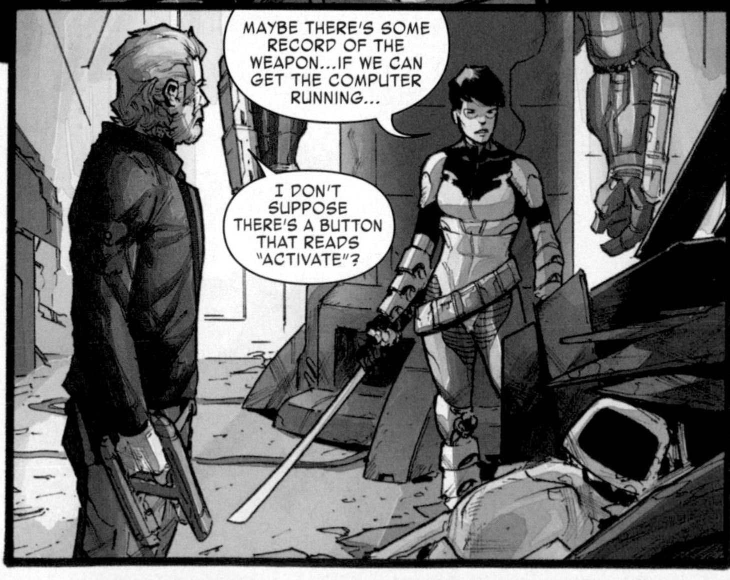
MAYBE THERE'S SOME RECORD OF THE WEAPON...IF WE CAN GET THE COMPUTER RUNNING...
I DON'T SUPPOSE THERE'S A BUTTON THAT READS "ACTIVATE"?

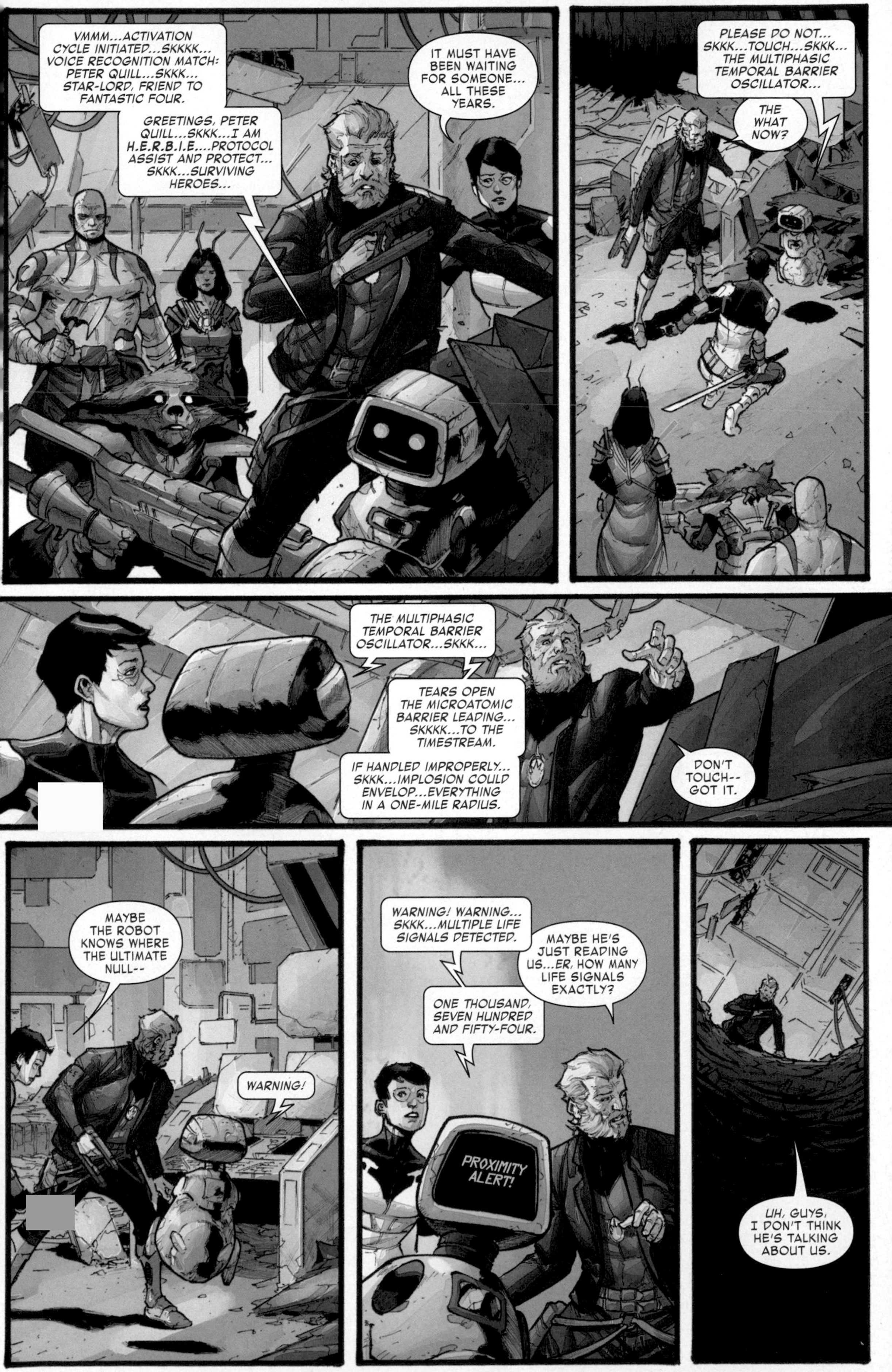
VMMM...ACTIVATION CYCLE INITIATED...SKKKK... VOICE RECOGNITION MATCH: PETER QUILL...SKKK... STAR-LORD, FRIEND TO FANTASTIC FOUR.
GREETINGS, PETER QUILL...SKKK...I AM H.E.R.B.I.E....PROTOCOL ASSIST AND PROTECT... SKKK...SURVIVING HEROES...
IT MUST HAVE BEEN WAITING FOR SOMEONE... ALL THESE YEARS.
PLEASE DO NOT... SKKK...TOUCH...SKKK... THE MULTIPHASIC TEMPORAL BARRIER OSCILLATOR...
THE WHAT NOW?
THE MULTIPHASIC TEMPORAL BARRIER OSCILLATOR...SKKK...
TEARS OPEN THE MICROATOMIC BARRIER LEADING... SKKKK...TO THE TIMESTREAM.
IF HANDLED IMPROPERLY... SKKK...IMPLOSION COULD ENVELOP...EVERYTHING IN A ONE-MILE RADIUS.
DON'T TOUCH-- GOT IT.
MAYBE THE ROBOT KNOWS WHERE THE ULTIMATE NULL--
WARNING!
WARNING! WARNING... SKKK...MULTIPLE LIFE SIGNALS DETECTED.
MAYBE HE'S JUST READING US...ER, HOW MANY LIFE SIGNALS EXACTLY?
ONE THOUSAND, SEVEN HUNDRED AND FIFTY-FOUR.
PROXIMITY ALERT!
UH, GUYS, I DON'T THINK HE'S TALKING ABOUT US.

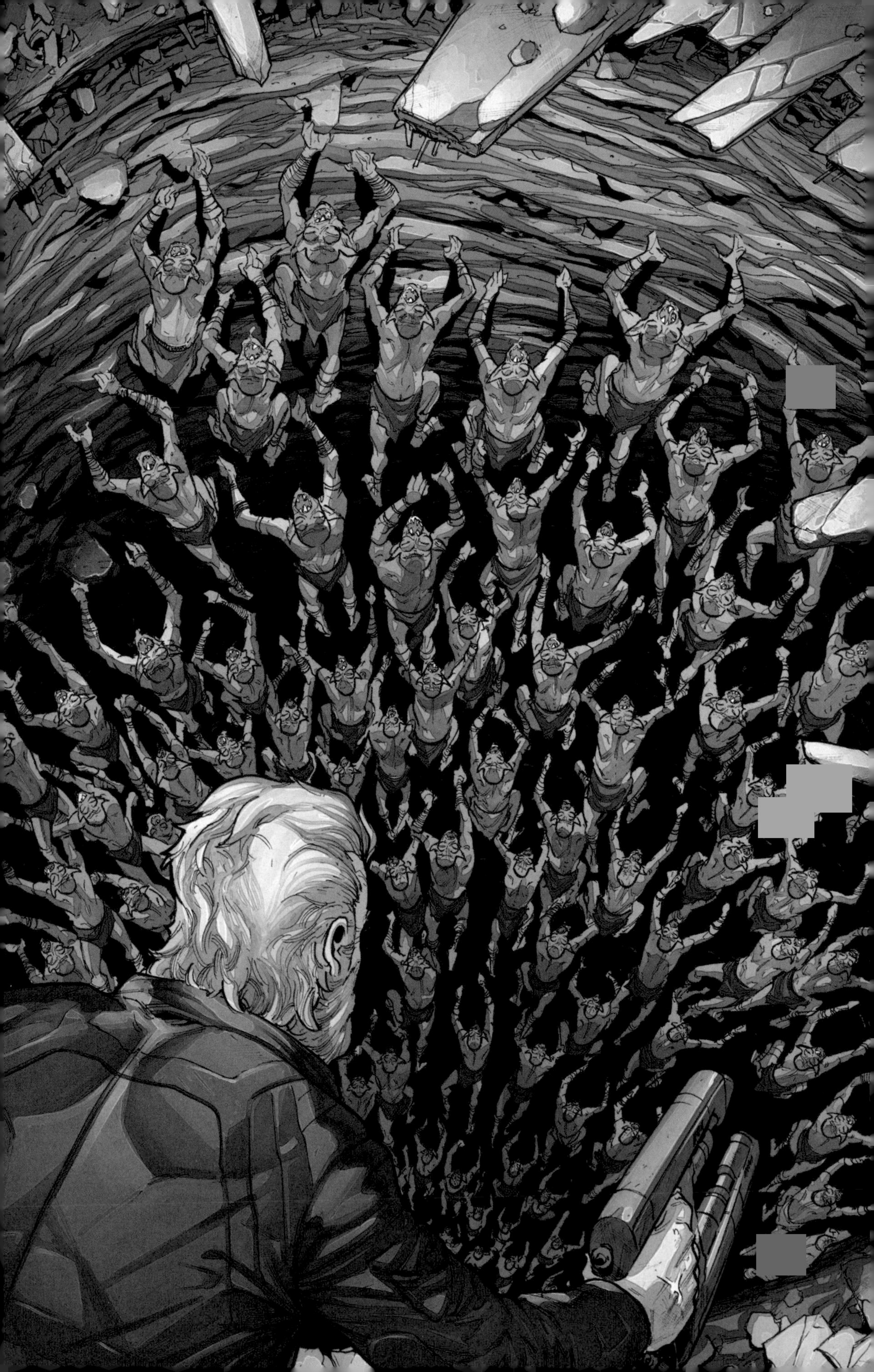

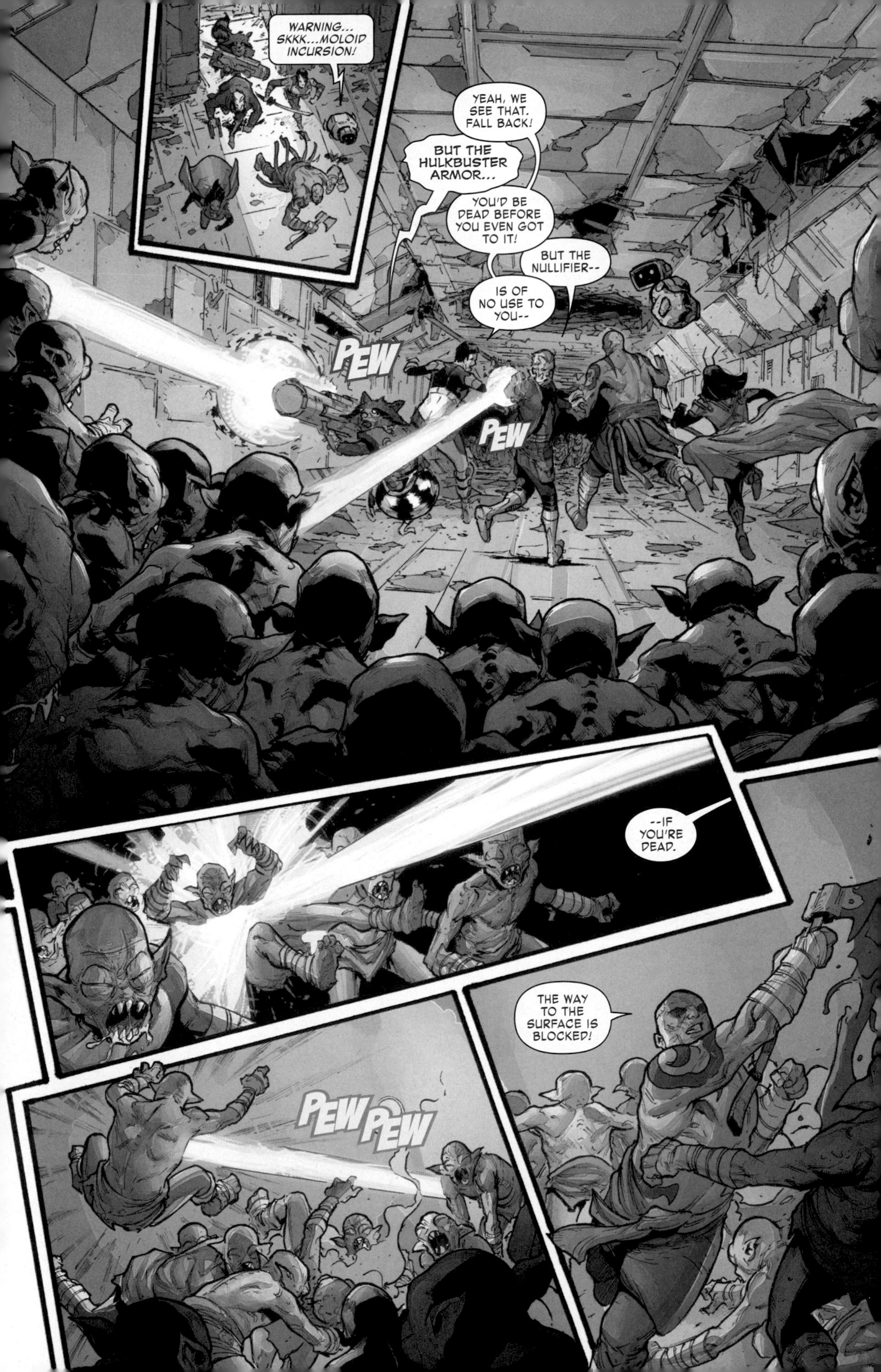
WARNING... SKKK...MOLOID INCURSION!
YEAH, WE SEE THAT. FALL BACK!
BUT THE HULKBUSTER ARMOR...
YOU'D BE DEAD BEFORE YOU EVEN GOT TO IT!
BUT THE NULLIFIER--
IS OF NO USE TO YOU--
PEW
PEW
--IF YOU'RE DEAD.
THE WAY TO THE SURFACE IS BLOCKED!
PEW PEW

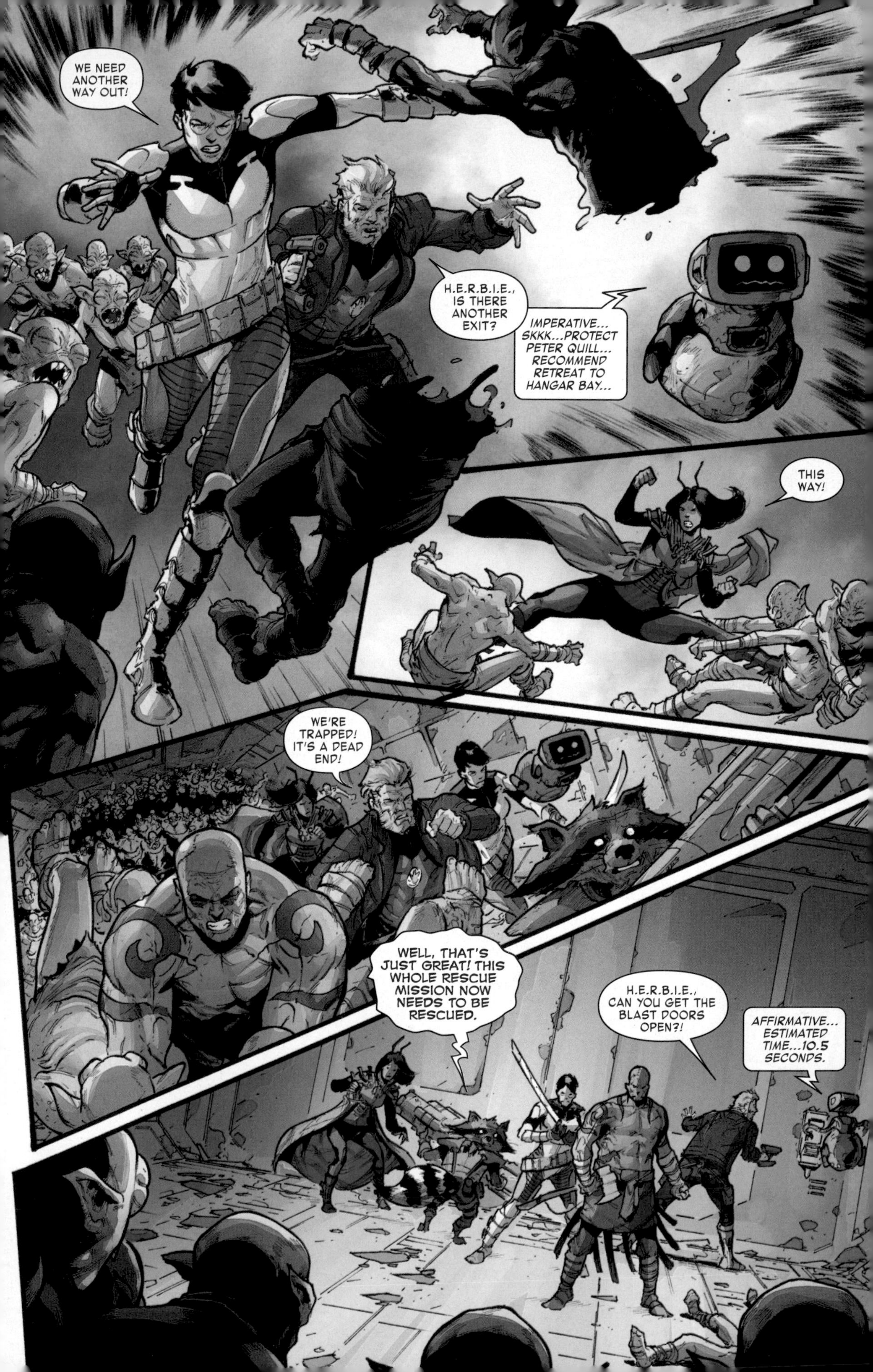
WE NEED ANOTHER WAY OUT!
H.E.R.B.I.E., IS THERE ANOTHER EXIT?
IMPERATIVE... SKKK...PROTECT PETER QUILL... RECOMMEND RETREAT TO HANGAR BAY...
THIS WAY!
WE'RE TRAPPED! IT'S A DEAD END!
WELL, THAT'S JUST GREAT! THIS WHOLE RESCUE MISSION NOW NEEDS TO BE RESCUED.
H.E.R.B.I.E., CAN YOU GET THE BLAST DOORS OPEN?!
AFFIRMATIVE... ESTIMATED TIME...10.5 SECONDS.

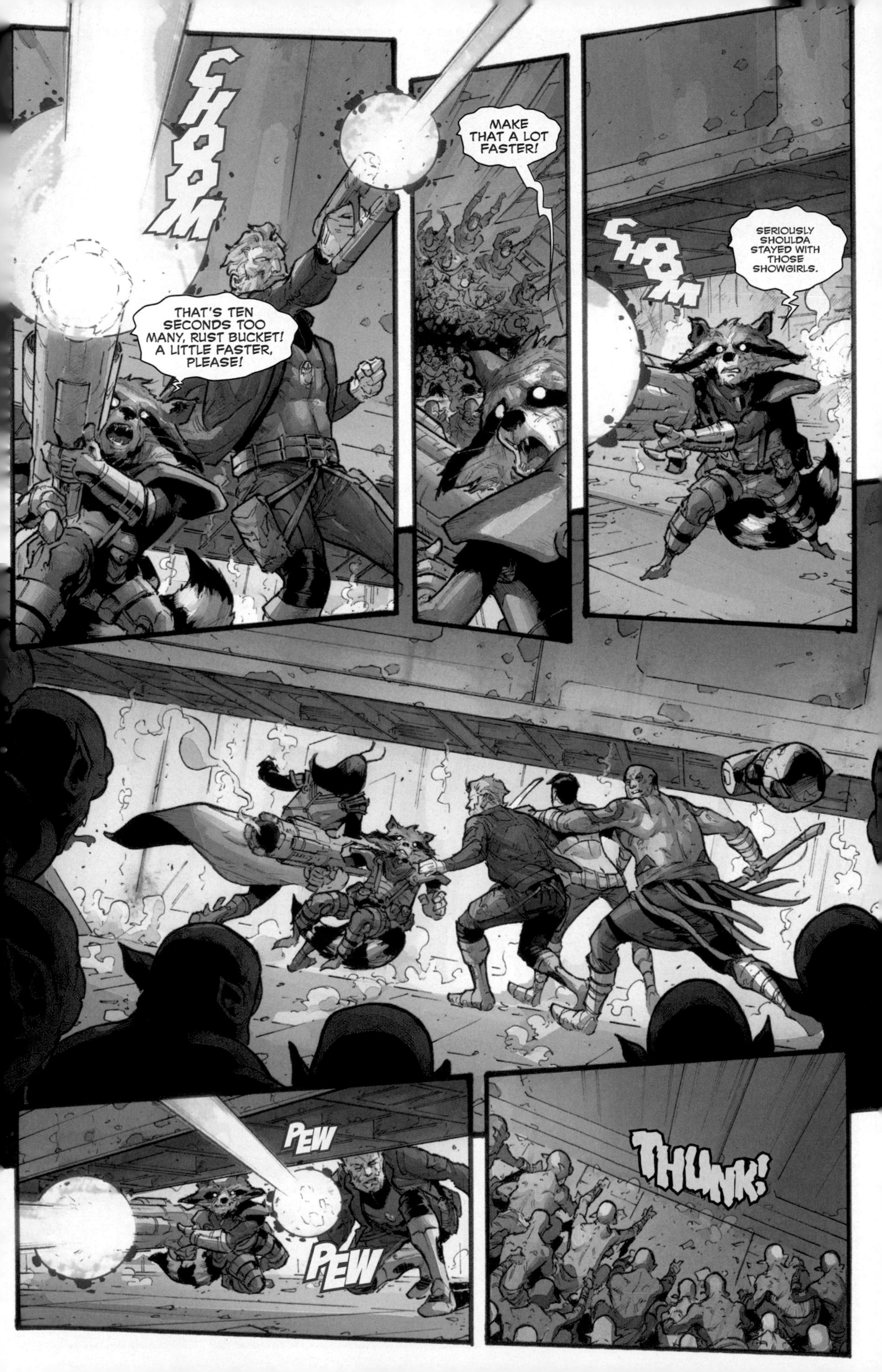
CHOOM
THAT'S TEN SECONDS TOO MANY, RUST BUCKET! A LITTLE FASTER, PLEASE!
MAKE THAT A LOT FASTER!
CHOOM
SERIOUSLY SHOULDA STAYED WITH THOSE SHOWGIRLS.
PEW
PEW
THUNK!

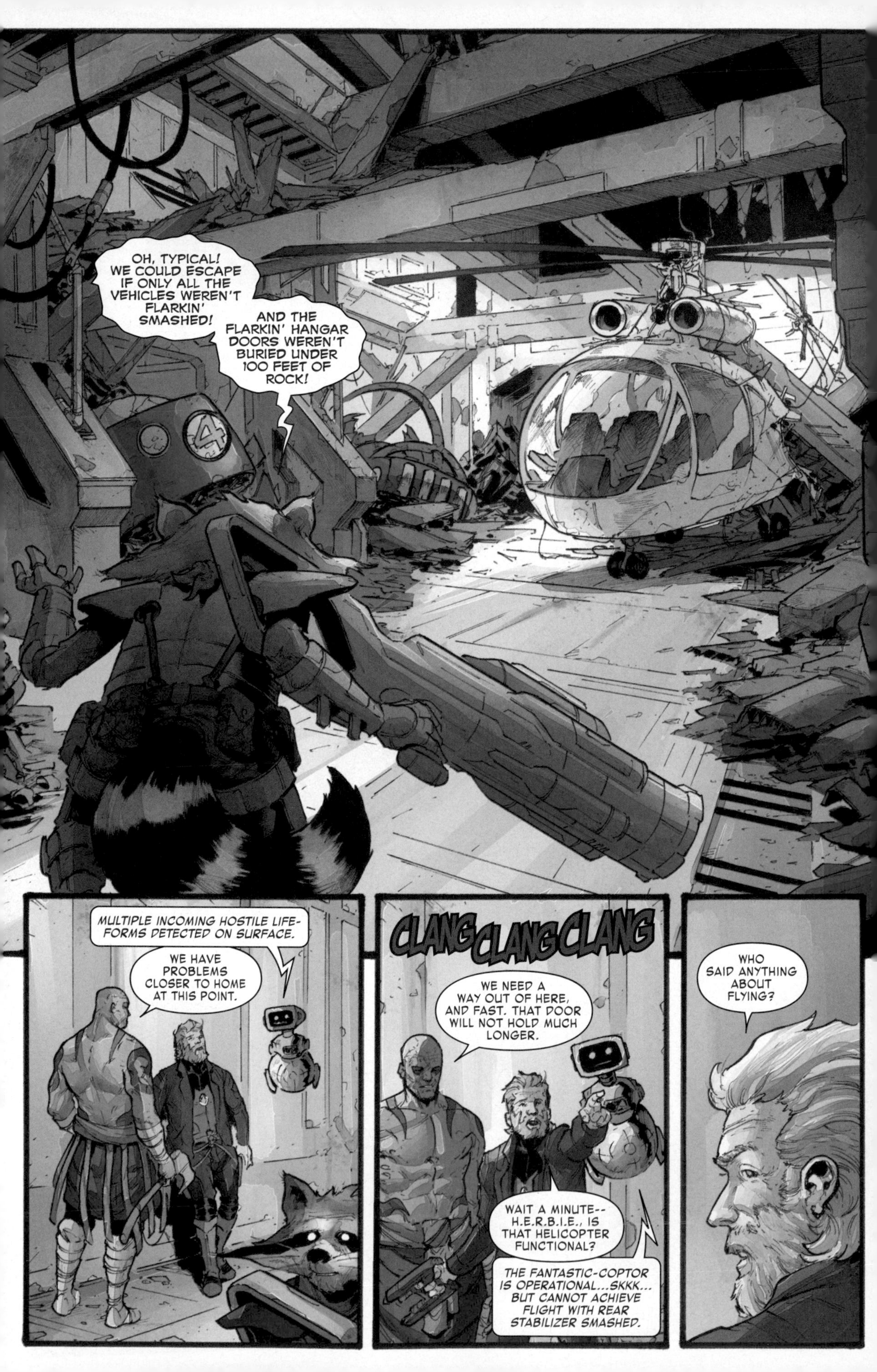

OH, TYPICAL! WE COULD ESCAPE IF ONLY ALL THE VEHICLES WEREN'T FLARKIN' SMASHED!
AND THE FLARKIN' HANGAR DOORS WEREN'T BURIED UNDER 100 FEET OF ROCK!
MULTIPLE INCOMING HOSTILE LIFE-FORMS DETECTED ON SURFACE.
WE HAVE PROBLEMS CLOSER TO HOME AT THIS POINT.
CLANG CLANG CLANG
WE NEED A WAY OUT OF HERE, AND FAST. THAT DOOR WILL NOT HOLD MUCH LONGER.
WAIT A MINUTE-- H.E.R.B.I.E., IS THAT HELICOPTER FUNCTIONAL?
THE FANTASTIC-COPTOR IS OPERATIONAL...SKKK... BUT CANNOT ACHIEVE FLIGHT WITH REAR STABILIZER SMASHED.
WHO SAID ANYTHING ABOUT FLYING?

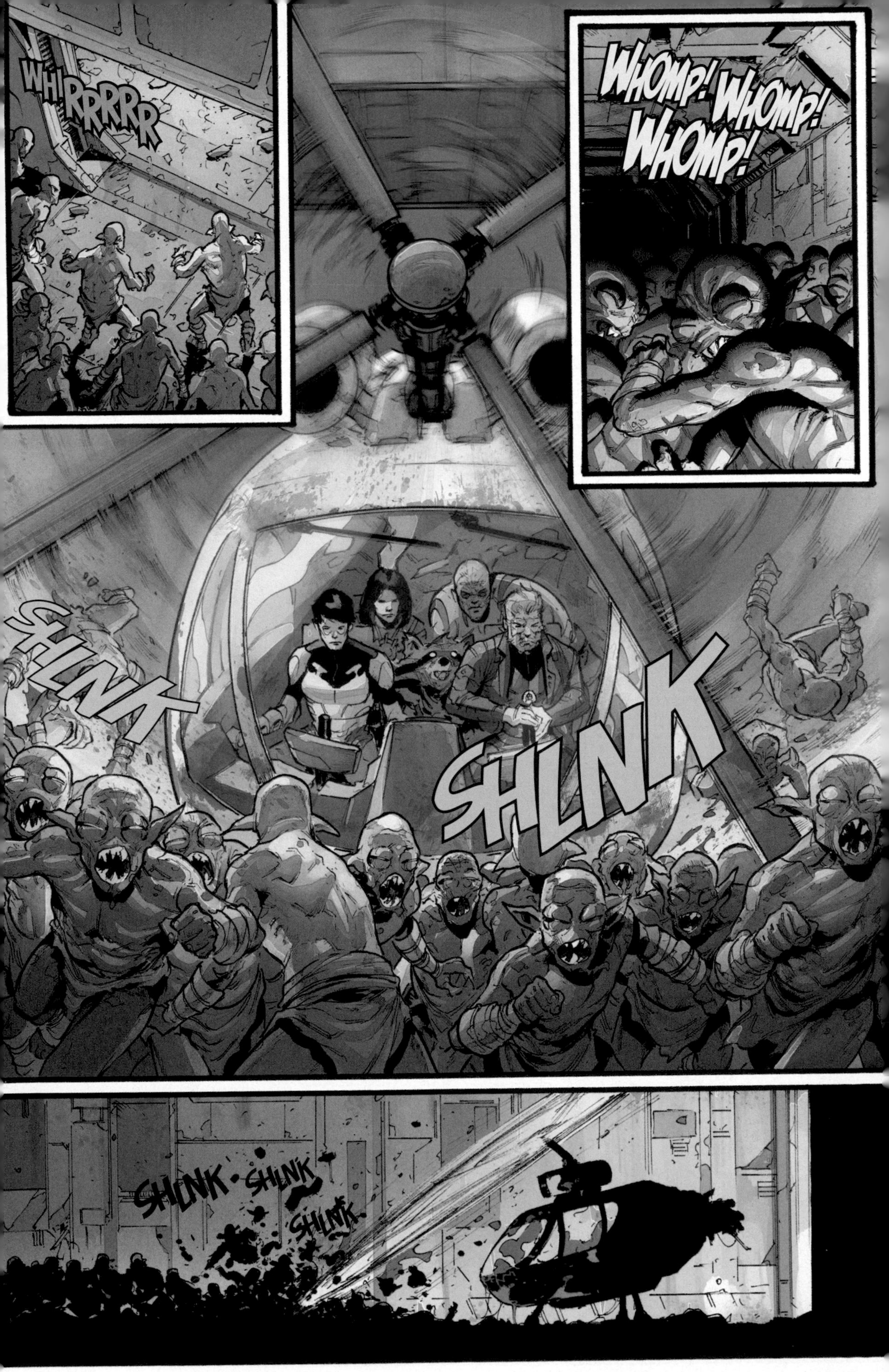
WHIRRRRR
WHOMP! WHOMP! WHOMP!
SHLNK
SHLNK
SHLNK SHLNK SHLNK

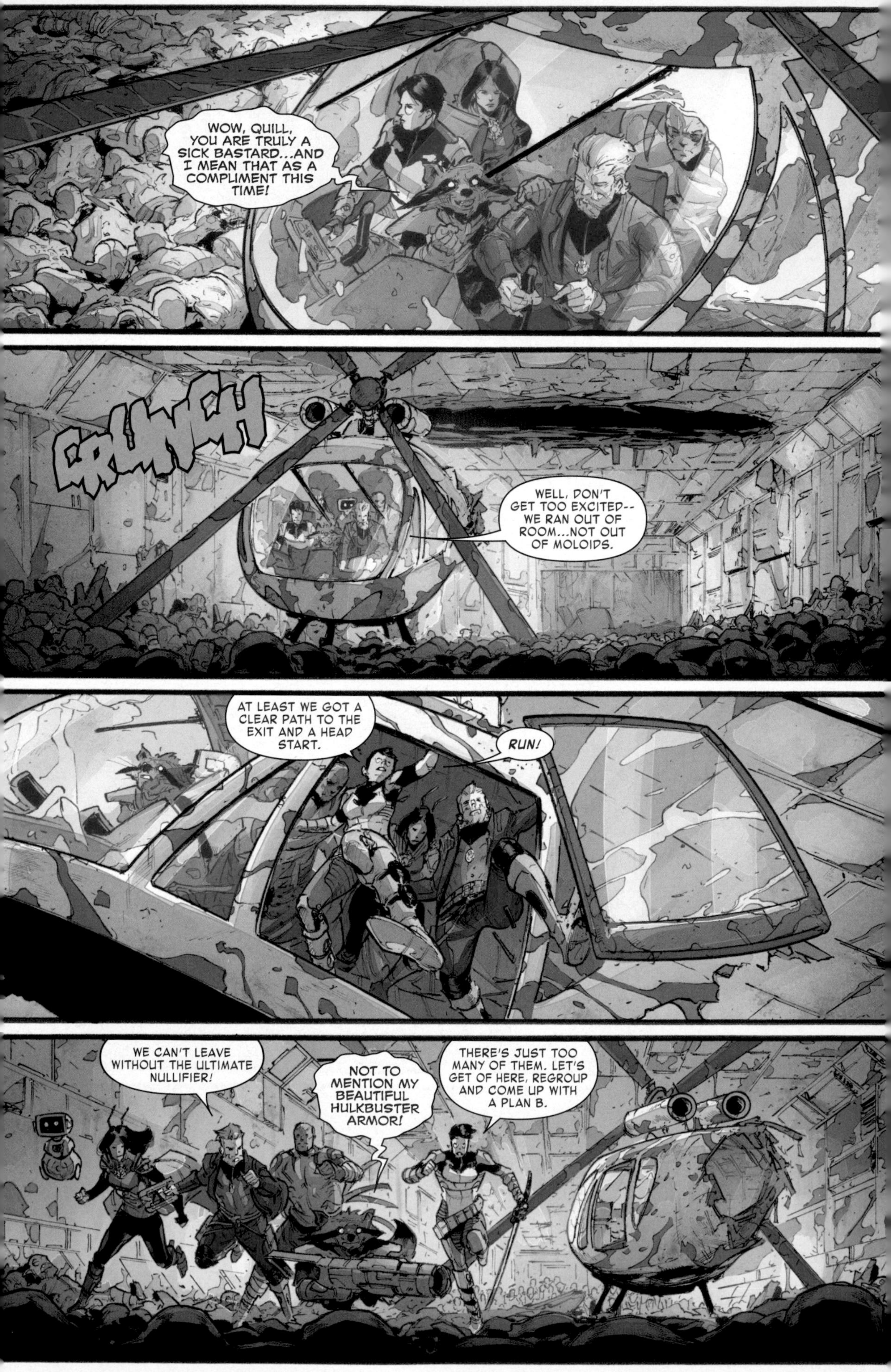
WOW, QUILL, YOU ARE TRULY A SICK BASTARD...AND I MEAN THAT AS A COMPLIMENT THIS TIME!
CRUNCH
WELL, DON'T GET TOO EXCITED-- WE RAN OUT OF ROOM...NOT OUT OF MOLOIDS.
AT LEAST WE GOT A CLEAR PATH TO THE EXIT AND A HEAD START.
RUN!
WE CAN'T LEAVE WITHOUT THE ULTIMATE NULLIFIER!
NOT TO MENTION MY BEAUTIFUL HULKBUSTER ARMOR!
THERE'S JUST TOO MANY OF THEM. LET'S GET OF HERE, REGROUP AND COME UP WITH A PLAN B.

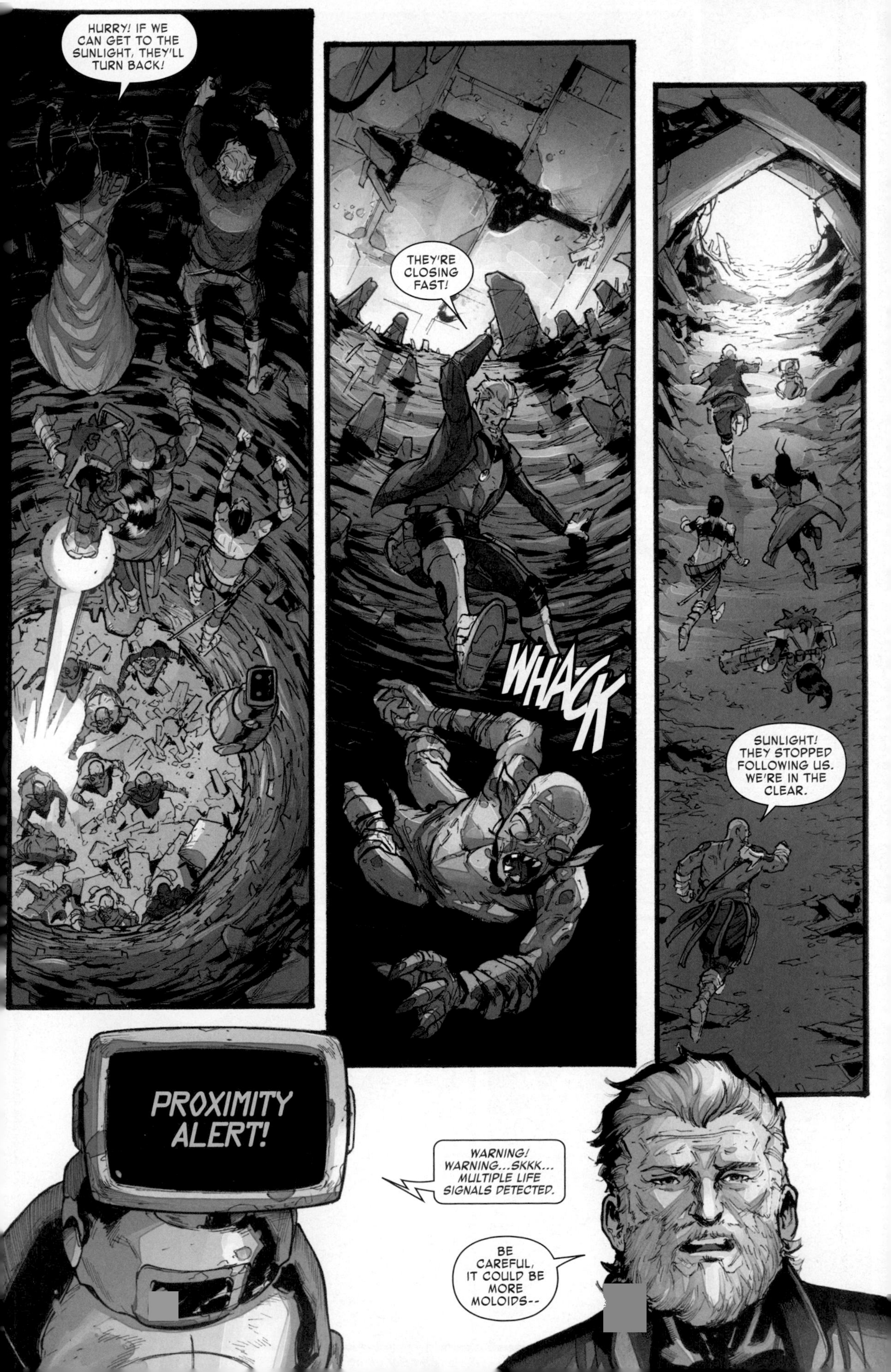
HURRY! IF WE CAN GET TO THE SUNLIGHT, THEY'LL TURN BACK!
THEY'RE CLOSING FAST!
WHACK
SUNLIGHT! THEY STOPPED FOLLOWING US. WE'RE IN THE CLEAR.
PROXIMITY ALERT!
WARNING! WARNING...SKKK... MULTIPLE LIFE SIGNALS DETECTED.
BE CAREFUL, IT COULD BE MORE MOLOIDS--

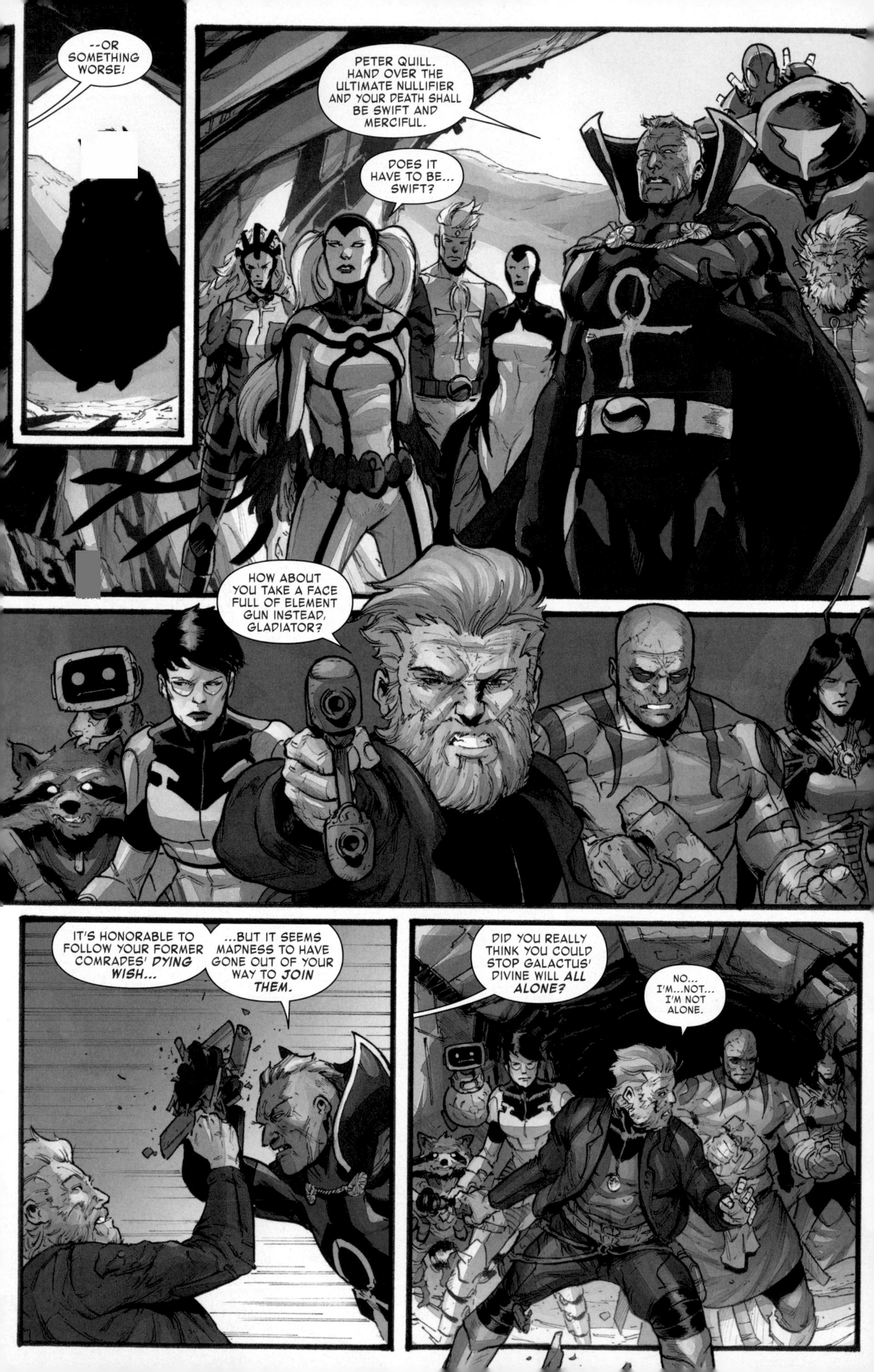
--OR SOMETHING WORSE!
PETER QUILL. HAND OVER THE ULTIMATE NULLIFIER AND YOUR DEATH SHALL BE SWIFT AND MERCIFUL.
DOES IT HAVE TO BE... SWIFT?
HOW ABOUT YOU TAKE A FACE FULL OF ELEMENT GUN INSTEAD, GLADIATOR?
IT'S HONORABLE TO FOLLOW YOUR FORMER COMRADES' DYING WISH...
...BUT IT SEEMS MADNESS TO HAVE GONE OUT OF YOUR WAY TO JOIN THEM.
DID YOU REALLY THINK YOU COULD STOP GALACTUS' DIVINE WILL ALL ALONE?
NO... I'M...NOT... I'M NOT ALONE.

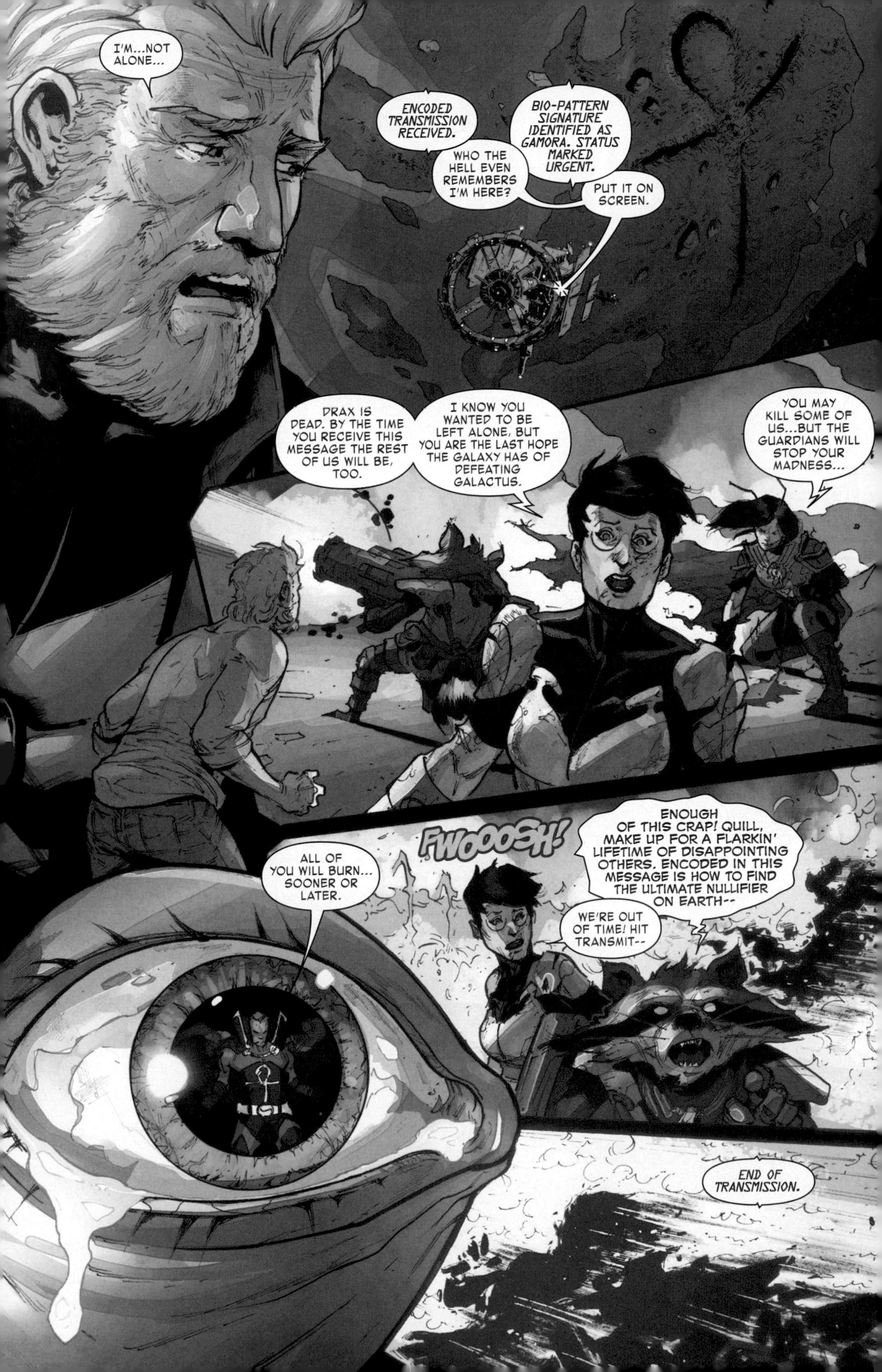
I'M...NOT ALONE...
ENCODED TRANSMISSION RECEIVED.
WHO THE HELL EVEN REMEMBERS I'M HERE?
BIO-PATTERN SIGNATURE IDENTIFIED AS GAMORA. STATUS MARKED URGENT.
PUT IT ON SCREEN.
DRAX IS DEAD. BY THE TIME YOU RECEIVE THIS MESSAGE THE REST OF US WILL BE, TOO.
I KNOW YOU WANTED TO BE LEFT ALONE, BUT YOU ARE THE LAST HOPE THE GALAXY HAS OF DEFEATING GALACTUS.
YOU MAY KILL SOME OF US...BUT THE GUARDIANS WILL STOP YOUR MADNESS...
ALL OF YOU WILL BURN... SOONER OR LATER.
FWOOOSH!
ENOUGH OF THIS CRAP! QUILL, MAKE UP FOR A FLARKIN' LIFETIME OF DISAPPOINTING OTHERS. ENCODED IN THIS MESSAGE IS HOW TO FIND THE ULTIMATE NULLIFIER ON EARTH--
WE'RE OUT OF TIME! HIT TRANSMIT--
END OF TRANSMISSION.

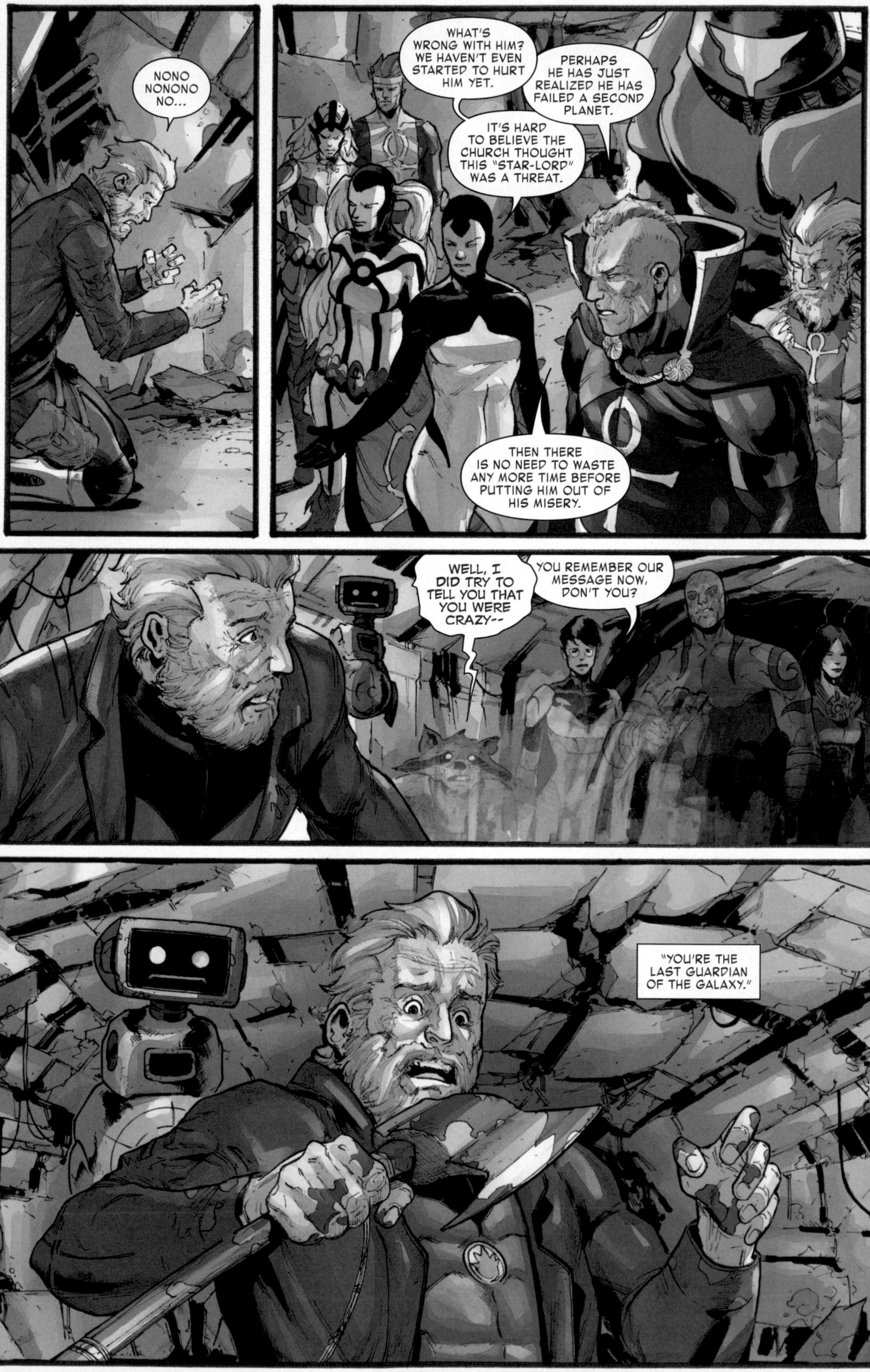
NONO NONONO NO...
WHAT'S WRONG WITH HIM? WE HAVEN'T EVEN STARTED TO HURT HIM YET.
PERHAPS HE HAS JUST REALIZED HE HAS FAILED A SECOND PLANET.
IT'S HARD TO BELIEVE THE CHURCH THOUGHT THIS "STAR-LORD" WAS A THREAT.
THEN THERE IS NO NEED TO WASTE ANY MORE TIME BEFORE PUTTING HIM OUT OF HIS MISERY.
WELL, I DID TRY TO TELL YOU THAT YOU WERE CRAZY--
YOU REMEMBER OUR MESSAGE NOW, DON'T YOU?
"YOU'RE THE LAST GUARDIAN OF THE GALAXY."

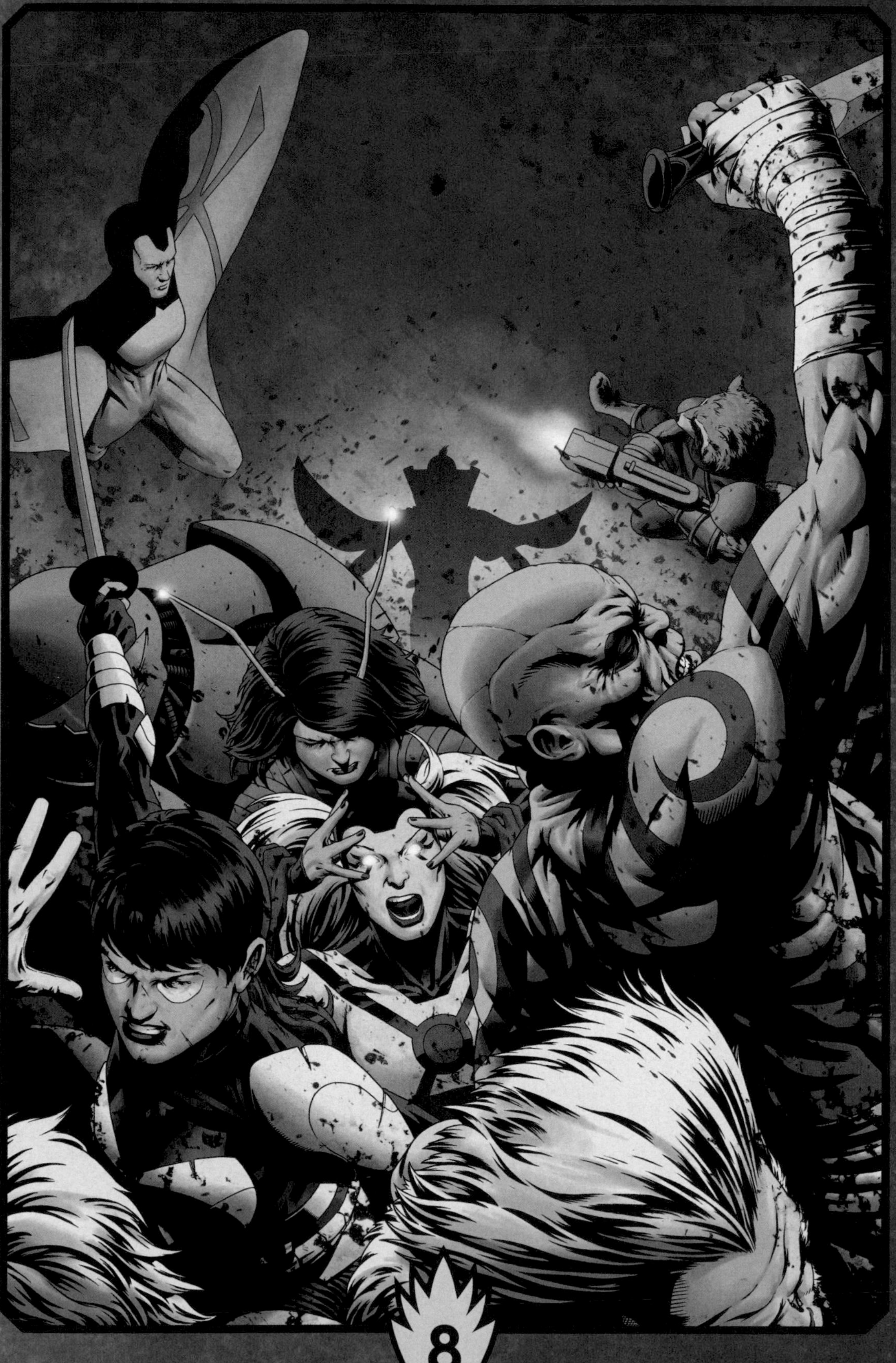

8

"DON'T FEAR THE REAPER"

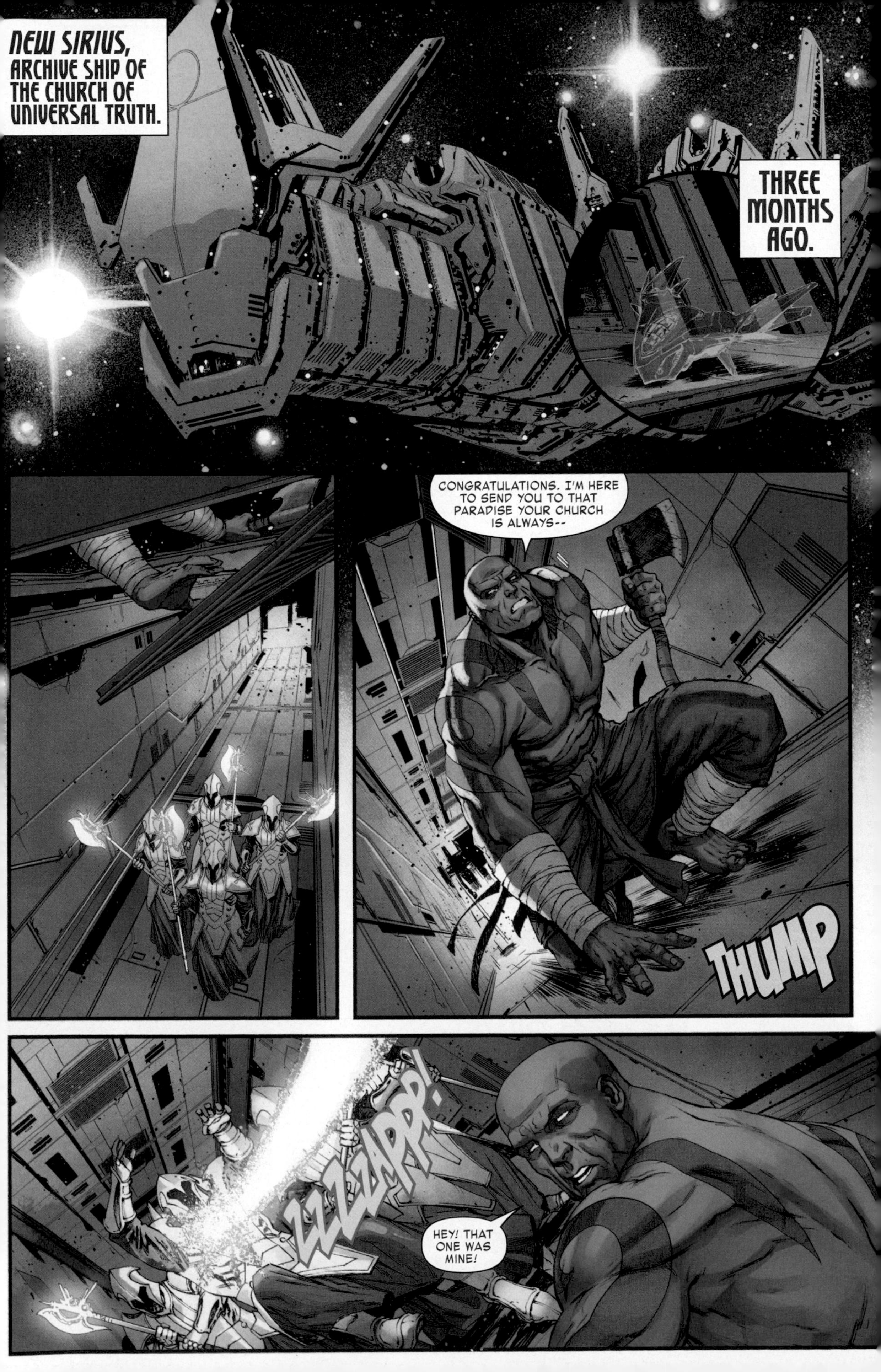
NEW SIRIUS, ARCHIVE SHIP OF THE CHURCH OF UNIVERSAL TRUTH.
THREE MONTHS AGO.
CONGRATULATIONS. I'M HERE TO SEND YOU TO THAT PARADISE YOUR CHURCH IS ALWAYS--
THUMP
ZZZZAPP!
HEY! THAT ONE WAS MINE!

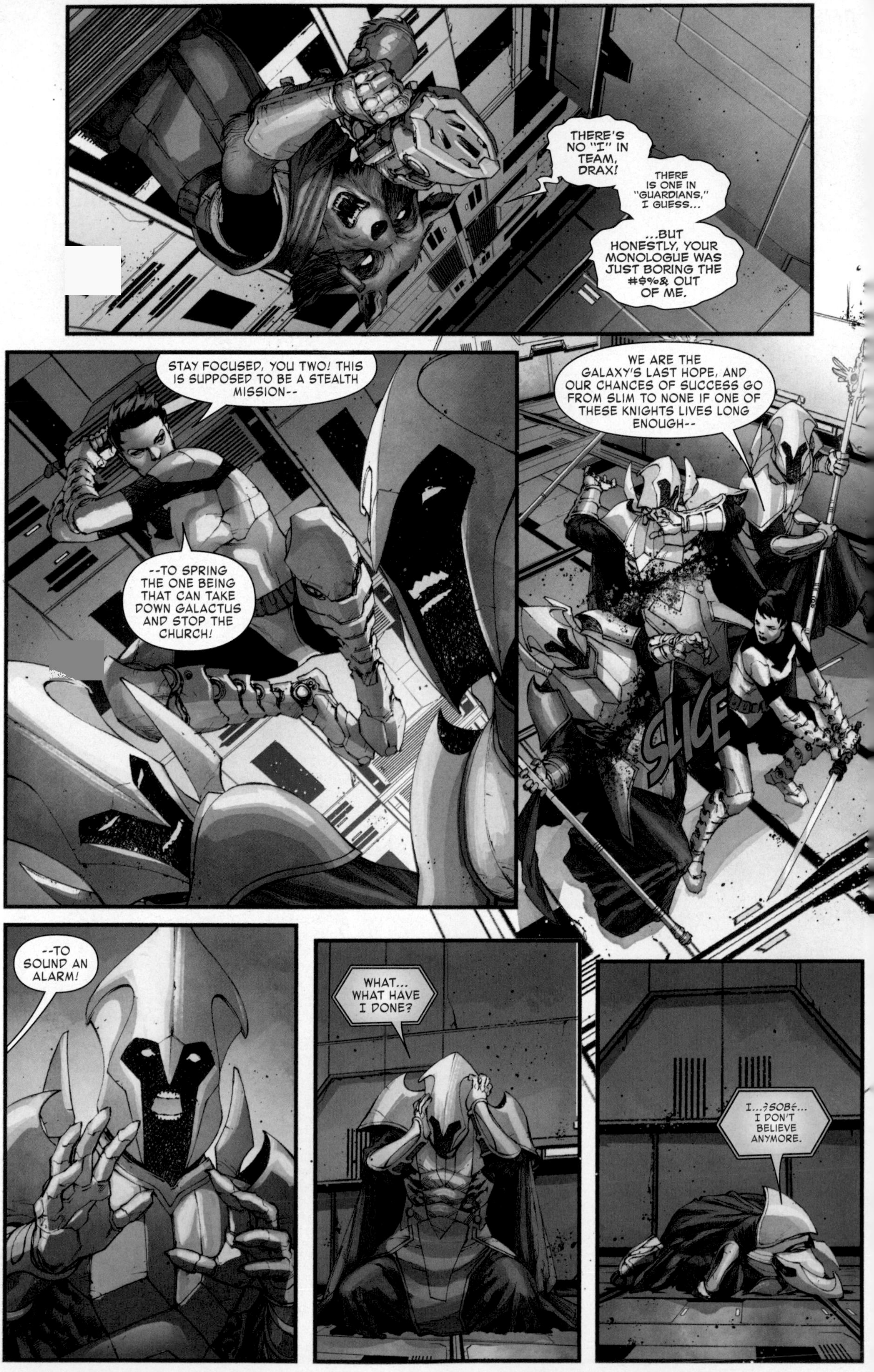
THERE'S NO "I" IN TEAM, DRAX!
THERE IS ONE IN "GUARDIANS," I GUESS...
...BUT HONESTLY, YOUR MONOLOGUE WAS JUST BORING THE #$%& OUT OF ME.
STAY FOCUSED, YOU TWO! THIS IS SUPPOSED TO BE A STEALTH MISSION--
--TO SPRING THE ONE BEING THAT CAN TAKE DOWN GALACTUS AND STOP THE CHURCH!
WE ARE THE GALAXY'S LAST HOPE, AND OUR CHANCES OF SUCCESS GO FROM SLIM TO NONE IF ONE OF THESE KNIGHTS LIVES LONG ENOUGH--
SLICE
--TO SOUND AN ALARM!
WHAT... WHAT HAVE I DONE?
I...SOB... I DON'T BELIEVE ANYMORE.

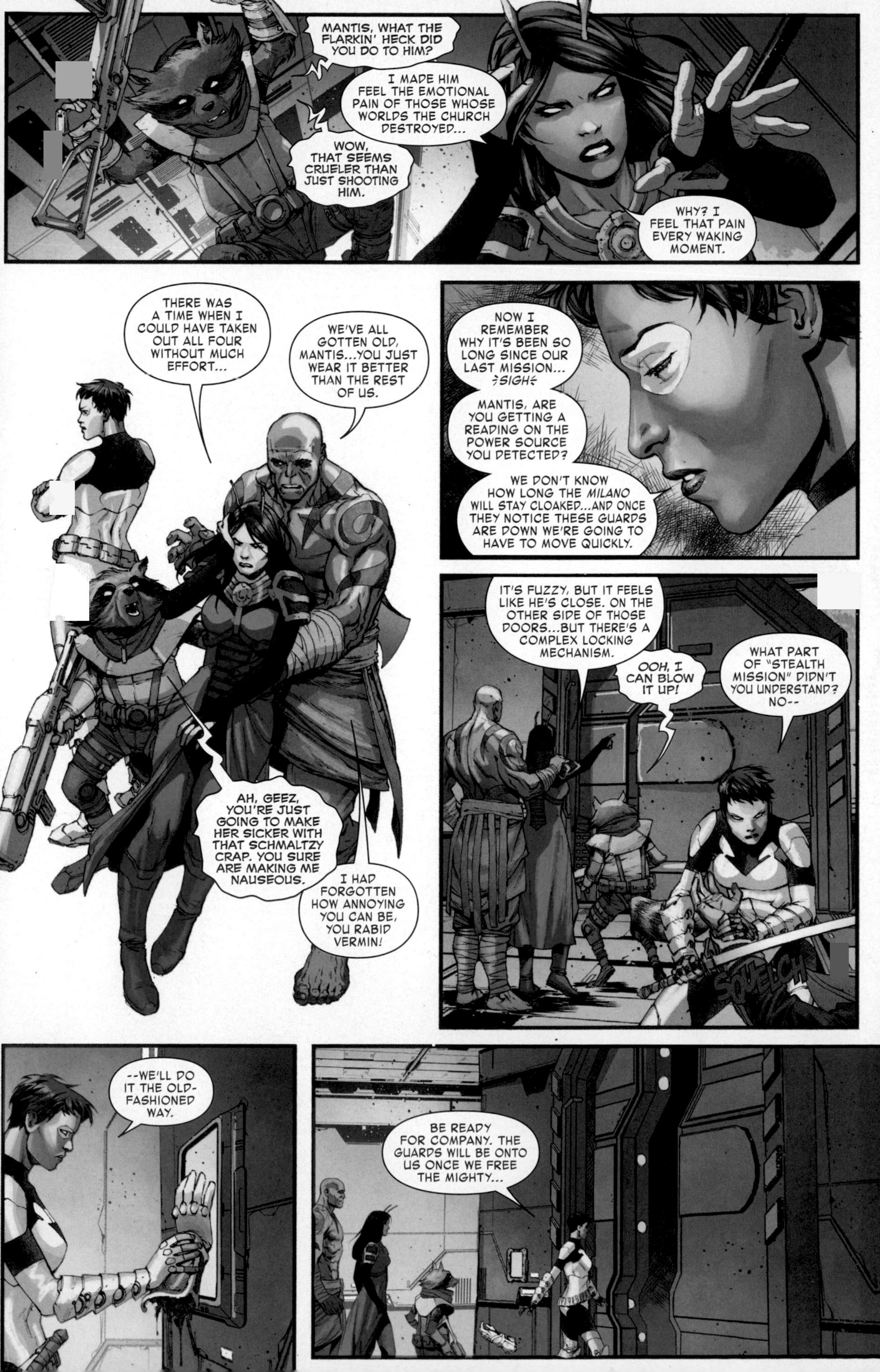
MANTIS, WHAT THE FLARKIN' HECK DID YOU DO TO HIM?
I MADE HIM FEEL THE EMOTIONAL PAIN OF THOSE WHOSE WORLDS THE CHURCH DESTROYED...
WOW, THAT SEEMS CRUELER THAN JUST SHOOTING HIM.
WHY? I FEEL THAT PAIN EVERY WAKING MOMENT.
THERE WAS A TIME WHEN I COULD HAVE TAKEN OUT ALL FOUR WITHOUT MUCH EFFORT...
WE'VE ALL GOTTEN OLD, MANTIS...YOU JUST WEAR IT BETTER THAN THE REST OF US.
AH, GEEZ, YOU'RE JUST GOING TO MAKE HER SICKER WITH THAT SCHMALTZY CRAP. YOU SURE ARE MAKING ME NAUSEOUS.
I HAD FORGOTTEN HOW ANNOYING YOU CAN BE, YOU RABID VERMIN!
NOW I REMEMBER WHY IT'S BEEN SO LONG SINCE OUR LAST MISSION... ⫶SIGH⫶
MANTIS, ARE YOU GETTING A READING ON THE POWER SOURCE YOU DETECTED?
WE DON'T KNOW HOW LONG THE *MILANO* WILL STAY CLOAKED...AND ONCE THEY NOTICE THESE GUARDS ARE DOWN WE'RE GOING TO HAVE TO MOVE QUICKLY.
IT'S FUZZY, BUT IT FEELS LIKE HE'S CLOSE. ON THE OTHER SIDE OF THOSE DOORS...BUT THERE'S A COMPLEX LOCKING MECHANISM.
OOH, I CAN BLOW IT UP!
WHAT PART OF "STEALTH MISSION" DIDN'T YOU UNDERSTAND? NO--
SQUELCH
--WE'LL DO IT THE OLD-FASHIONED WAY.
BE READY FOR COMPANY. THE GUARDS WILL BE ONTO US ONCE WE FREE THE MIGHTY...

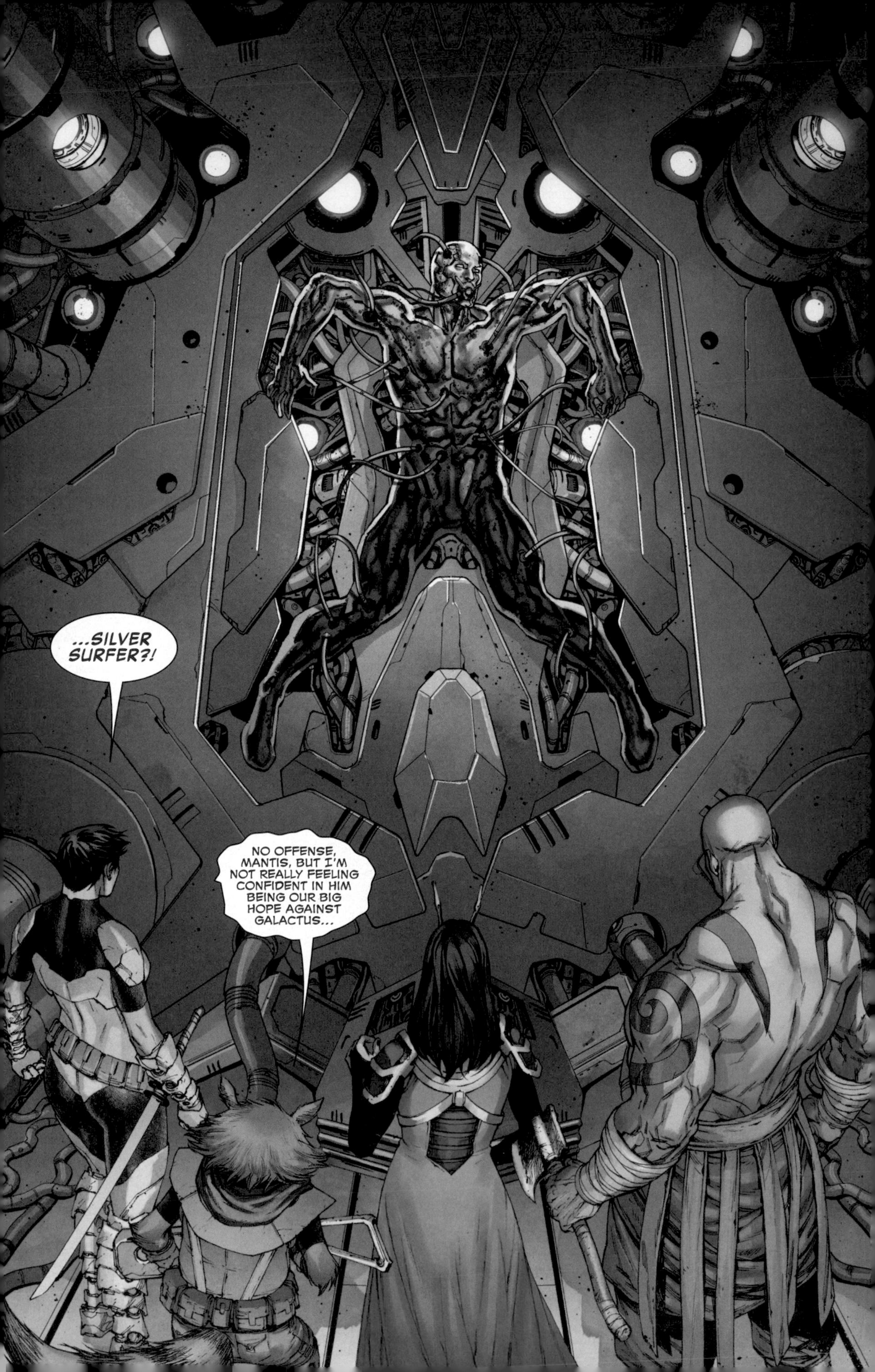
...SILVER SURFER?!
NO OFFENSE, MANTIS, BUT I'M NOT REALLY FEELING CONFIDENT IN HIM BEING OUR BIG HOPE AGAINST GALACTUS...

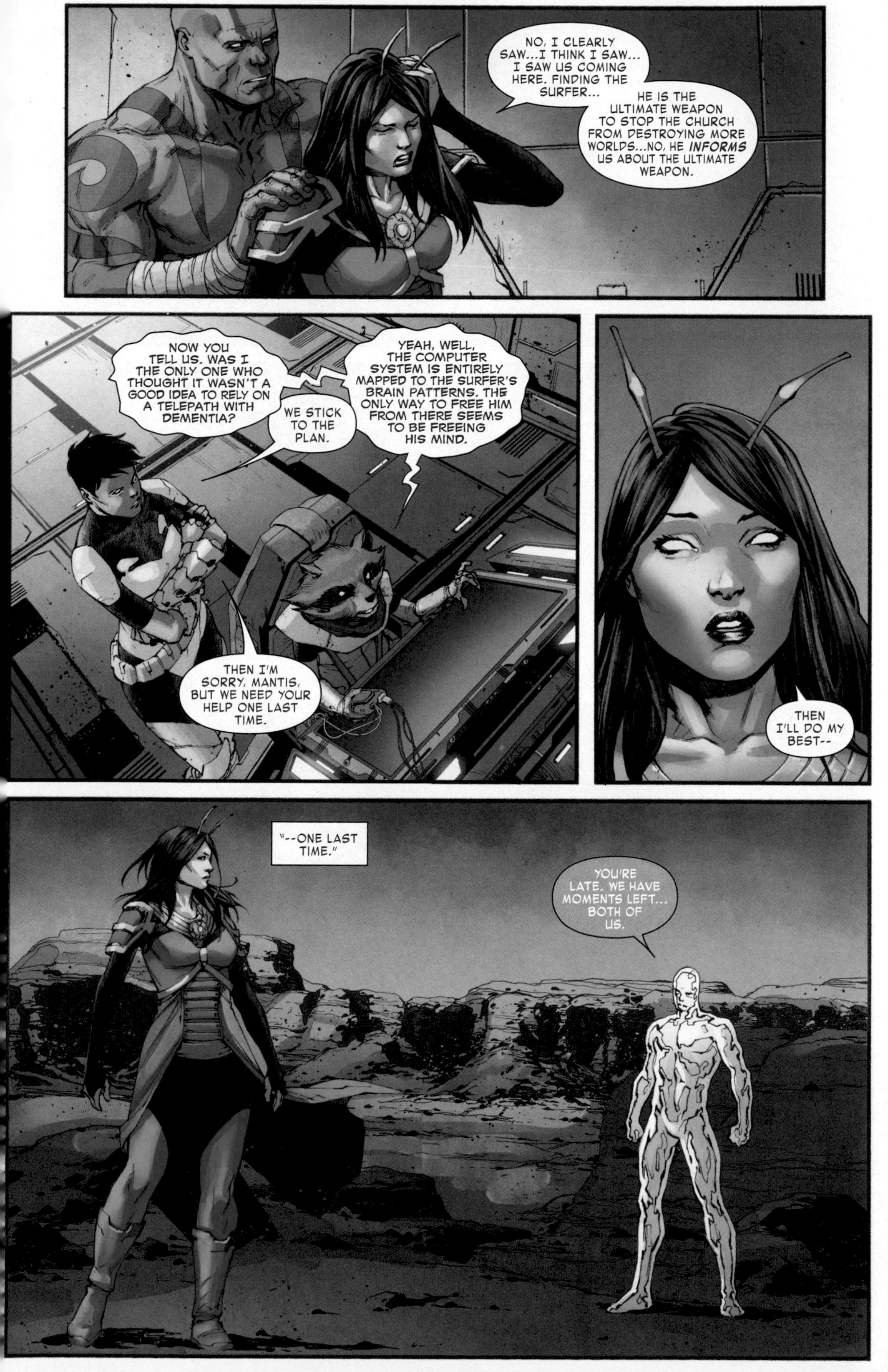
NO, I CLEARLY SAW...I THINK I SAW... I SAW US COMING HERE. FINDING THE SURFER...
HE IS THE ULTIMATE WEAPON TO STOP THE CHURCH FROM DESTROYING MORE WORLDS...NO, HE *INFORMS* US ABOUT THE ULTIMATE WEAPON.
NOW YOU TELL US. WAS I THE ONLY ONE WHO THOUGHT IT WASN'T A GOOD IDEA TO RELY ON A TELEPATH WITH DEMENTIA?
WE STICK TO THE PLAN.
YEAH, WELL, THE COMPUTER SYSTEM IS ENTIRELY MAPPED TO THE SURFER'S BRAIN PATTERNS. THE ONLY WAY TO FREE HIM FROM THERE SEEMS TO BE FREEING HIS MIND.
THEN I'M SORRY, MANTIS, BUT WE NEED YOUR HELP ONE LAST TIME.
THEN I'LL DO MY BEST--
"--ONE LAST TIME."
YOU'RE LATE. WE HAVE MOMENTS LEFT... BOTH OF US.

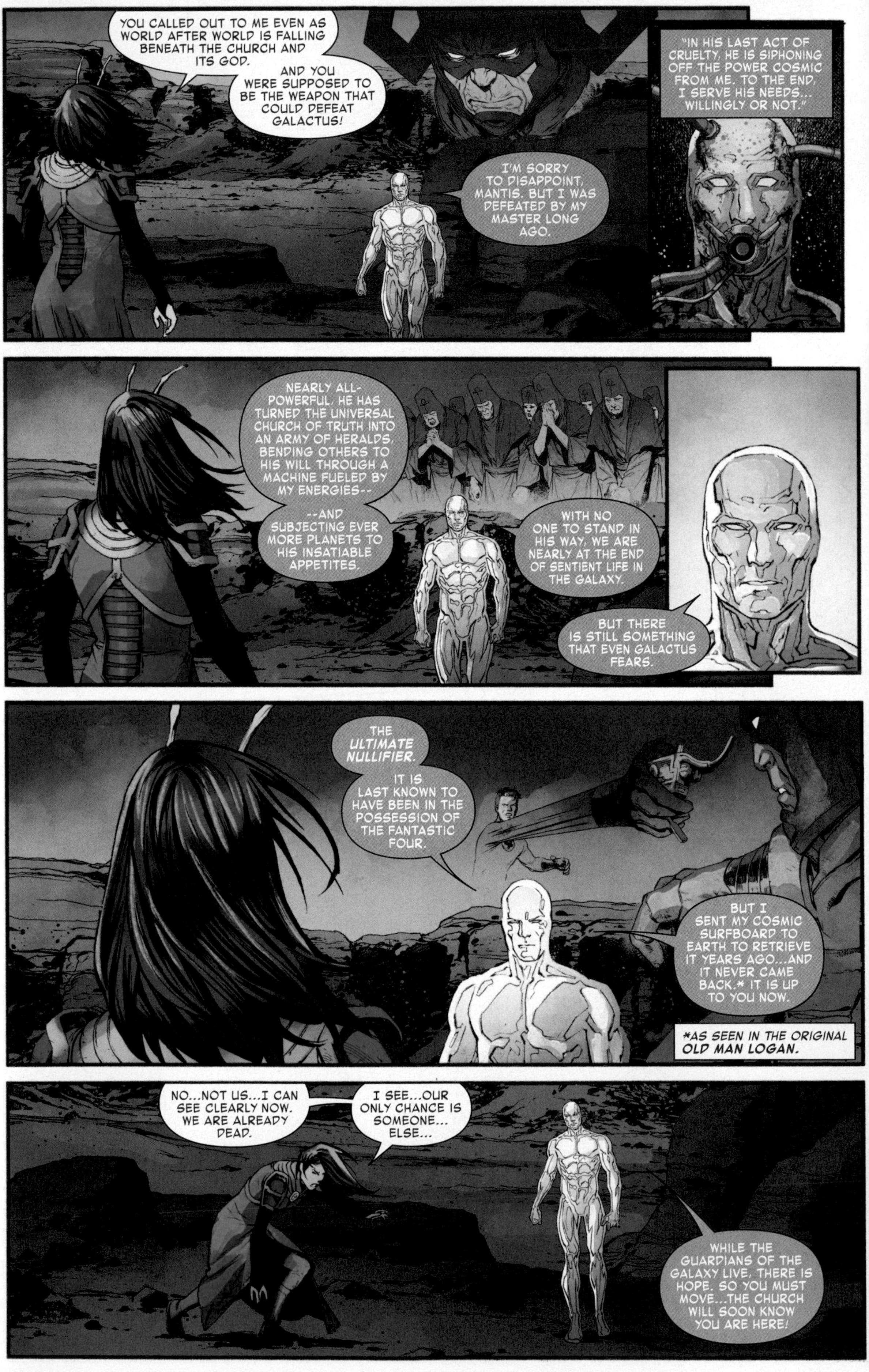

YOU CALLED OUT TO ME EVEN AS WORLD AFTER WORLD IS FALLING BENEATH THE CHURCH AND ITS GOD.
AND YOU WERE SUPPOSED TO BE THE WEAPON THAT COULD DEFEAT GALACTUS!
I'M SORRY TO DISAPPOINT, MANTIS. BUT I WAS DEFEATED BY MY MASTER LONG AGO.
"IN HIS LAST ACT OF CRUELTY, HE IS SIPHONING OFF THE POWER COSMIC FROM ME. TO THE END, I SERVE HIS NEEDS... WILLINGLY OR NOT."
NEARLY ALL-POWERFUL, HE HAS TURNED THE UNIVERSAL CHURCH OF TRUTH INTO AN ARMY OF HERALDS, BENDING OTHERS TO HIS WILL THROUGH A MACHINE FUELED BY MY ENERGIES--
--AND SUBJECTING EVER MORE PLANETS TO HIS INSATIABLE APPETITES.
WITH NO ONE TO STAND IN HIS WAY, WE ARE NEARLY AT THE END OF SENTIENT LIFE IN THE GALAXY.
BUT THERE IS STILL SOMETHING THAT EVEN GALACTUS FEARS.
THE ULTIMATE NULLIFIER.
IT IS LAST KNOWN TO HAVE BEEN IN THE POSSESSION OF THE FANTASTIC FOUR.
BUT I SENT MY COSMIC SURFBOARD TO EARTH TO RETRIEVE IT YEARS AGO...AND IT NEVER CAME BACK.* IT IS UP TO YOU NOW.
*AS SEEN IN THE ORIGINAL OLD MAN LOGAN.
NO...NOT US...I CAN SEE CLEARLY NOW. WE ARE ALREADY DEAD.
I SEE...OUR ONLY CHANCE IS SOMEONE... ELSE...
WHILE THE GUARDIANS OF THE GALAXY LIVE, THERE IS HOPE. SO YOU MUST MOVE...THE CHURCH WILL SOON KNOW YOU ARE HERE!

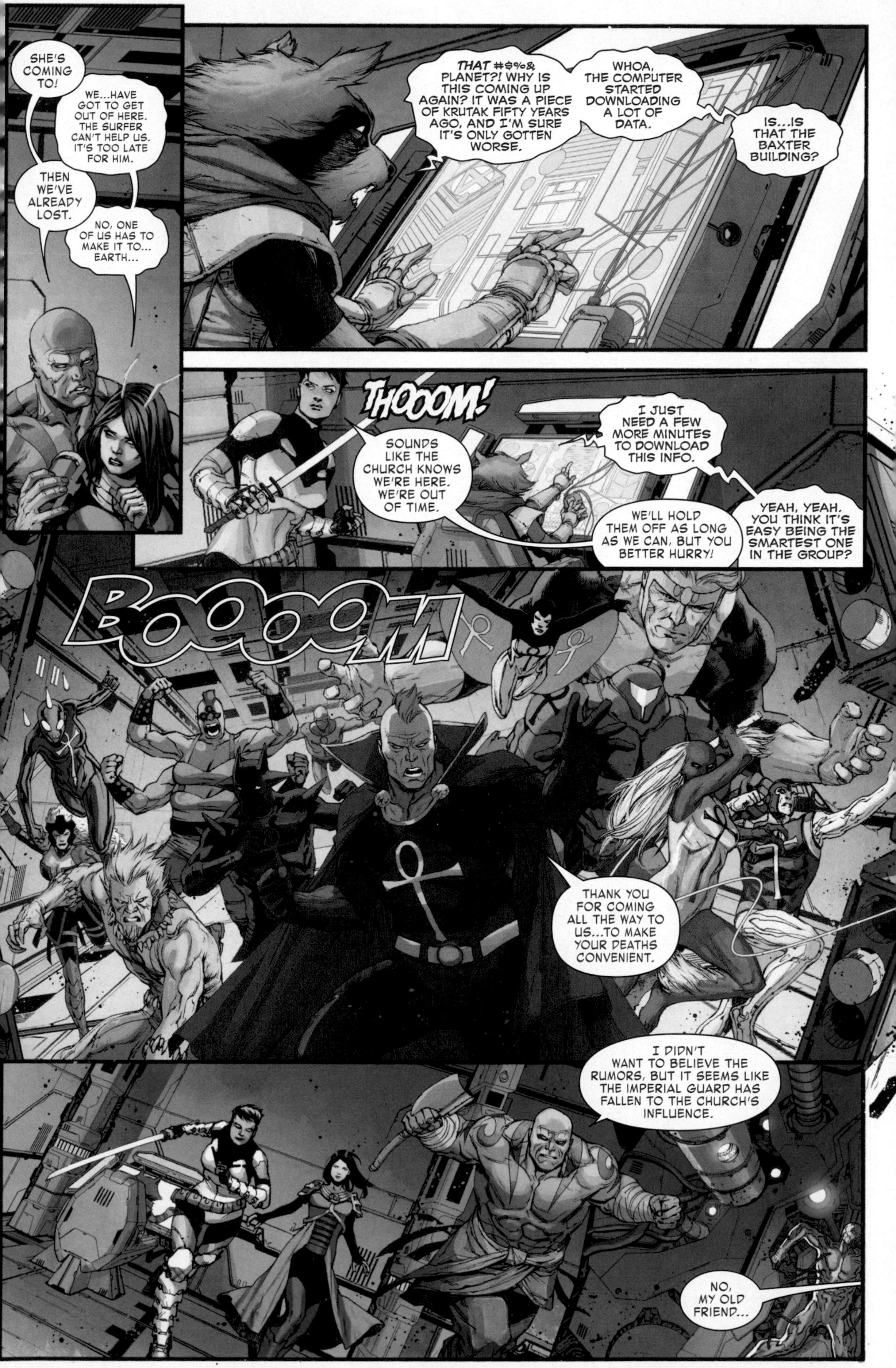
SHE'S COMING TO!
WE...HAVE GOT TO GET OUT OF HERE. THE SURFER CAN'T HELP US. IT'S TOO LATE FOR HIM.
THEN WE'VE ALREADY LOST.
NO, ONE OF US HAS TO MAKE IT TO... EARTH...
THAT #$%& PLANET?! WHY IS THIS COMING UP AGAIN? IT WAS A PIECE OF KRUTAK FIFTY YEARS AGO, AND I'M SURE IT'S ONLY GOTTEN WORSE.
WHOA, THE COMPUTER STARTED DOWNLOADING A LOT OF DATA.
IS...IS THAT THE BAXTER BUILDING?
THOOOM!
SOUNDS LIKE THE CHURCH KNOWS WE'RE HERE. WE'RE OUT OF TIME.
I JUST NEED A FEW MORE MINUTES TO DOWNLOAD THIS INFO.
WE'LL HOLD THEM OFF AS LONG AS WE CAN, BUT YOU BETTER HURRY!
YEAH, YEAH. YOU THINK IT'S EASY BEING THE SMARTEST ONE IN THE GROUP?
BOOOOM
THANK YOU FOR COMING ALL THE WAY TO US...TO MAKE YOUR DEATHS CONVENIENT.
I DIDN'T WANT TO BELIEVE THE RUMORS, BUT IT SEEMS LIKE THE IMPERIAL GUARD HAS FALLEN TO THE CHURCH'S INFLUENCE.
NO, MY OLD FRIEND...

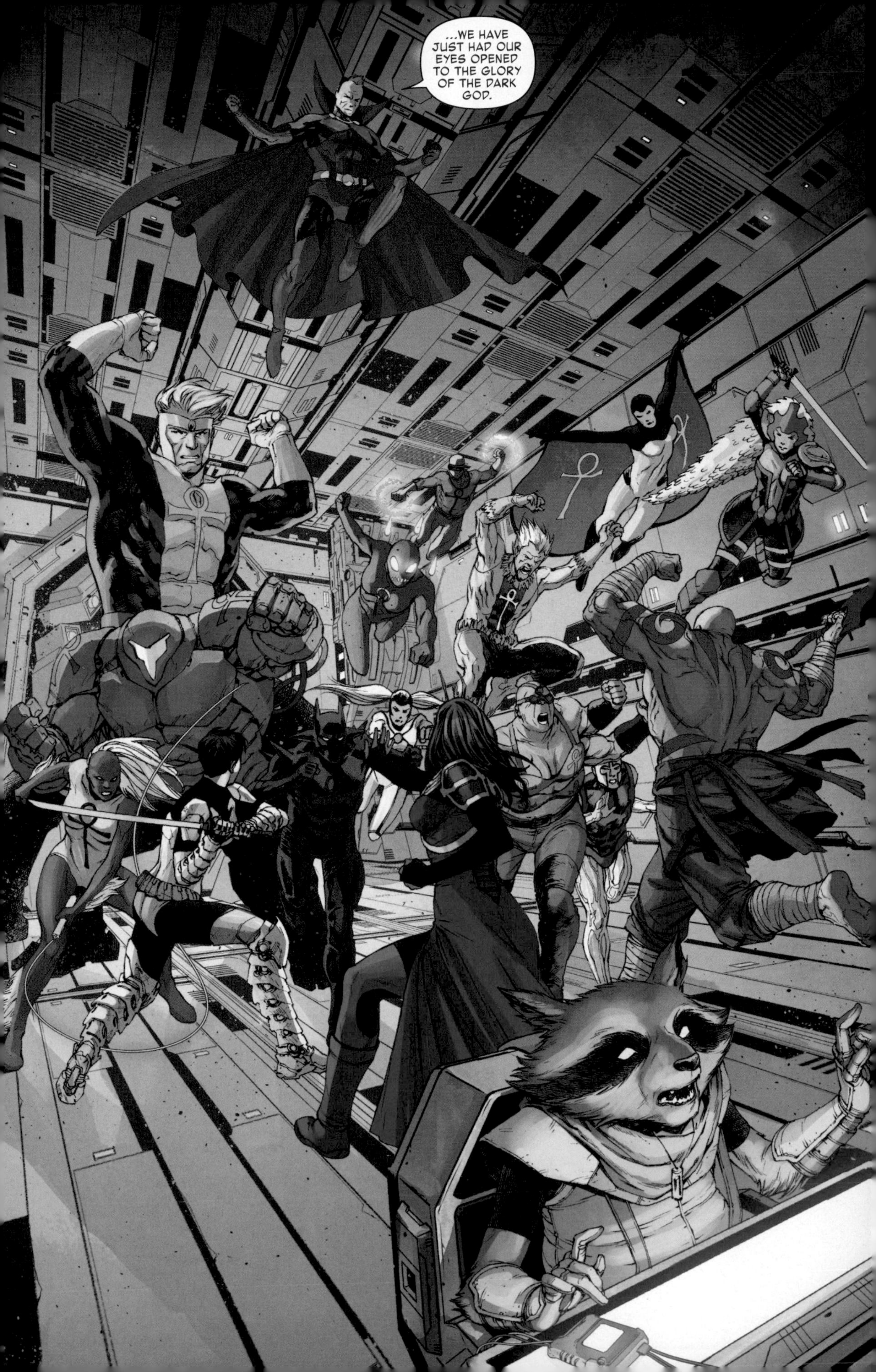
...WE HAVE JUST HAD OUR EYES OPENED TO THE GLORY OF THE DARK GOD.

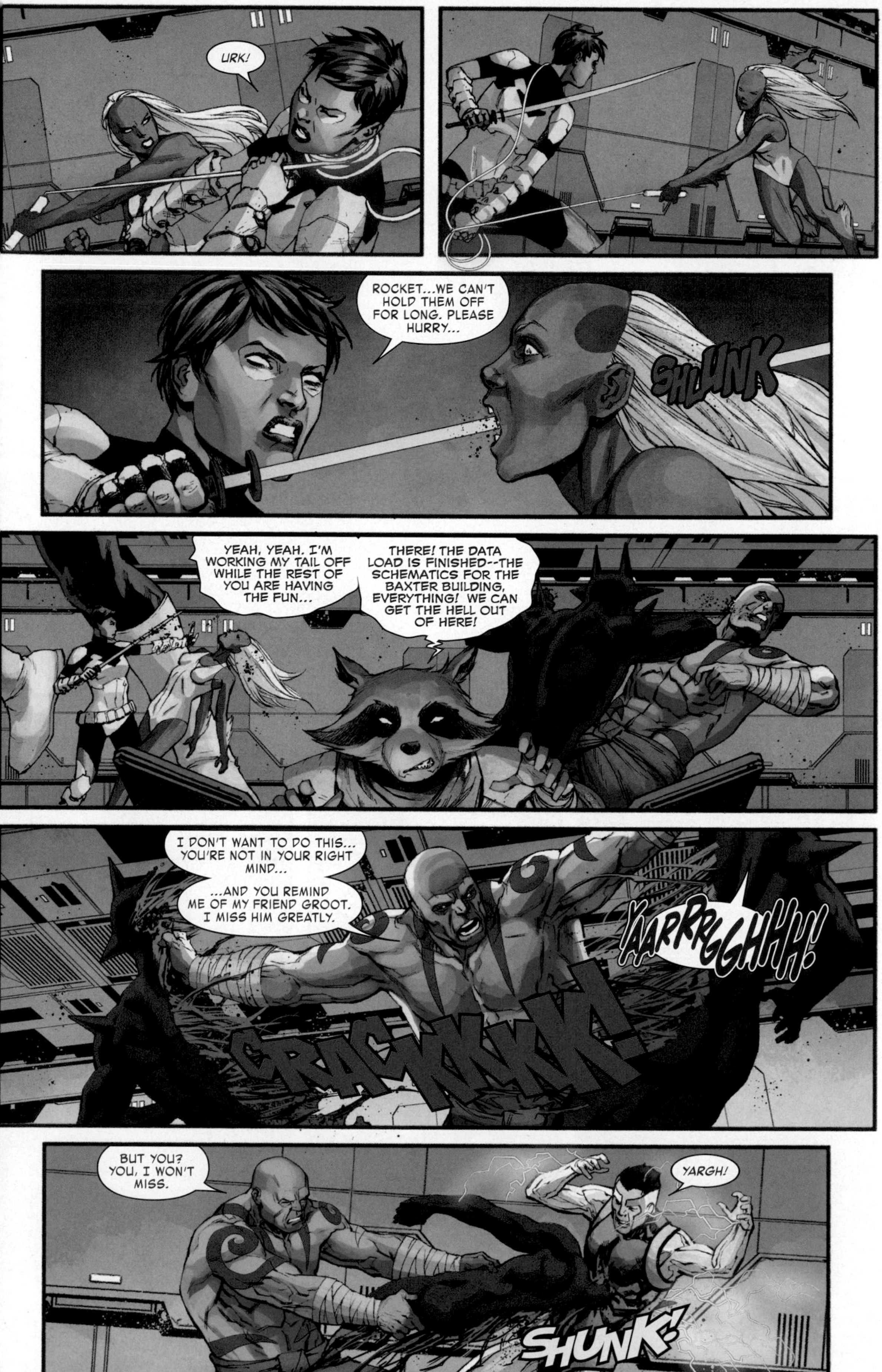
URK!
ROCKET...WE CAN'T HOLD THEM OFF FOR LONG. PLEASE HURRY...
SHLUNK
YEAH, YEAH. I'M WORKING MY TAIL OFF WHILE THE REST OF YOU ARE HAVING THE FUN...
THERE! THE DATA LOAD IS FINISHED--THE SCHEMATICS FOR THE BAXTER BUILDING, EVERYTHING! WE CAN GET THE HELL OUT OF HERE!
I DON'T WANT TO DO THIS... YOU'RE NOT IN YOUR RIGHT MIND...
...AND YOU REMIND ME OF MY FRIEND GROOT. I MISS HIM GREATLY.
YAARRRGGHHH!
CRACKKKKK!
BUT YOU? YOU, I WON'T MISS.
YARGH!
SHUNK!

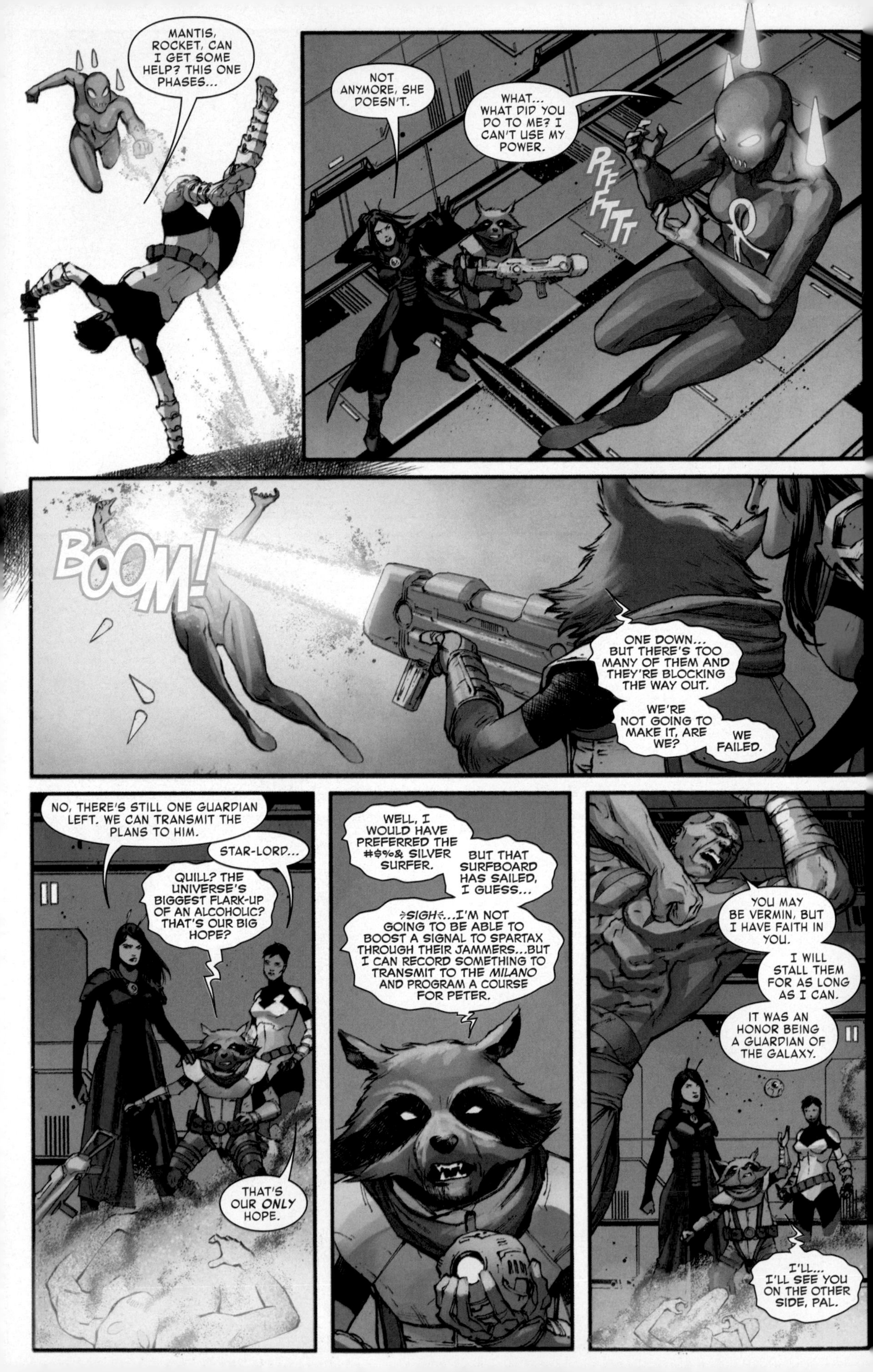
MANTIS, ROCKET, CAN I GET SOME HELP? THIS ONE PHASES...
NOT ANYMORE, SHE DOESN'T.
WHAT... WHAT DID YOU DO TO ME? I CAN'T USE MY POWER.
PFFFTTT
BOOM!
ONE DOWN... BUT THERE'S TOO MANY OF THEM AND THEY'RE BLOCKING THE WAY OUT.
WE'RE NOT GOING TO MAKE IT, ARE WE?
WE FAILED.
NO, THERE'S STILL ONE GUARDIAN LEFT. WE CAN TRANSMIT THE PLANS TO HIM.
STAR-LORD...
QUILL? THE UNIVERSE'S BIGGEST FLARK-UP OF AN ALCOHOLIC? THAT'S OUR BIG HOPE?
THAT'S OUR ONLY HOPE.
WELL, I WOULD HAVE PREFERRED THE #$%& SILVER SURFER.
BUT THAT SURFBOARD HAS SAILED, I GUESS...
SIGH...I'M NOT GOING TO BE ABLE TO BOOST A SIGNAL TO SPARTAX THROUGH THEIR JAMMERS...BUT I CAN RECORD SOMETHING TO TRANSMIT TO THE MILANO AND PROGRAM A COURSE FOR PETER.
YOU MAY BE VERMIN, BUT I HAVE FAITH IN YOU.
I WILL STALL THEM FOR AS LONG AS I CAN.
IT WAS AN HONOR BEING A GUARDIAN OF THE GALAXY.
I'LL... I'LL SEE YOU ON THE OTHER SIDE, PAL.

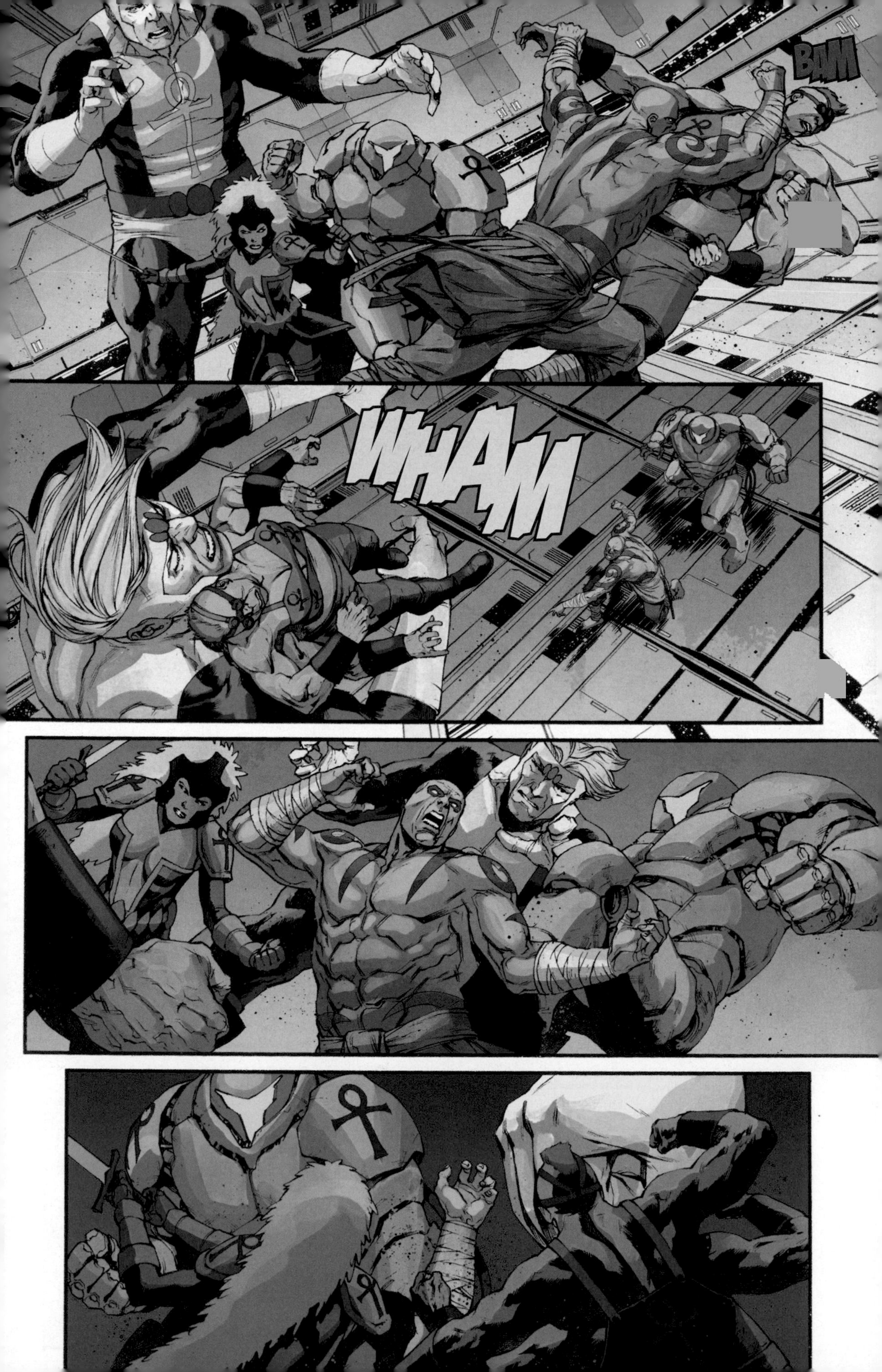
BAM
WHAM

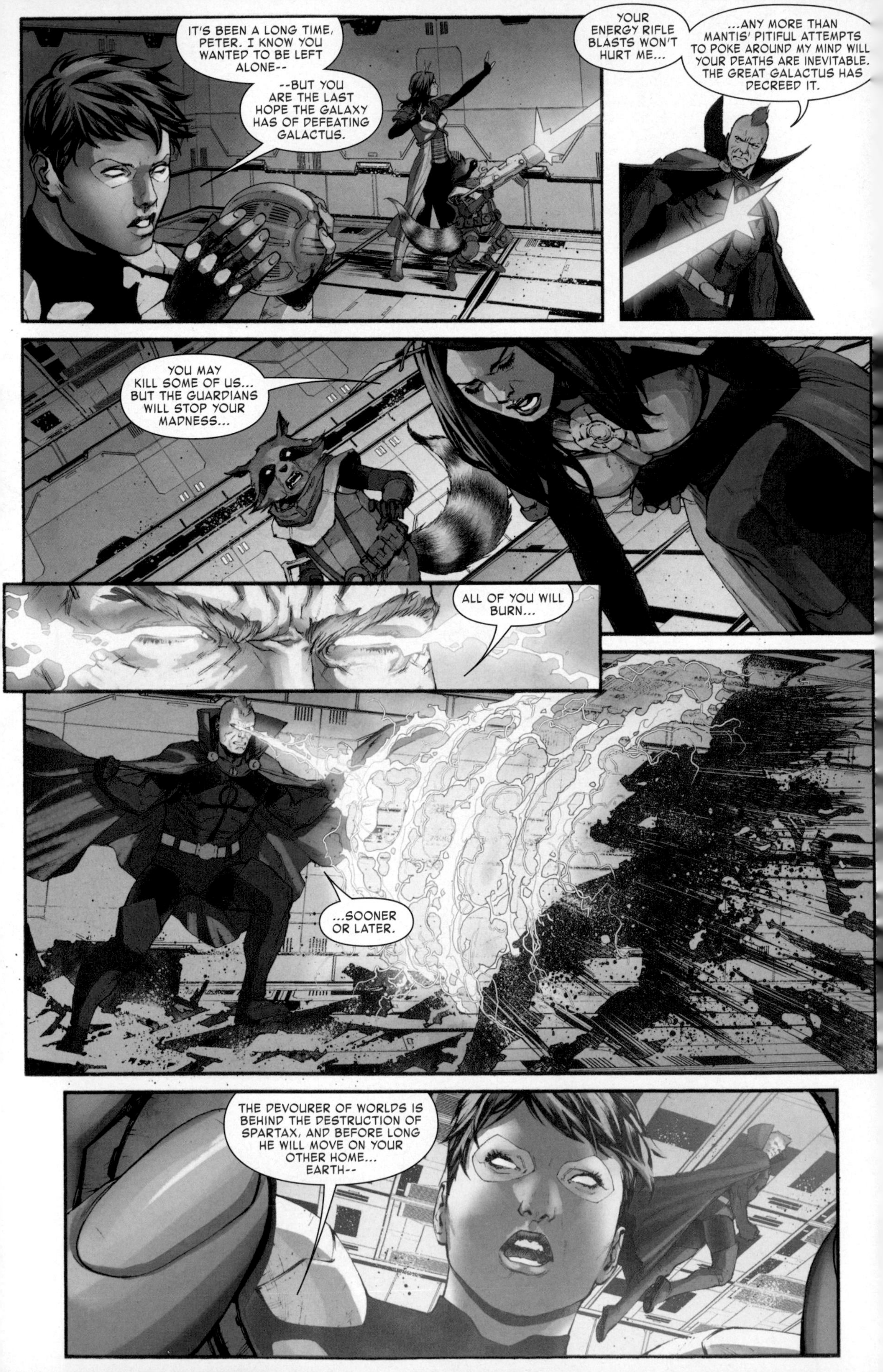
IT'S BEEN A LONG TIME, PETER. I KNOW YOU WANTED TO BE LEFT ALONE--
--BUT YOU ARE THE LAST HOPE THE GALAXY HAS OF DEFEATING GALACTUS.
YOUR ENERGY RIFLE BLASTS WON'T HURT ME...
...ANY MORE THAN MANTIS' PITIFUL ATTEMPTS TO POKE AROUND MY MIND WILL. YOUR DEATHS ARE INEVITABLE. THE GREAT GALACTUS HAS DECREED IT.
YOU MAY KILL SOME OF US... BUT THE GUARDIANS WILL STOP YOUR MADNESS...
ALL OF YOU WILL BURN...
...SOONER OR LATER.
THE DEVOURER OF WORLDS IS BEHIND THE DESTRUCTION OF SPARTAX, AND BEFORE LONG HE WILL MOVE ON YOUR OTHER HOME... EARTH--

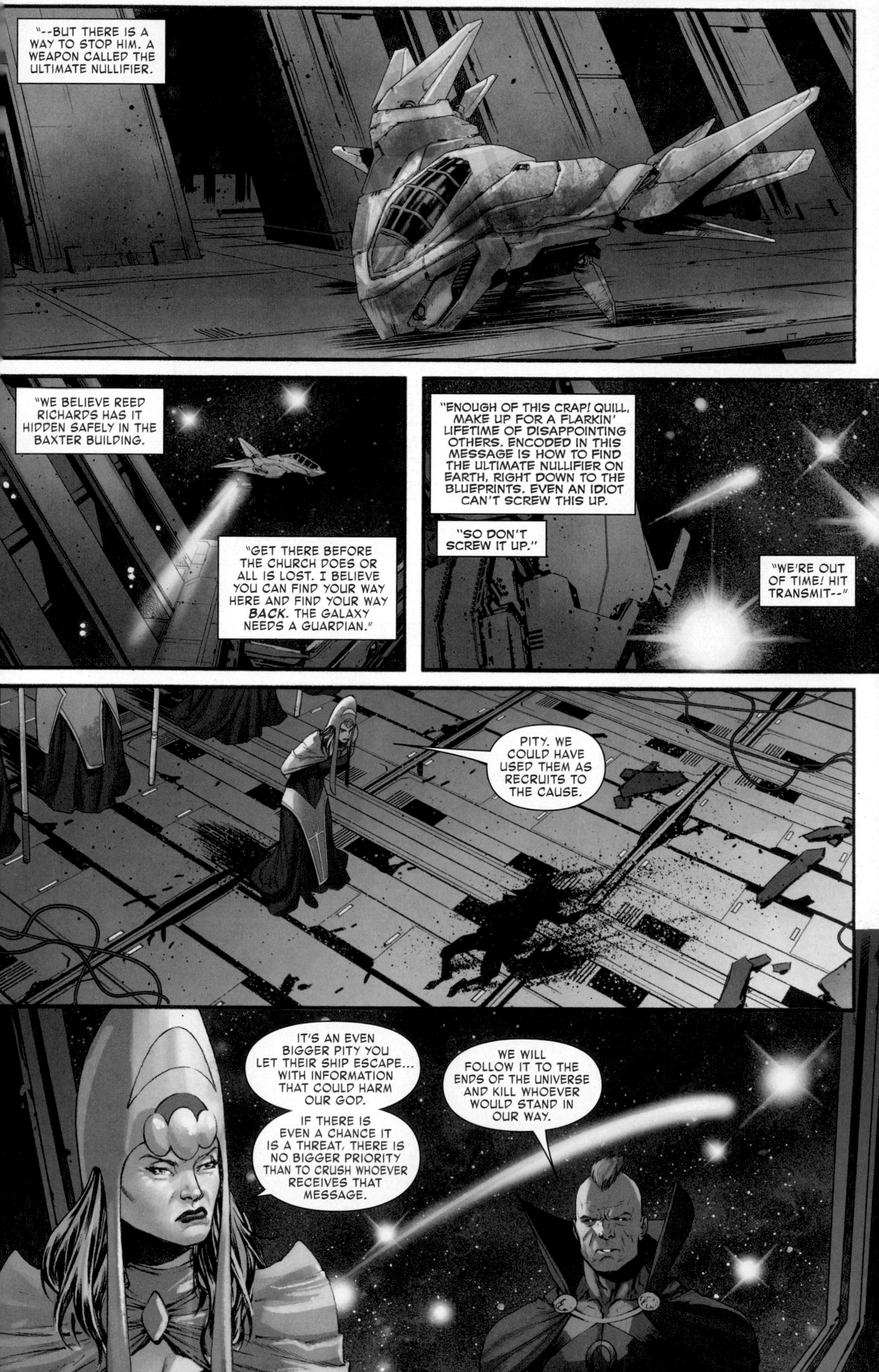
"--BUT THERE IS A WAY TO STOP HIM. A WEAPON CALLED THE ULTIMATE NULLIFIER.
"WE BELIEVE REED RICHARDS HAS IT HIDDEN SAFELY IN THE BAXTER BUILDING.
"GET THERE BEFORE THE CHURCH DOES OR ALL IS LOST. I BELIEVE YOU CAN FIND YOUR WAY HERE AND FIND YOUR WAY BACK. THE GALAXY NEEDS A GUARDIAN."
"ENOUGH OF THIS CRAP! QUILL, MAKE UP FOR A FLARKIN' LIFETIME OF DISAPPOINTING OTHERS. ENCODED IN THIS MESSAGE IS HOW TO FIND THE ULTIMATE NULLIFIER ON EARTH, RIGHT DOWN TO THE BLUEPRINTS. EVEN AN IDIOT CAN'T SCREW THIS UP.
"SO DON'T SCREW IT UP."
"WE'RE OUT OF TIME! HIT TRANSMIT--"
PITY. WE COULD HAVE USED THEM AS RECRUITS TO THE CAUSE.
IT'S AN EVEN BIGGER PITY YOU LET THEIR SHIP ESCAPE... WITH INFORMATION THAT COULD HARM OUR GOD.
IF THERE IS EVEN A CHANCE IT IS A THREAT, THERE IS NO BIGGER PRIORITY THAN TO CRUSH WHOEVER RECEIVES THAT MESSAGE.
WE WILL FOLLOW IT TO THE ENDS OF THE UNIVERSE AND KILL WHOEVER WOULD STAND IN OUR WAY.

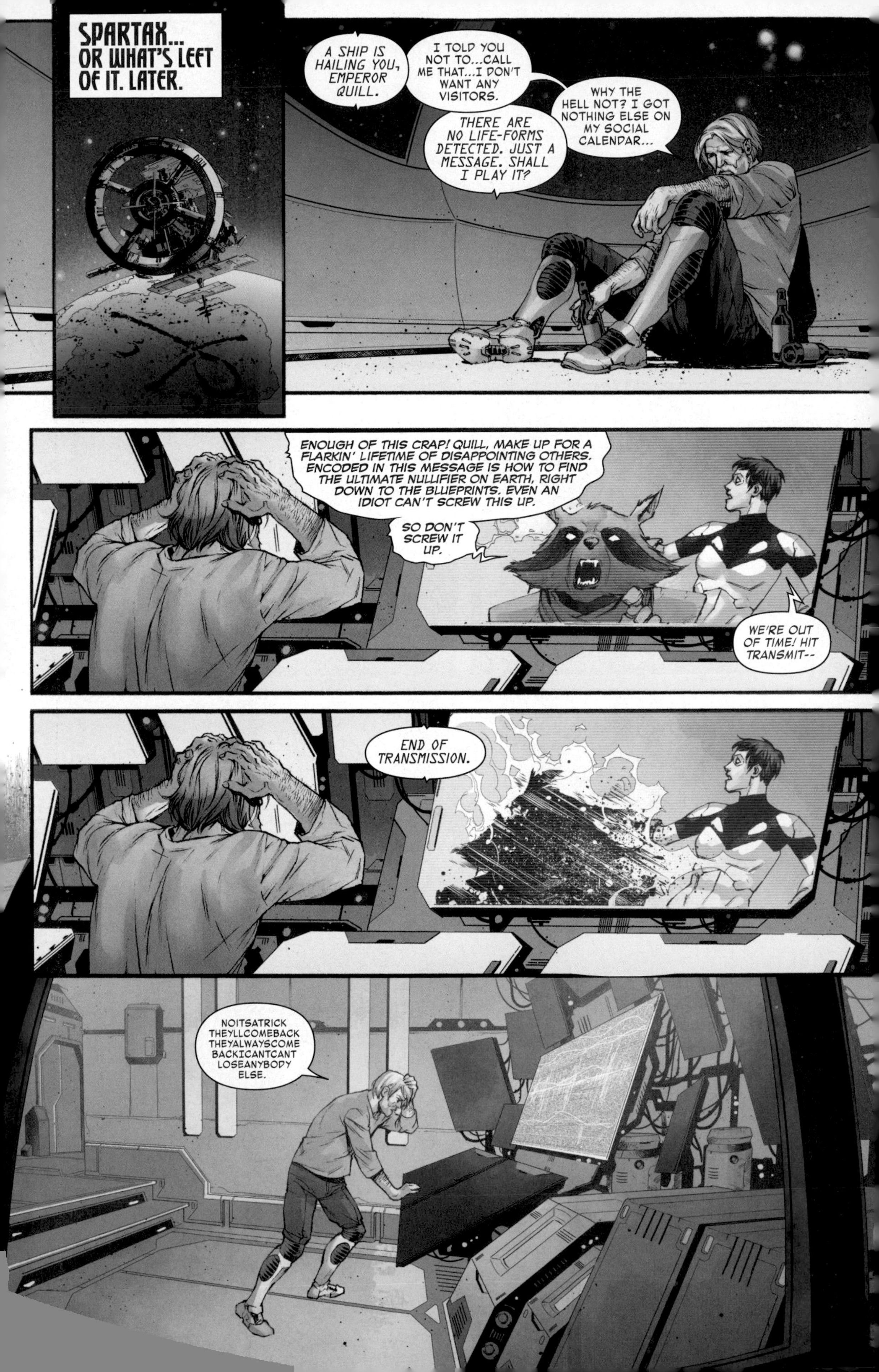

SPARTAX... OR WHAT'S LEFT OF IT. LATER.
A SHIP IS HAILING YOU, EMPEROR QUILL.
I TOLD YOU NOT TO...CALL ME THAT...I DON'T WANT ANY VISITORS.
THERE ARE NO LIFE-FORMS DETECTED. JUST A MESSAGE. SHALL I PLAY IT?
WHY THE HELL NOT? I GOT NOTHING ELSE ON MY SOCIAL CALENDAR...
ENOUGH OF THIS CRAP! QUILL, MAKE UP FOR A FLARKIN' LIFETIME OF DISAPPOINTING OTHERS. ENCODED IN THIS MESSAGE IS HOW TO FIND THE ULTIMATE NULLIFIER ON EARTH, RIGHT DOWN TO THE BLUEPRINTS. EVEN AN IDIOT CAN'T SCREW THIS UP.
SO DON'T SCREW IT UP.
WE'RE OUT OF TIME! HIT TRANSMIT--
END OF TRANSMISSION.
NOITSATRICK THEYLLCOMEBACK THEYALWAYSCOME BACKICANTCANT LOSEANYBODY ELSE.

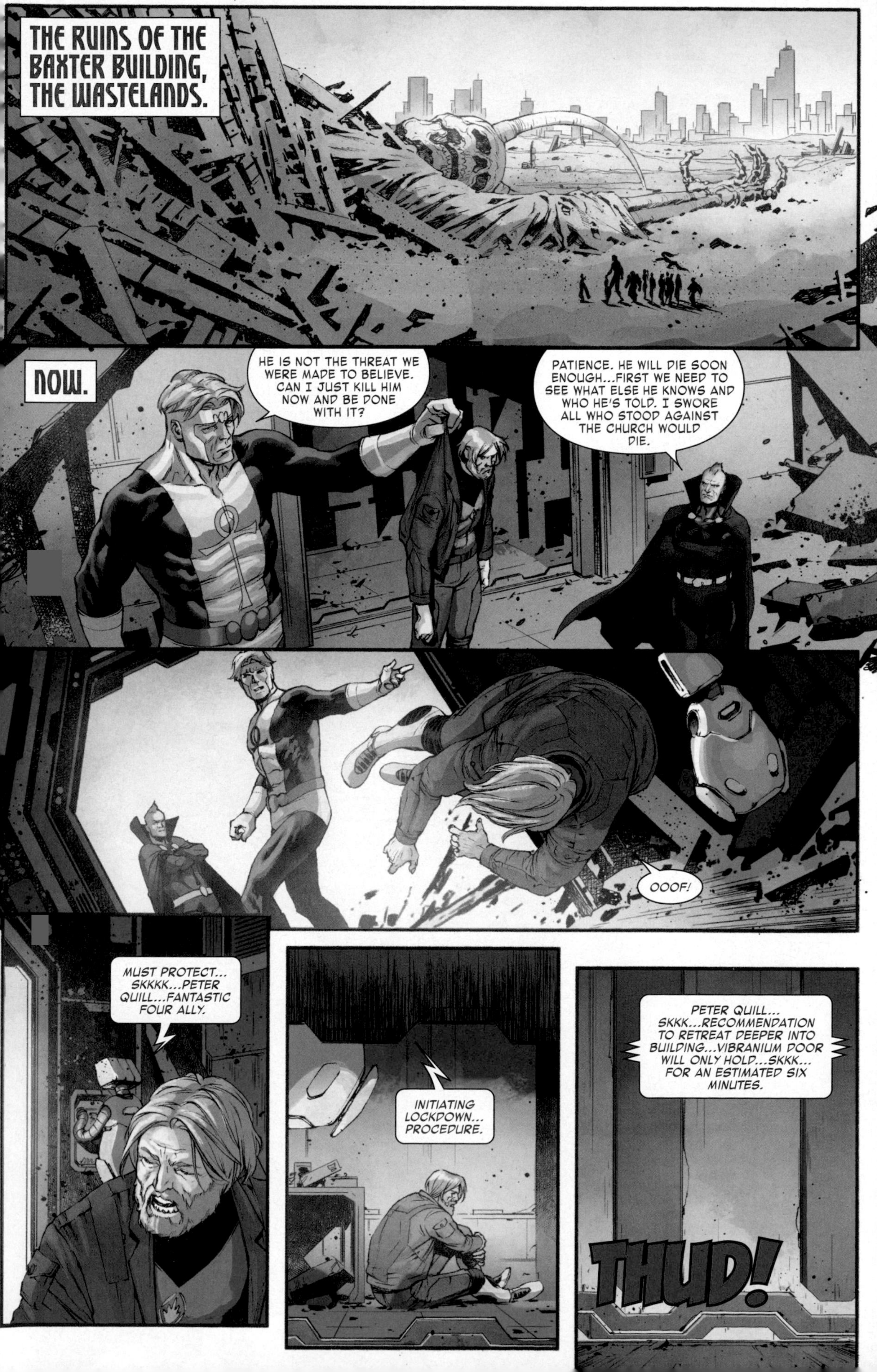
THE RUINS OF THE BAXTER BUILDING, THE WASTELANDS.
NOW.
HE IS NOT THE THREAT WE WERE MADE TO BELIEVE. CAN I JUST KILL HIM NOW AND BE DONE WITH IT?
PATIENCE. HE WILL DIE SOON ENOUGH...FIRST WE NEED TO SEE WHAT ELSE HE KNOWS AND WHO HE'S TOLD. I SWORE ALL WHO STOOD AGAINST THE CHURCH WOULD DIE.
OOOF!
MUST PROTECT... SKKKK...PETER QUILL...FANTASTIC FOUR ALLY.
INITIATING LOCKDOWN... PROCEDURE.
PETER QUILL... SKKK...RECOMMENDATION TO RETREAT DEEPER INTO BUILDING...VIBRANIUM DOOR WILL ONLY HOLD...SKKK... FOR AN ESTIMATED SIX MINUTES.
THUD!

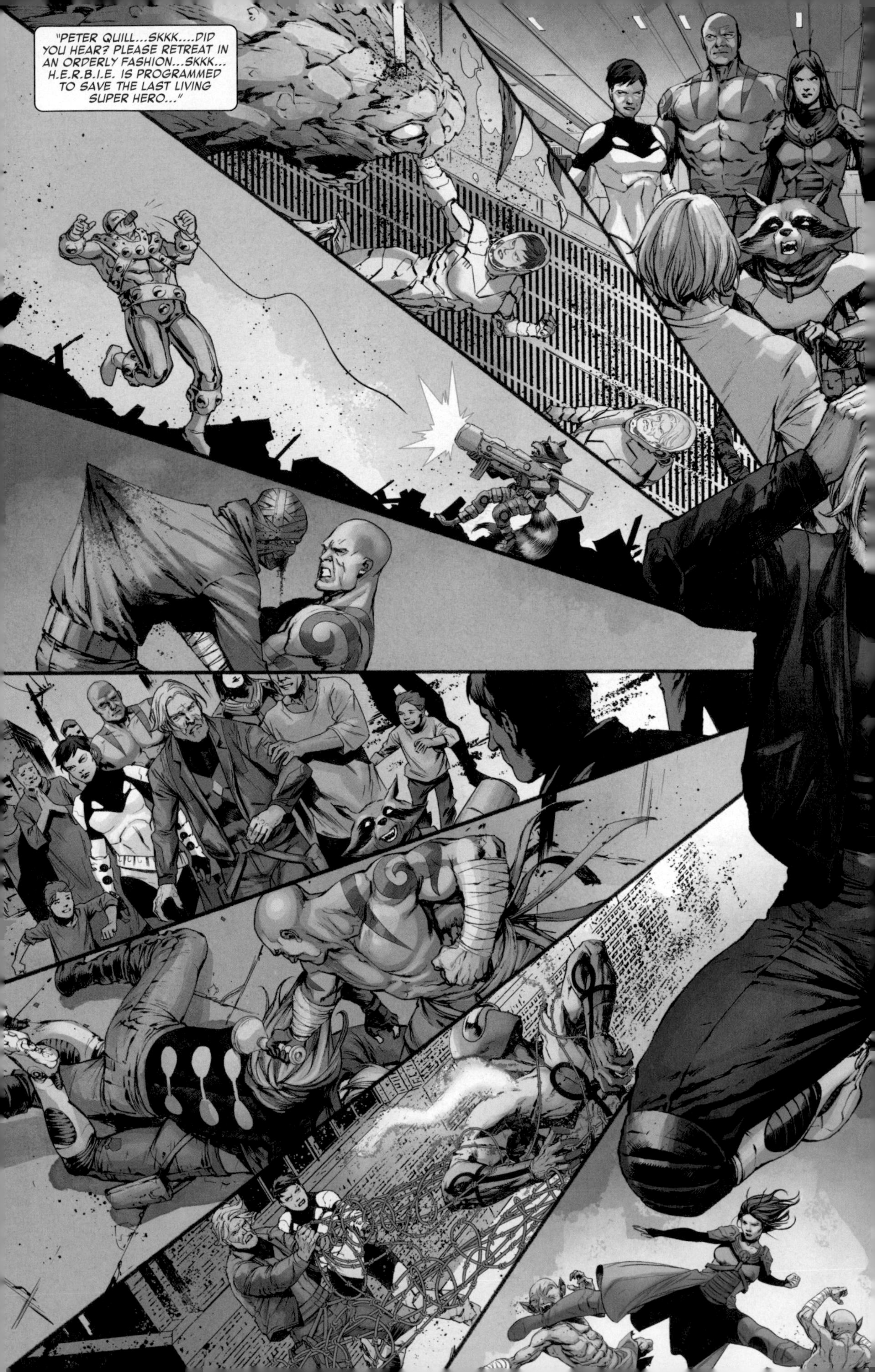
"PETER QUILL...SKKK....DID YOU HEAR? PLEASE RETREAT IN AN ORDERLY FASHION...SKKK... H.E.R.B.I.E. IS PROGRAMMED TO SAVE THE LAST LIVING SUPER HERO..."

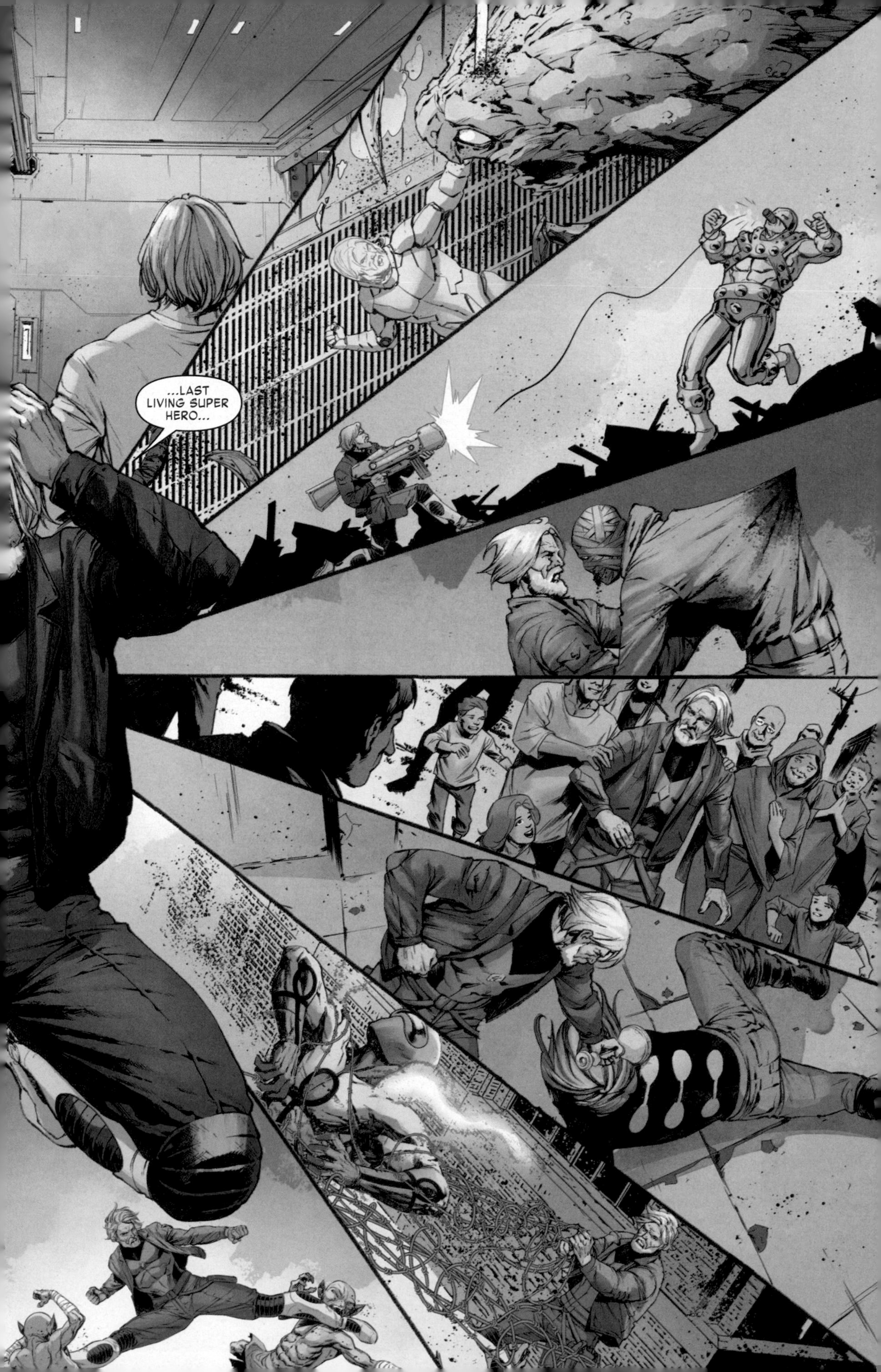
...LAST LIVING SUPER HERO...

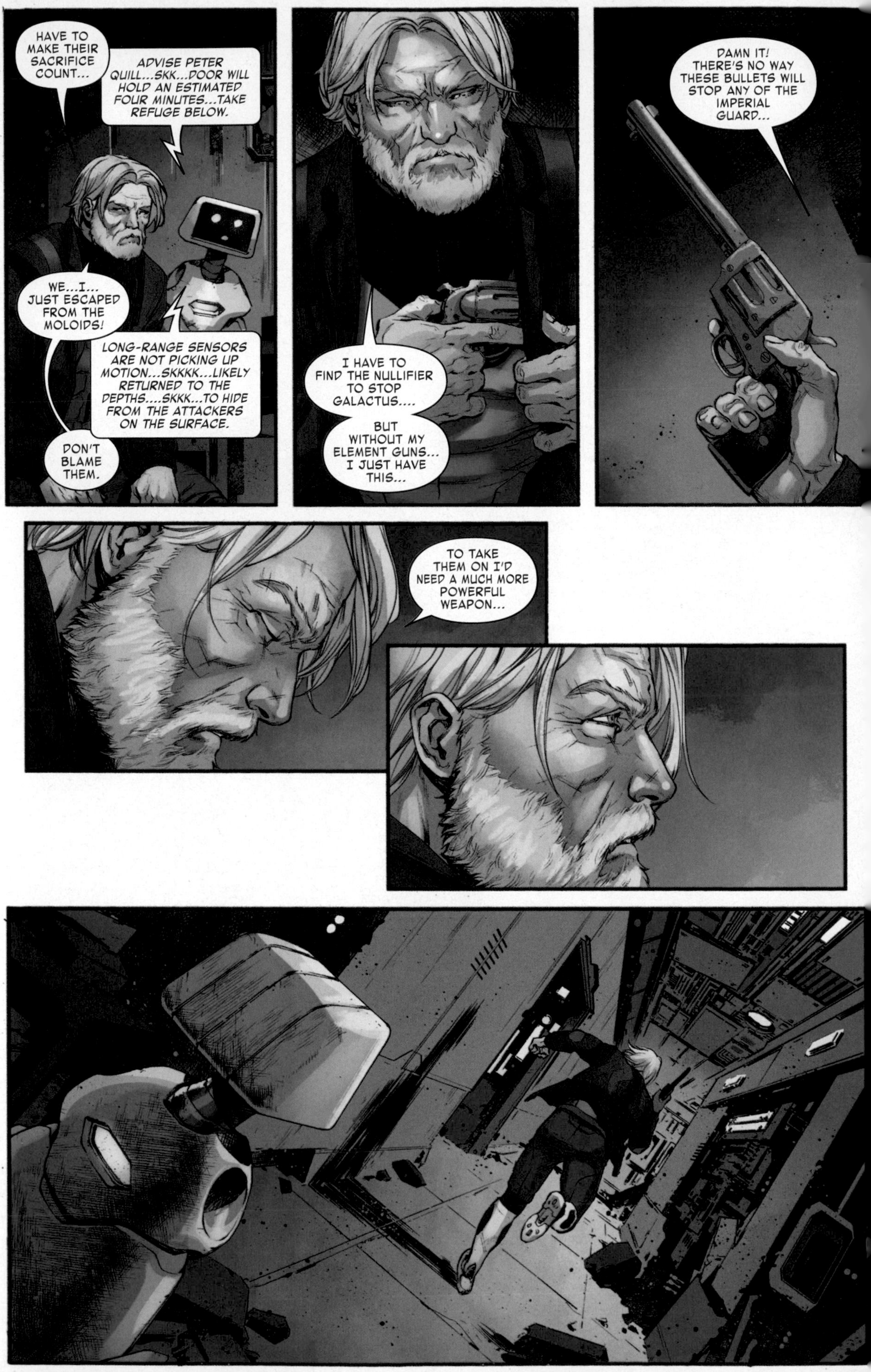
HAVE TO MAKE THEIR SACRIFICE COUNT...
ADVISE PETER QUILL...SKK...DOOR WILL HOLD AN ESTIMATED FOUR MINUTES...TAKE REFUGE BELOW.
WE...I... JUST ESCAPED FROM THE MOLOIDS!
LONG-RANGE SENSORS ARE NOT PICKING UP MOTION...SKKKK...LIKELY RETURNED TO THE DEPTHS....SKKK...TO HIDE FROM THE ATTACKERS ON THE SURFACE.
DON'T BLAME THEM.
I HAVE TO FIND THE NULLIFIER TO STOP GALACTUS....
BUT WITHOUT MY ELEMENT GUNS... I JUST HAVE THIS...
DAMN IT! THERE'S NO WAY THESE BULLETS WILL STOP ANY OF THE IMPERIAL GUARD...
TO TAKE THEM ON I'D NEED A MUCH MORE POWERFUL WEAPON...

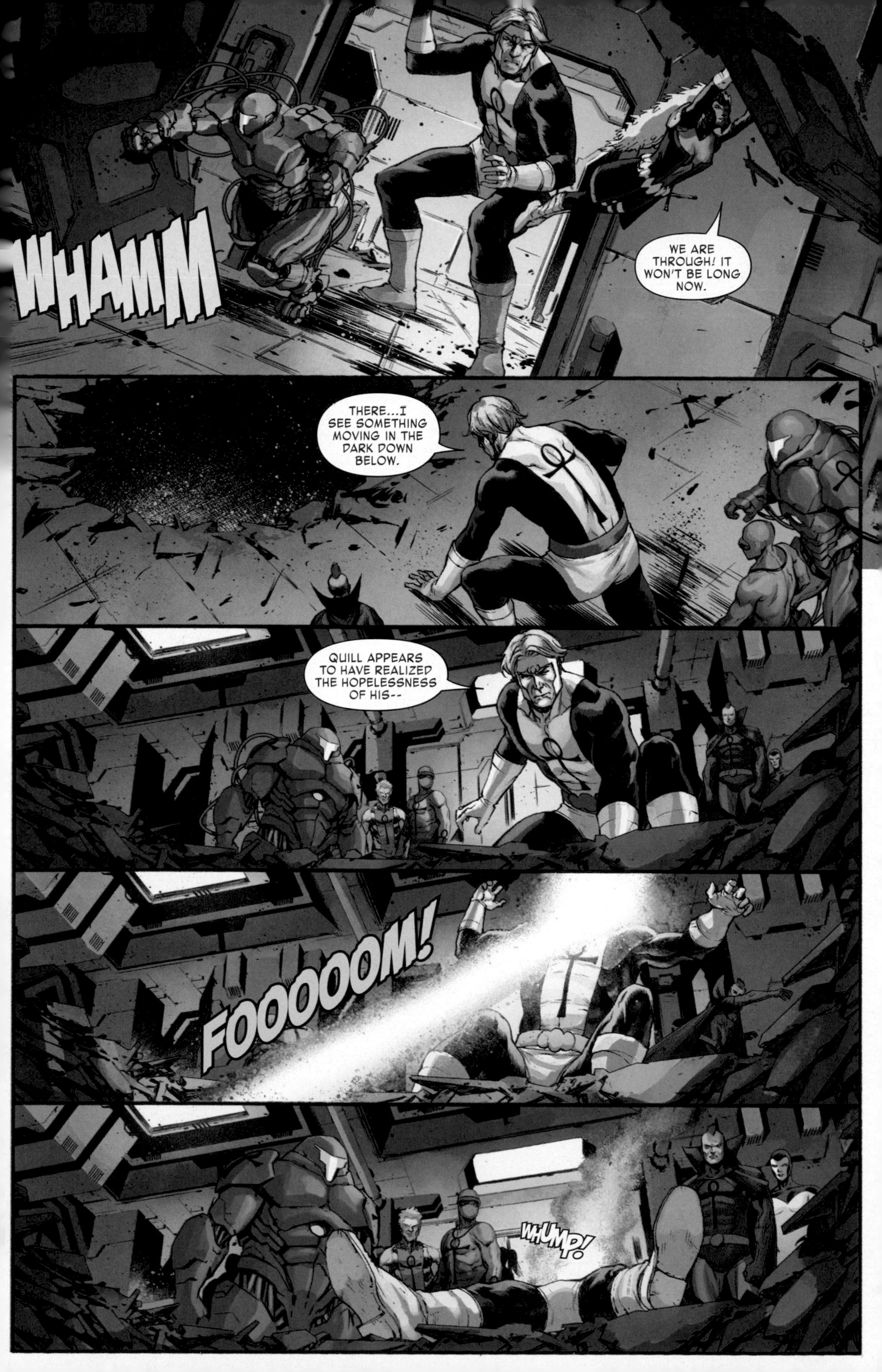
WHAMM
WE ARE THROUGH! IT WON'T BE LONG NOW.
THERE...I SEE SOMETHING MOVING IN THE DARK DOWN BELOW.
QUILL APPEARS TO HAVE REALIZED THE HOPELESSNESS OF HIS--
FOOOOOM!
WHUMP!

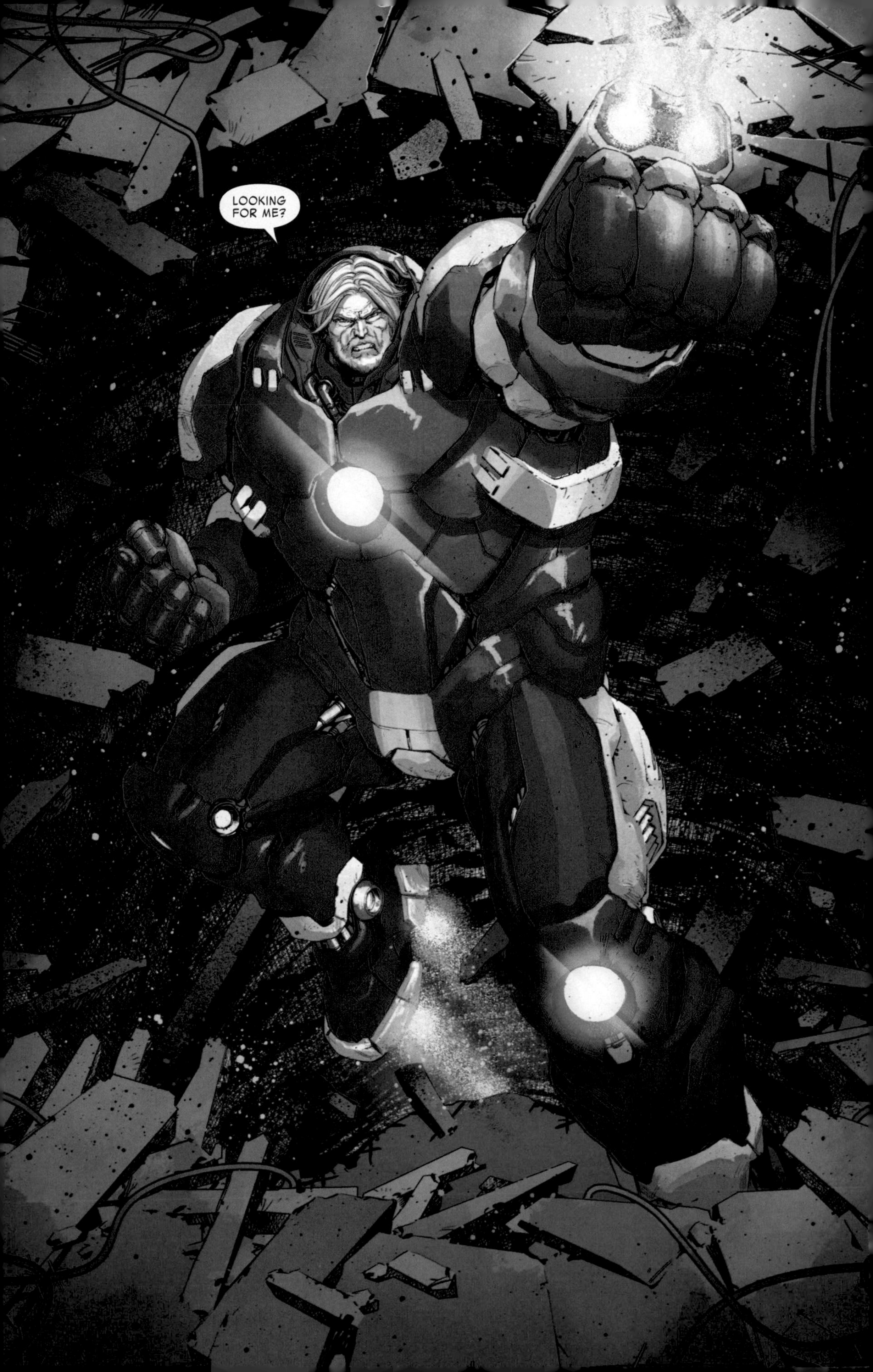
LOOKING FOR ME?

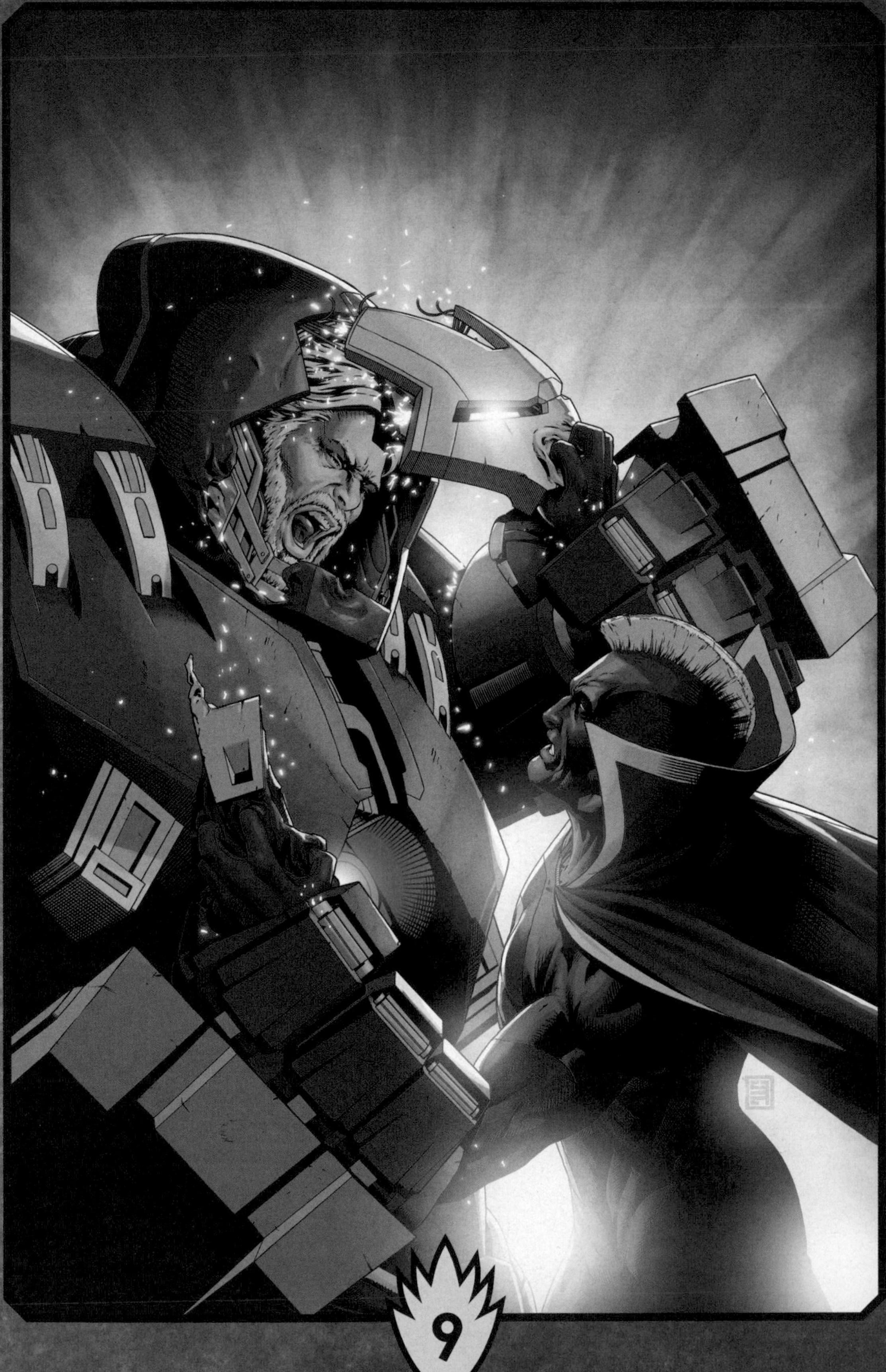

9

"GO YOUR OWN WAY"

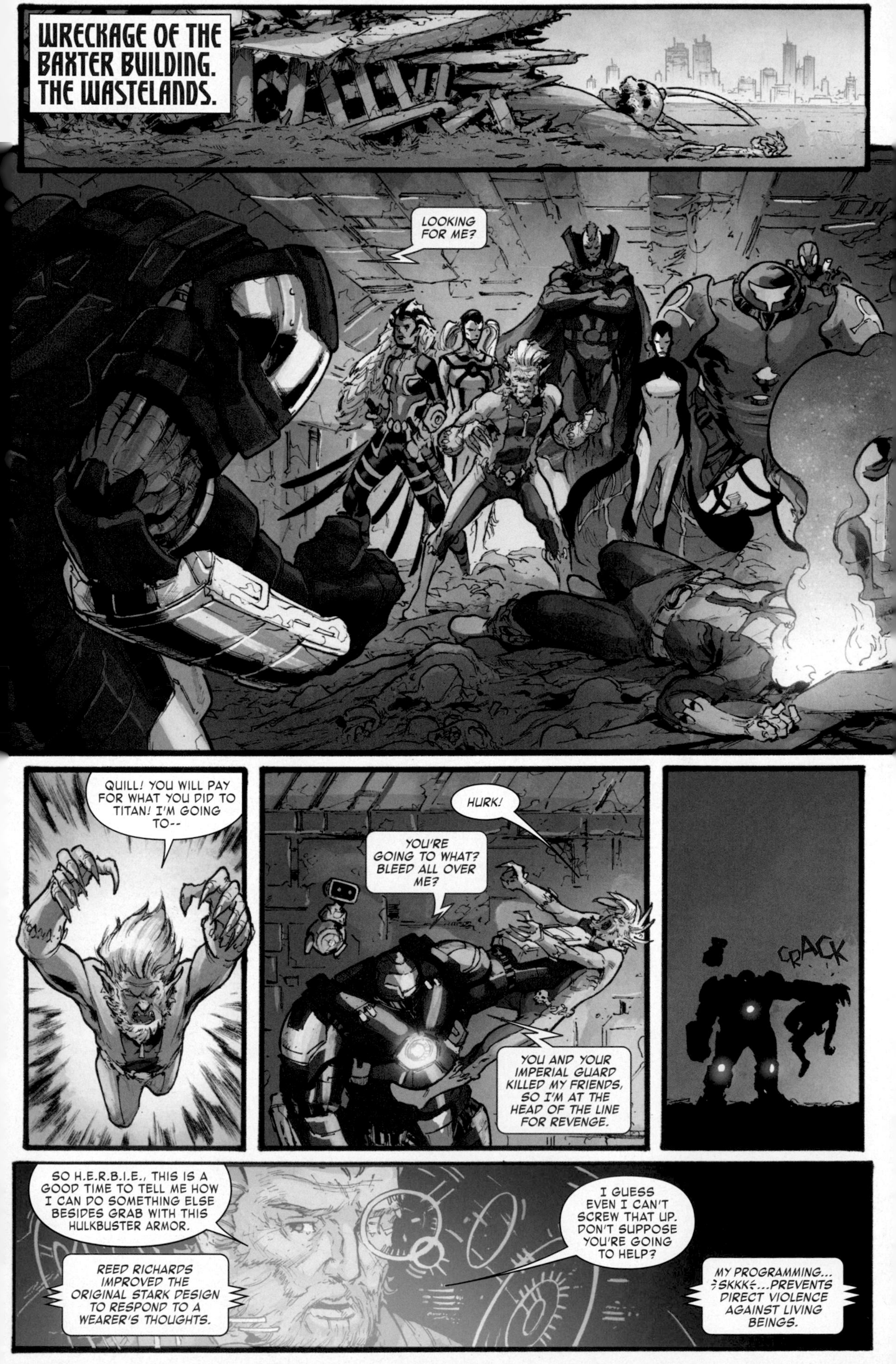

WRECKAGE OF THE BAXTER BUILDING. THE WASTELANDS.
LOOKING FOR ME?
QUILL! YOU WILL PAY FOR WHAT YOU DID TO TITAN! I'M GOING TO--
HURK!
YOU'RE GOING TO WHAT? BLEED ALL OVER ME?
YOU AND YOUR IMPERIAL GUARD KILLED MY FRIENDS, SO I'M AT THE HEAD OF THE LINE FOR REVENGE.
CRACK
SO H.E.R.B.I.E., THIS IS A GOOD TIME TO TELL ME HOW I CAN DO SOMETHING ELSE BESIDES GRAB WITH THIS HULKBUSTER ARMOR.
REED RICHARDS IMPROVED THE ORIGINAL STARK DESIGN TO RESPOND TO A WEARER'S THOUGHTS.
I GUESS EVEN I CAN'T SCREW THAT UP. DON'T SUPPOSE YOU'RE GOING TO HELP?
MY PROGRAMMING... SKKK...PREVENTS DIRECT VIOLENCE AGAINST LIVING BEINGS.

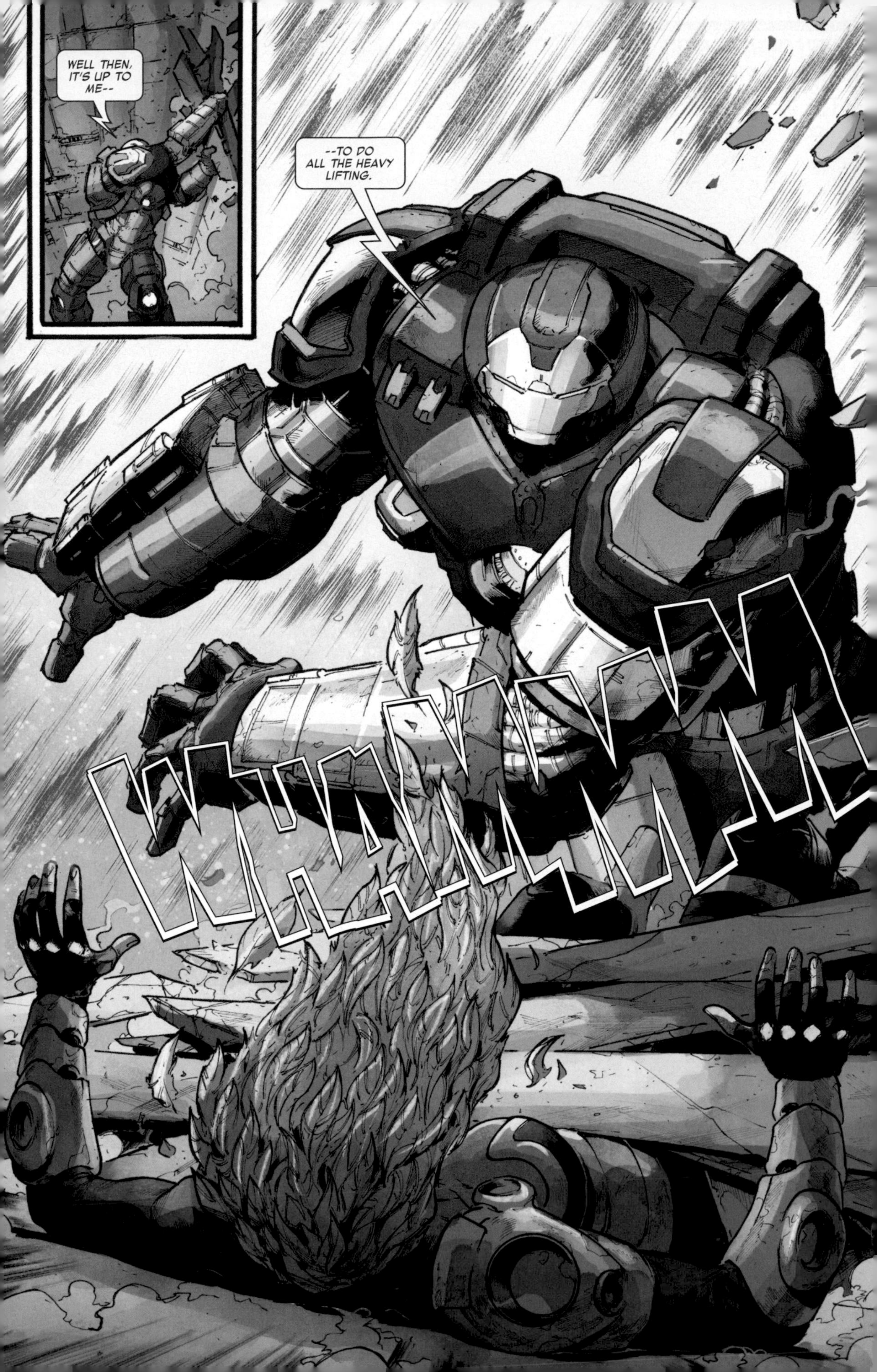
WELL THEN, IT'S UP TO ME--
--TO DO ALL THE HEAVY LIFTING.
WHAMMM

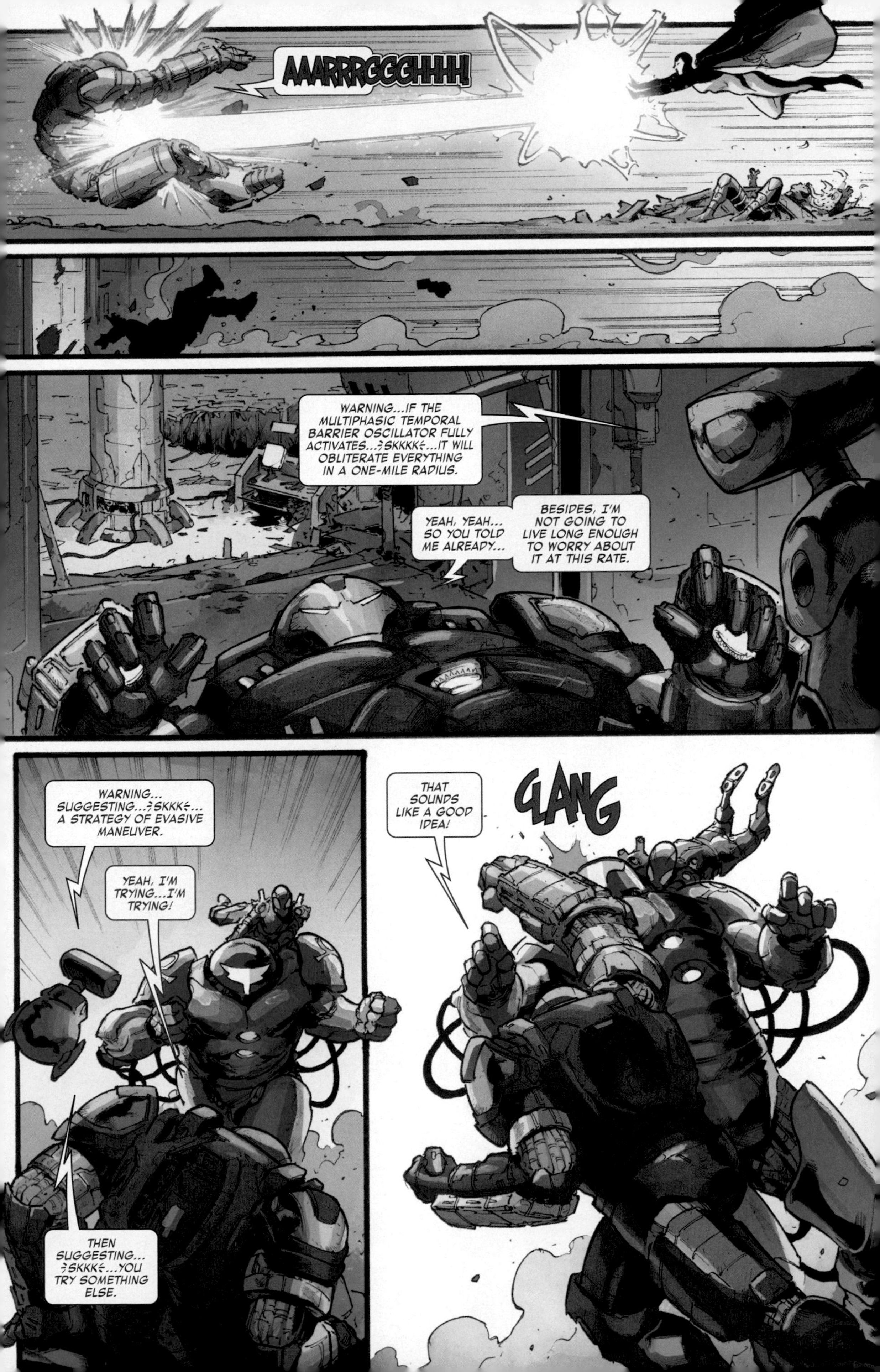
AAARRRGGGHHH!
WARNING...IF THE MULTIPHASIC TEMPORAL BARRIER OSCILLATOR FULLY ACTIVATES...>SKKKK<...IT WILL OBLITERATE EVERYTHING IN A ONE-MILE RADIUS.
YEAH, YEAH... SO YOU TOLD ME ALREADY...
BESIDES, I'M NOT GOING TO LIVE LONG ENOUGH TO WORRY ABOUT IT AT THIS RATE.
WARNING... SUGGESTING...>SKKK<... A STRATEGY OF EVASIVE MANEUVER.
YEAH, I'M TRYING...I'M TRYING!
THEN SUGGESTING... >SKKK<...YOU TRY SOMETHING ELSE.
THAT SOUNDS LIKE A GOOD IDEA!
CLANG

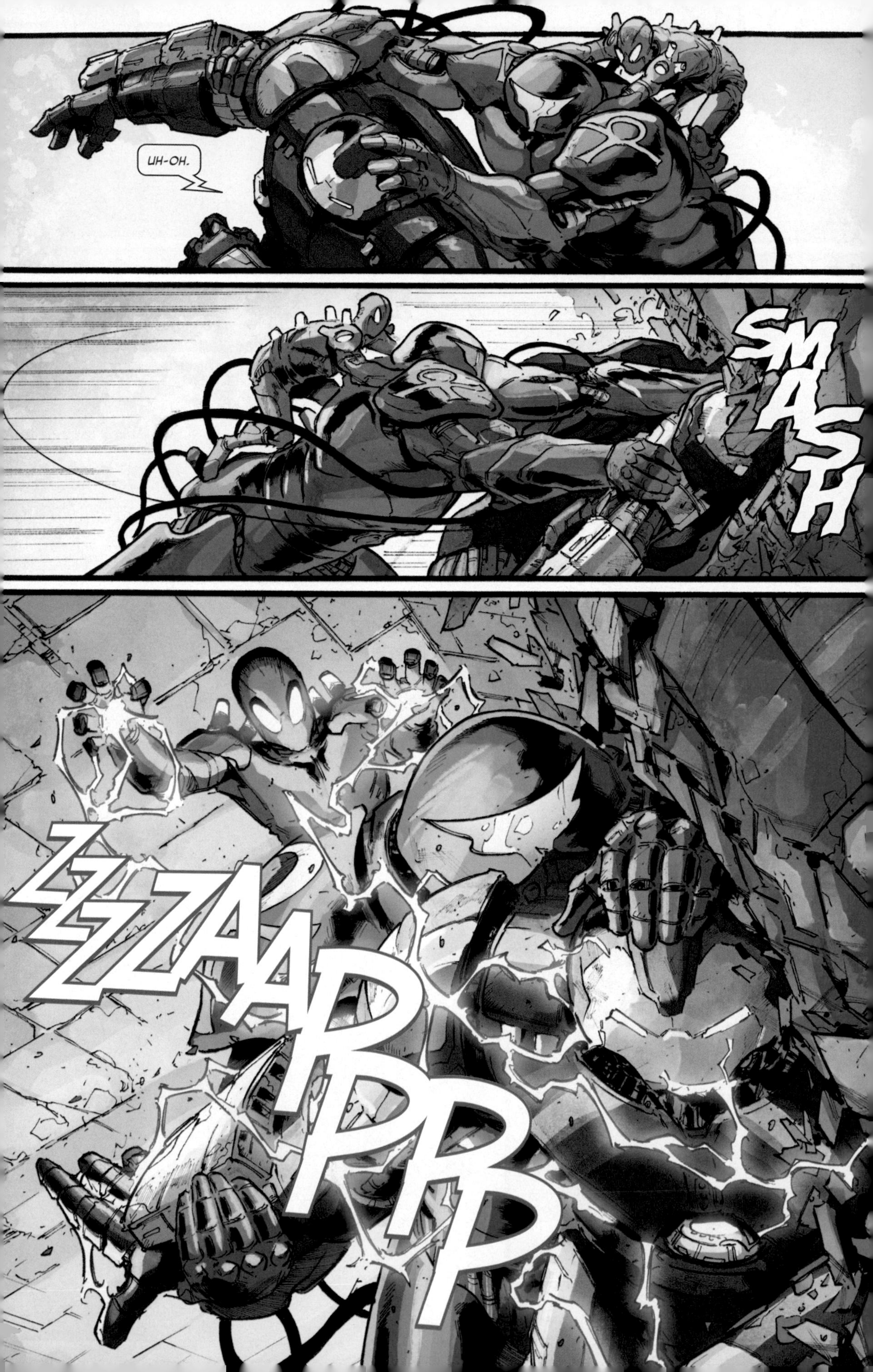
UH-OH.
SMASH
ZZZAAPPP

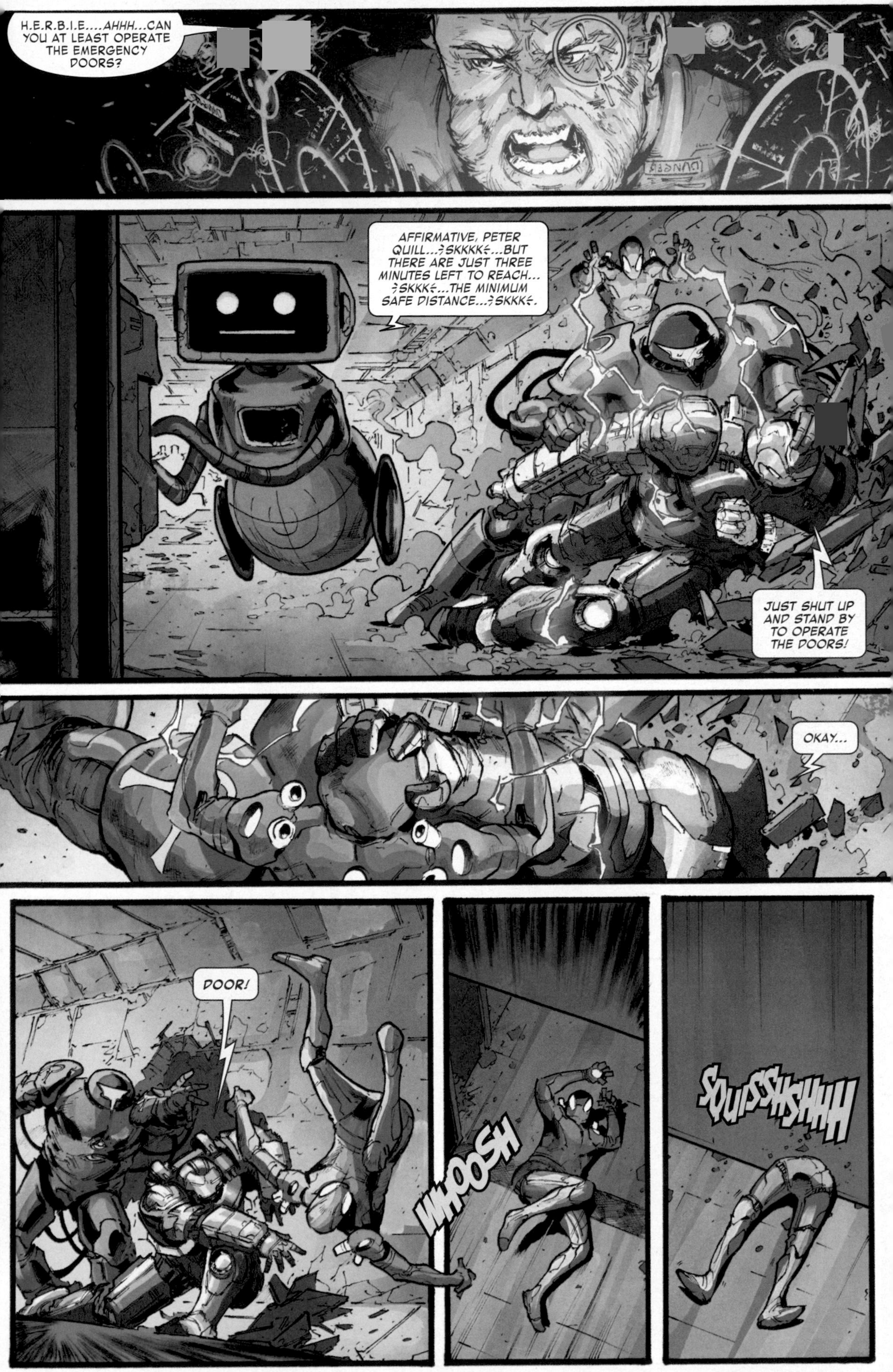

H.E.R.B.I.E....AHHH...CAN YOU AT LEAST OPERATE THE EMERGENCY DOORS?
AFFIRMATIVE, PETER QUILL...SKKKK...BUT THERE ARE JUST THREE MINUTES LEFT TO REACH...SKKK...THE MINIMUM SAFE DISTANCE...SKKK.
JUST SHUT UP AND STAND BY TO OPERATE THE DOORS!
OKAY...
DOOR!
WHOOSH
SQUISSHSHHH

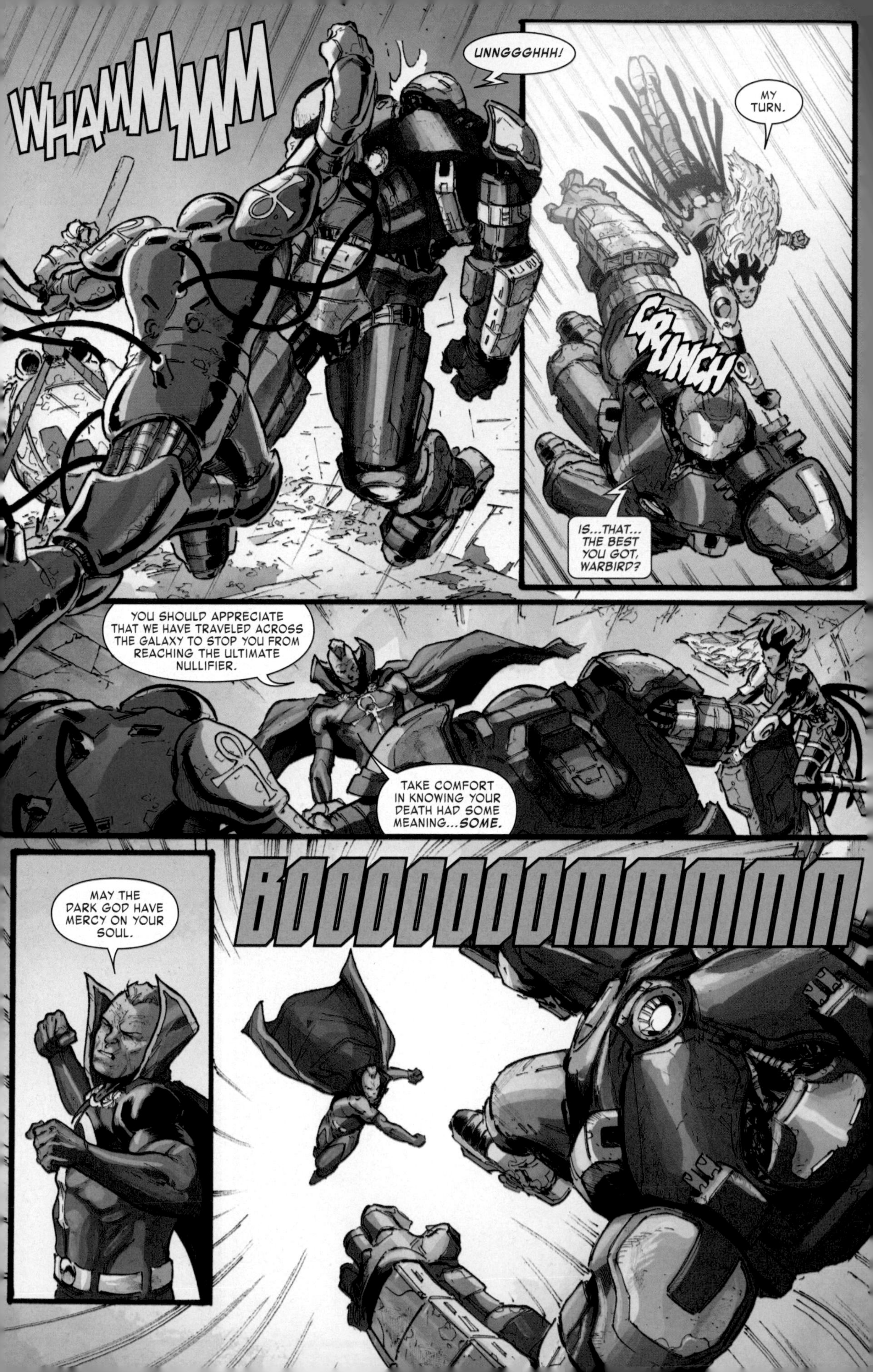
WHAMMMMM
UNNGGGHHH!
MY TURN.
CRUNCH
IS...THAT... THE BEST YOU GOT, WARBIRD?
YOU SHOULD APPRECIATE THAT WE HAVE TRAVELED ACROSS THE GALAXY TO STOP YOU FROM REACHING THE ULTIMATE NULLIFIER.
TAKE COMFORT IN KNOWING YOUR DEATH HAD SOME MEANING...SOME.
MAY THE DARK GOD HAVE MERCY ON YOUR SOUL.
BOOOOOOOMMMMMM

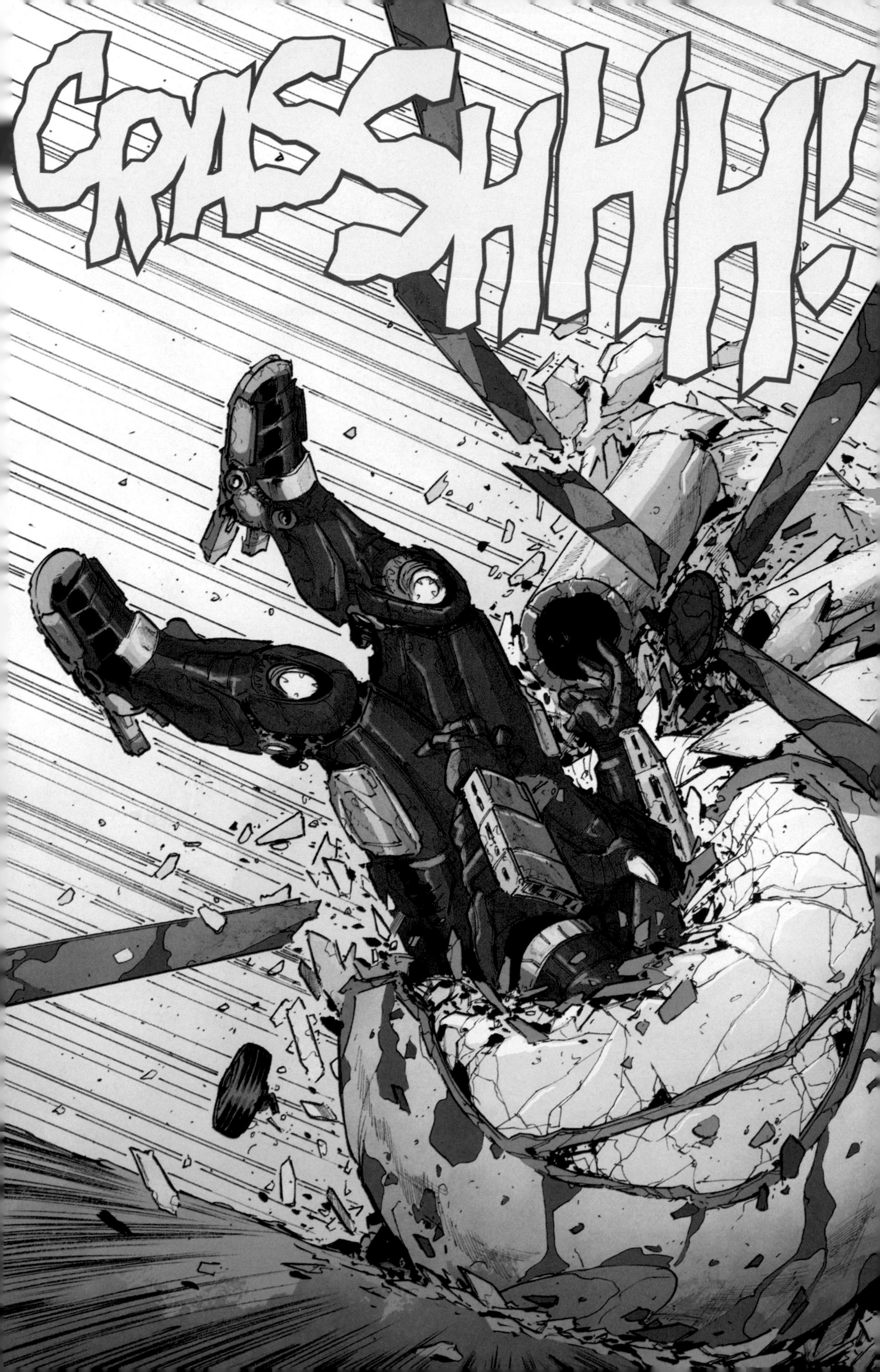
CRASSHHH!

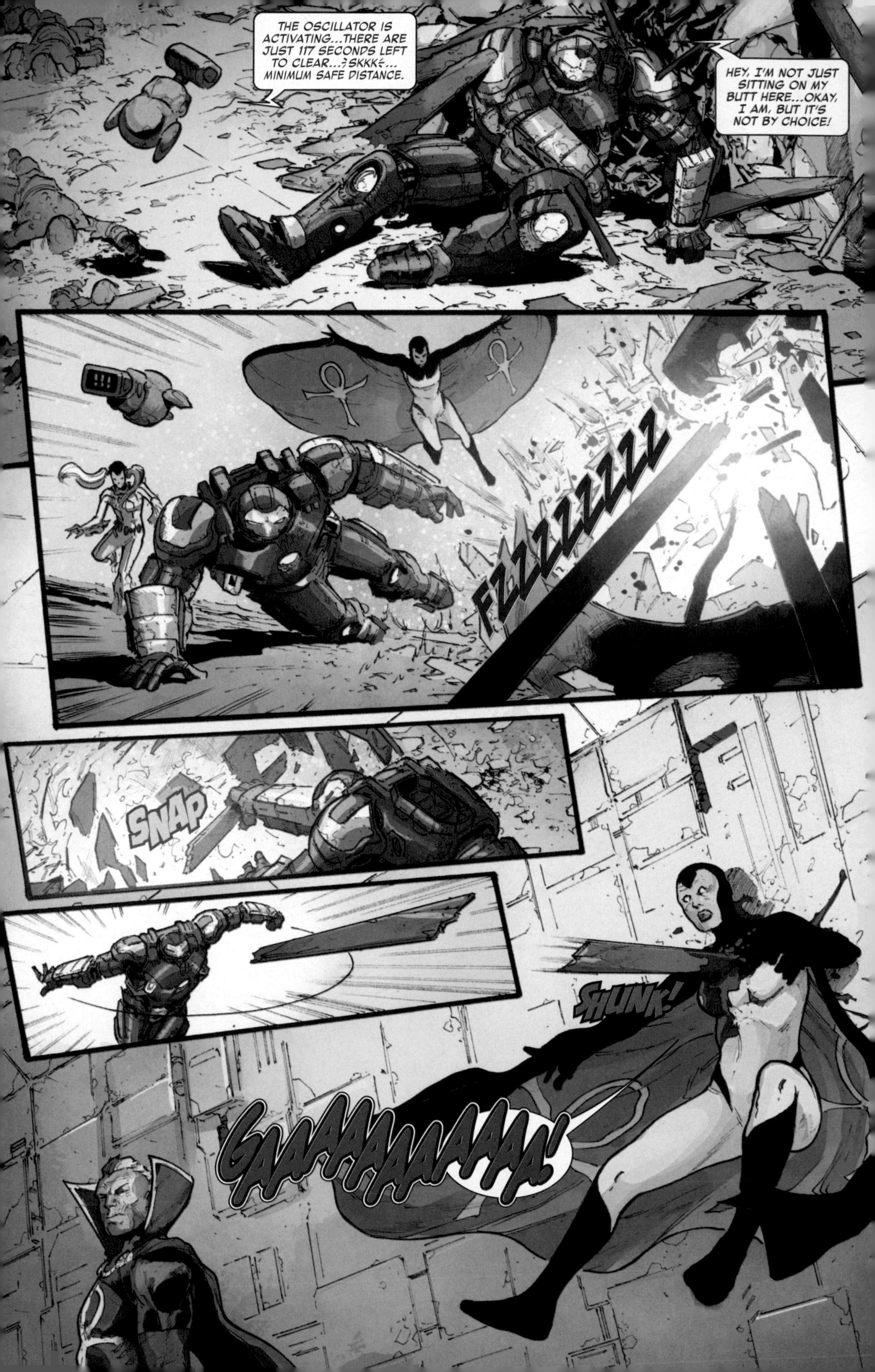
THE OSCILLATOR IS ACTIVATING...THERE ARE JUST 117 SECONDS LEFT TO CLEAR...ƒSKKKƒ... MINIMUM SAFE DISTANCE.
HEY, I'M NOT JUST SITTING ON MY BUTT HERE...OKAY, I AM, BUT IT'S NOT BY CHOICE!
FZZZZZZZZZ
SNAP
SHUNK!
GAAAAAAAAAAA!

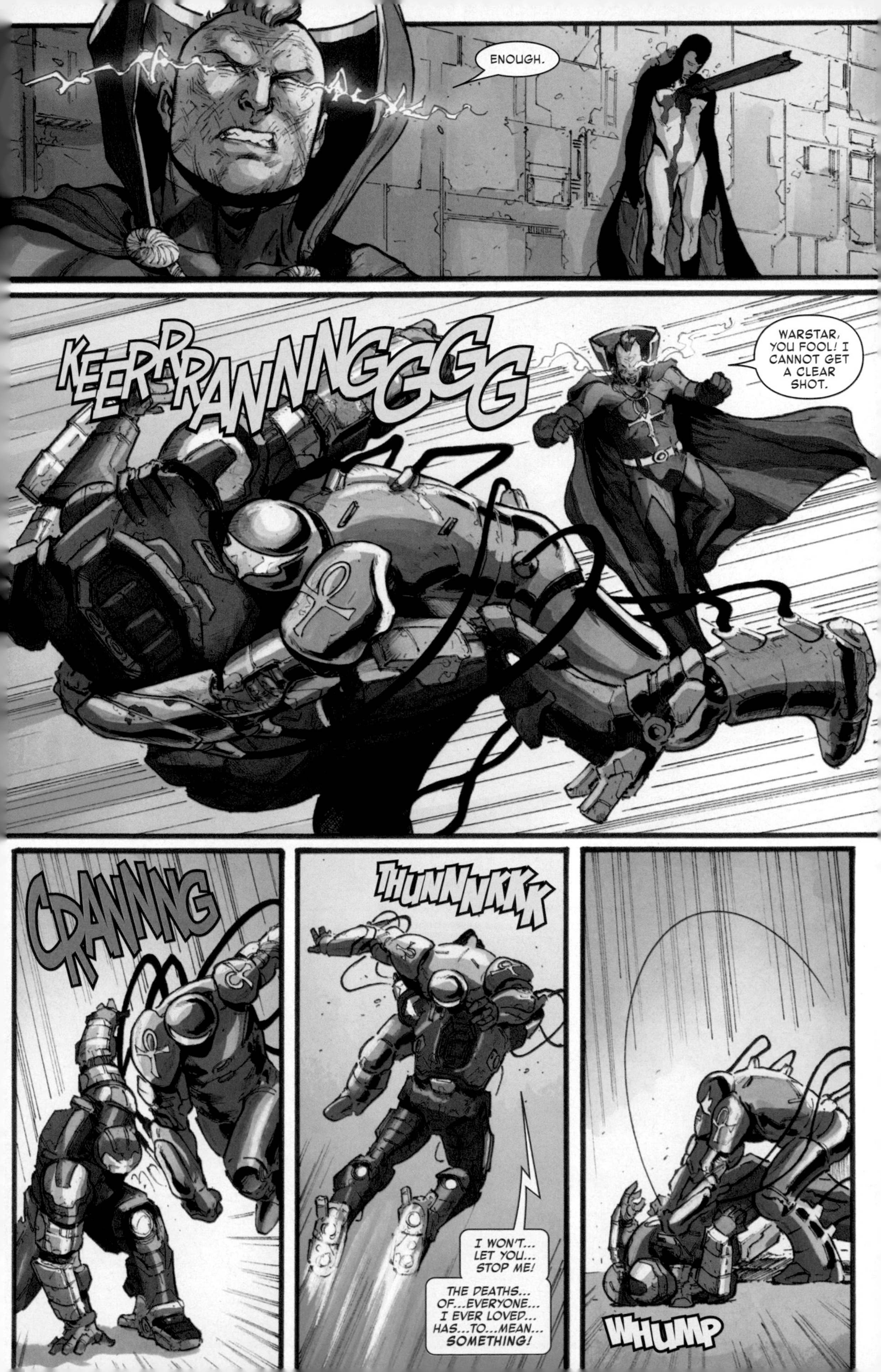
ENOUGH.
KEERRRANNNGGGG
WARSTAR, YOU FOOL! I CANNOT GET A CLEAR SHOT.
CRANNNG
THUNNNKKK
I WON'T... LET YOU... STOP ME!
THE DEATHS... OF...EVERYONE... I EVER LOVED... HAS...TO...MEAN... SOMETHING!
WHUMP

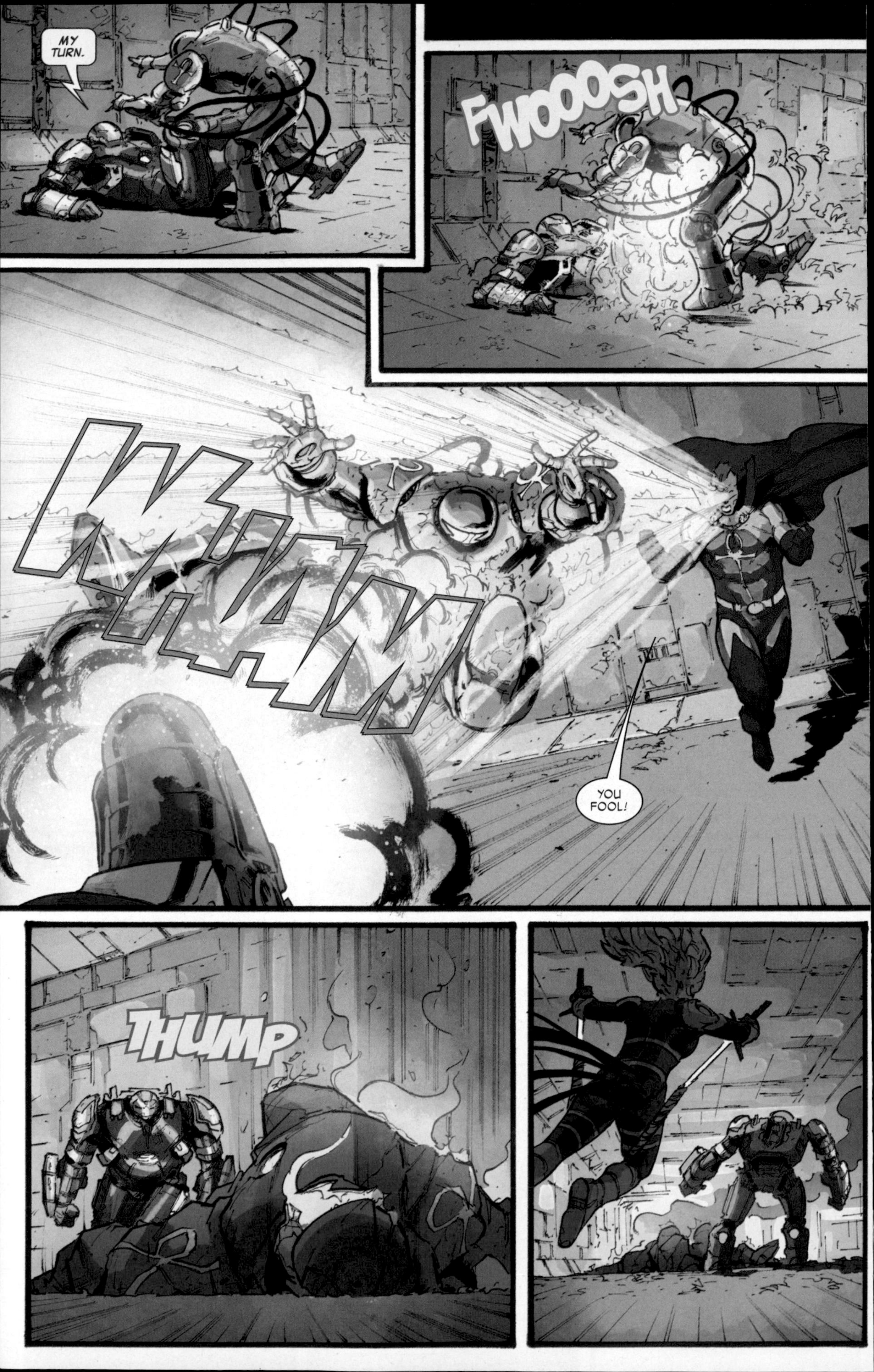
MY TURN.
FWOOOSH
WHAM
YOU FOOL!
THUMP

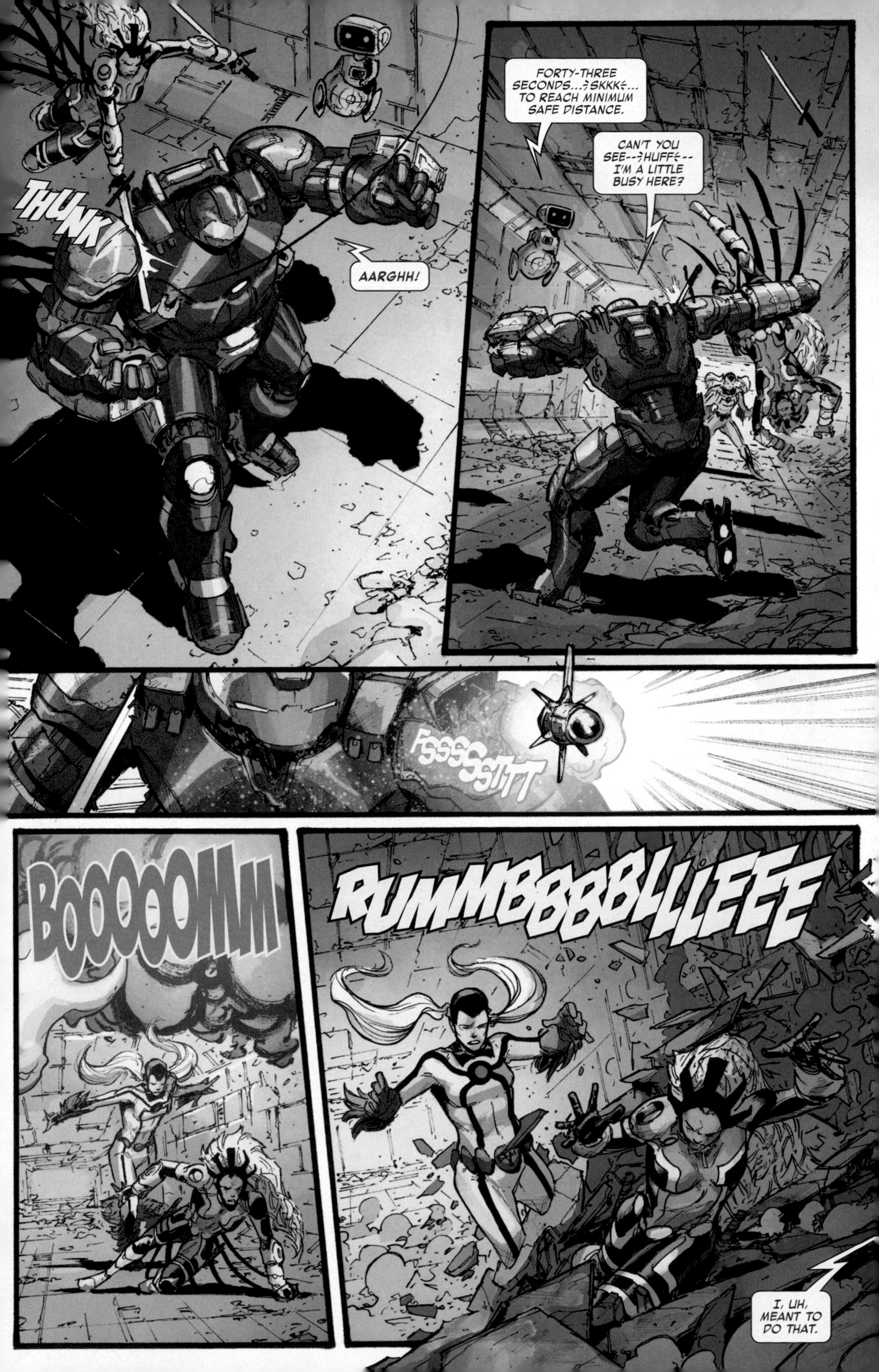
THUNK
AARGHH!
FORTY-THREE SECONDS...⟩SKKK⟨... TO REACH MINIMUM SAFE DISTANCE.
CAN'T YOU SEE--⟩HUFF⟨-- I'M A LITTLE BUSY HERE?
FSSSSSTTT
BOOOOOMM
RUMMBBBBLLEEE
I, UH, MEANT TO DO THAT.

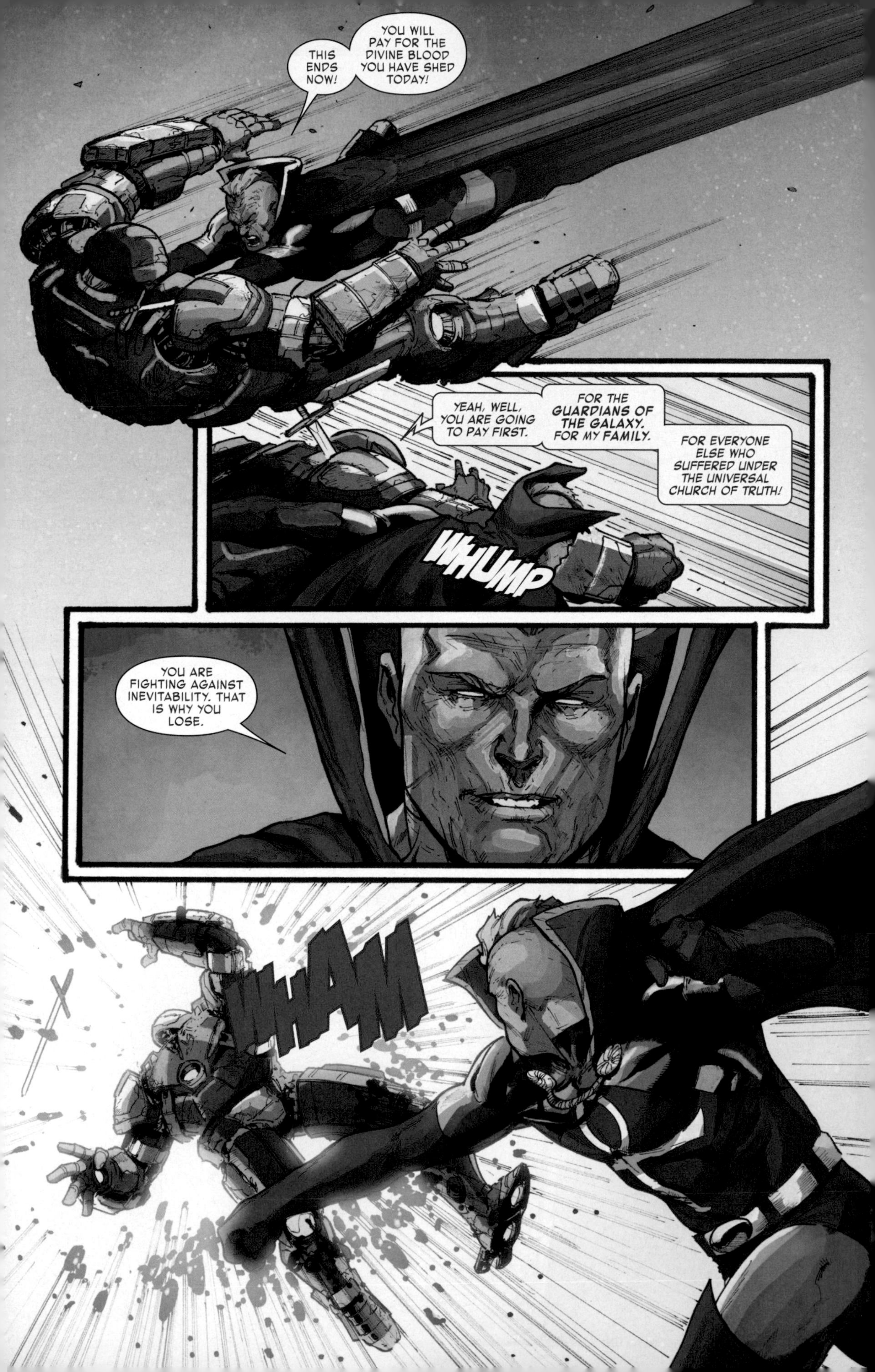
THIS ENDS NOW!
YOU WILL PAY FOR THE DIVINE BLOOD YOU HAVE SHED TODAY!
YEAH, WELL, YOU ARE GOING TO PAY FIRST.
FOR THE GUARDIANS OF THE GALAXY. FOR MY FAMILY.
FOR EVERYONE ELSE WHO SUFFERED UNDER THE UNIVERSAL CHURCH OF TRUTH!
WHUMP
YOU ARE FIGHTING AGAINST INEVITABILITY. THAT IS WHY YOU LOSE.
WHAM

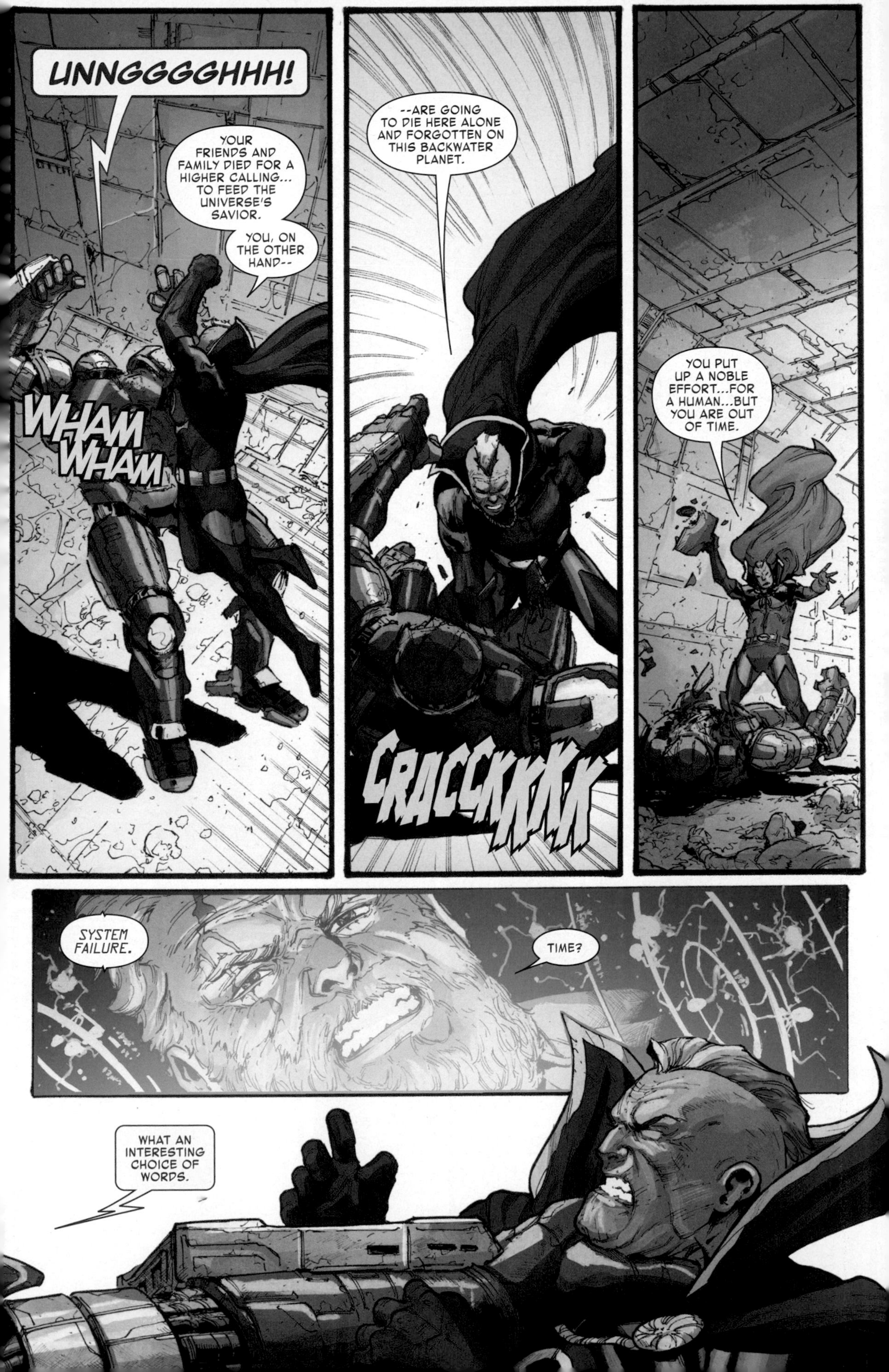
UNNGGGGHHH!
YOUR FRIENDS AND FAMILY DIED FOR A HIGHER CALLING... TO FEED THE UNIVERSE'S SAVIOR.
YOU, ON THE OTHER HAND--
WHAM WHAM
--ARE GOING TO DIE HERE ALONE AND FORGOTTEN ON THIS BACKWATER PLANET.
CRACCKKKKK
YOU PUT UP A NOBLE EFFORT...FOR A HUMAN...BUT YOU ARE OUT OF TIME.
SYSTEM FAILURE.
TIME?
WHAT AN INTERESTING CHOICE OF WORDS.

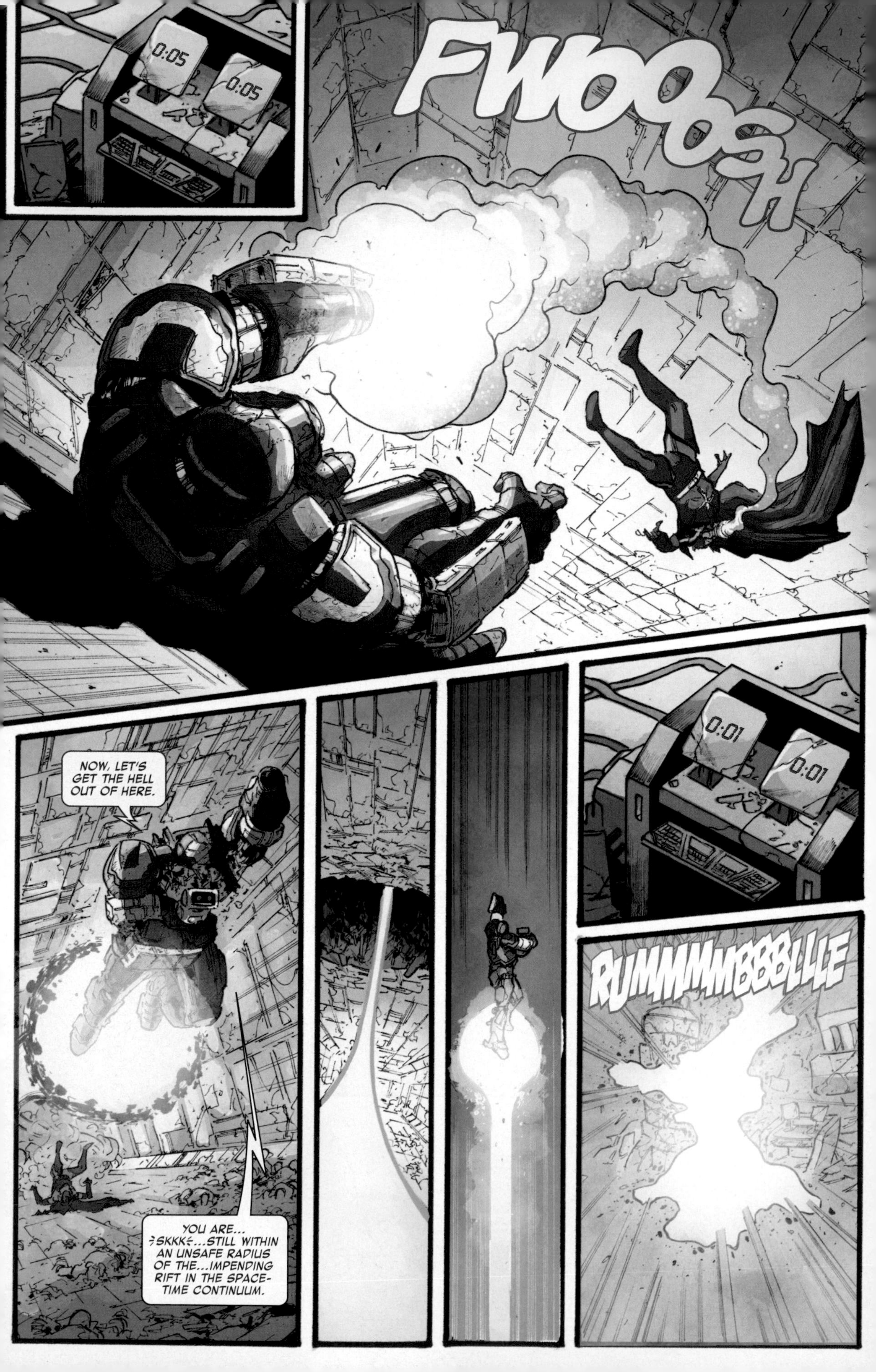
0:05
0:05
FWOOOSH
NOW, LET'S GET THE HELL OUT OF HERE.
YOU ARE... ≠SKKK≠...STILL WITHIN AN UNSAFE RADIUS OF THE...IMPENDING RIFT IN THE SPACE-TIME CONTINUUM.
0:01
0:01
RUMMMMBBBLLLE

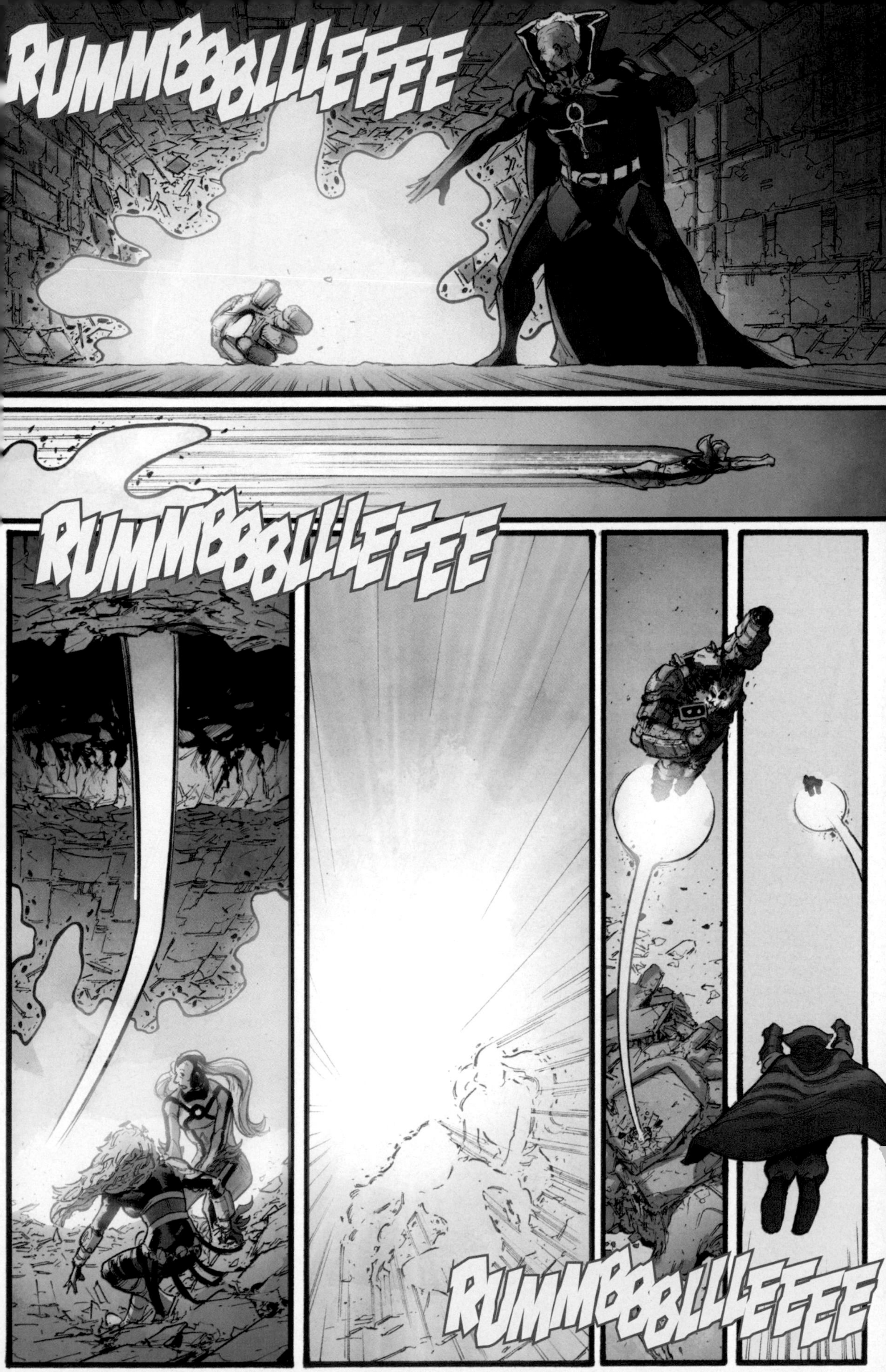
RUMMBBBLLLEEEE
RUMMBBBLLLEEEE
RUMMBBBLLLEEEE

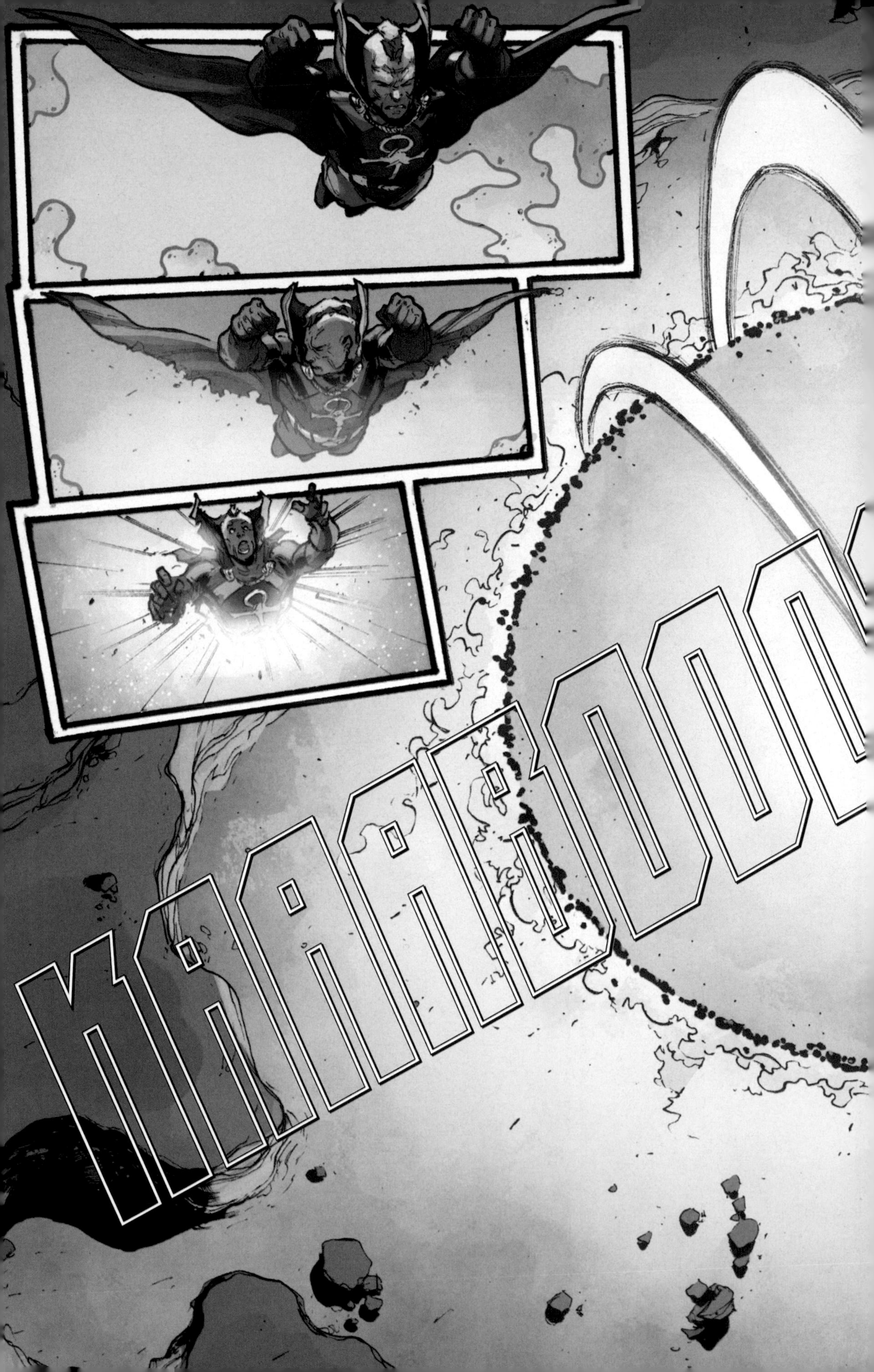

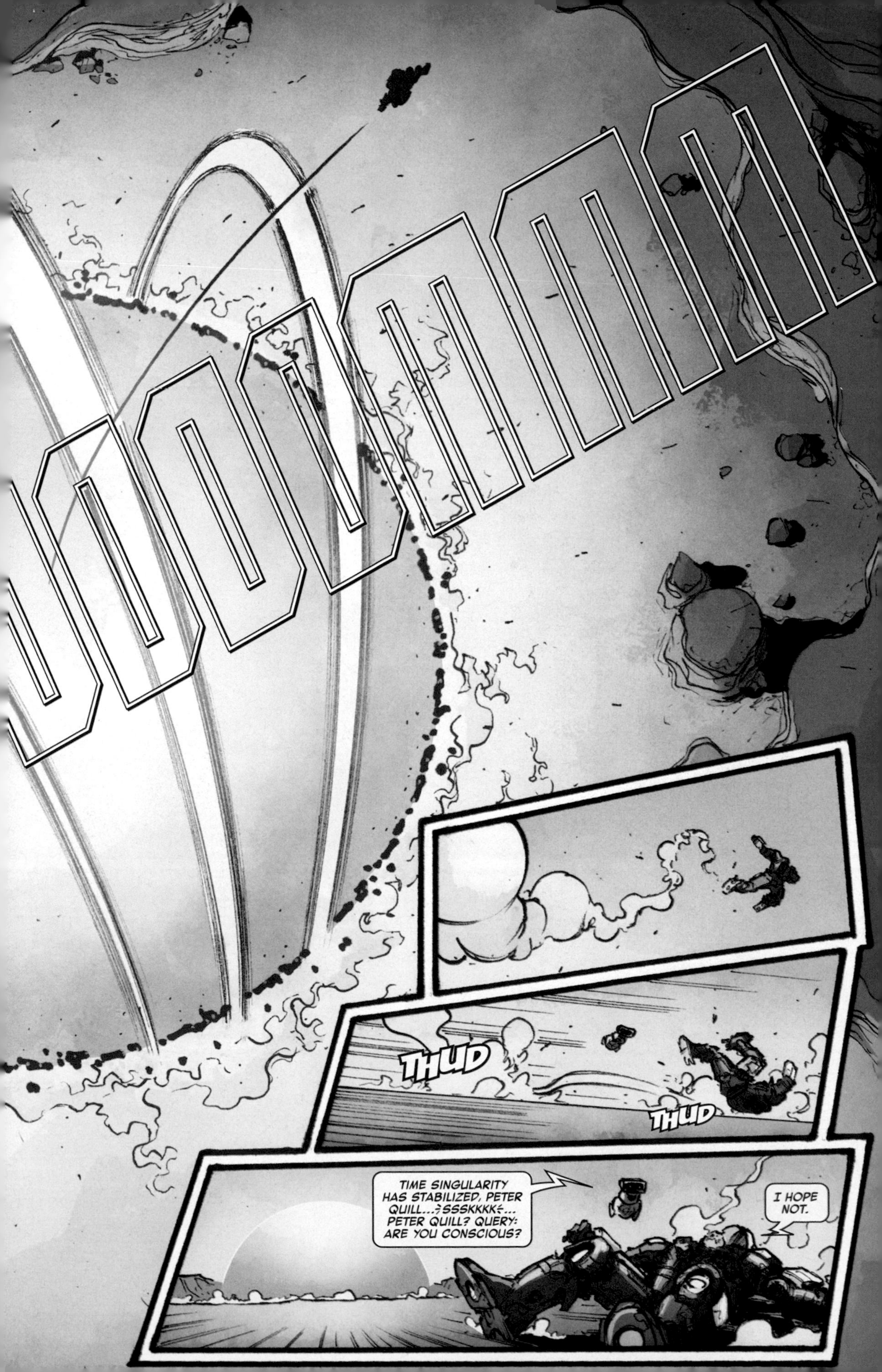
THUD
THUD
TIME SINGULARITY HAS STABILIZED, PETER QUILL...⋟SSSKKKK⋞... PETER QUILL? QUERY: ARE YOU CONSCIOUS?
I HOPE NOT.

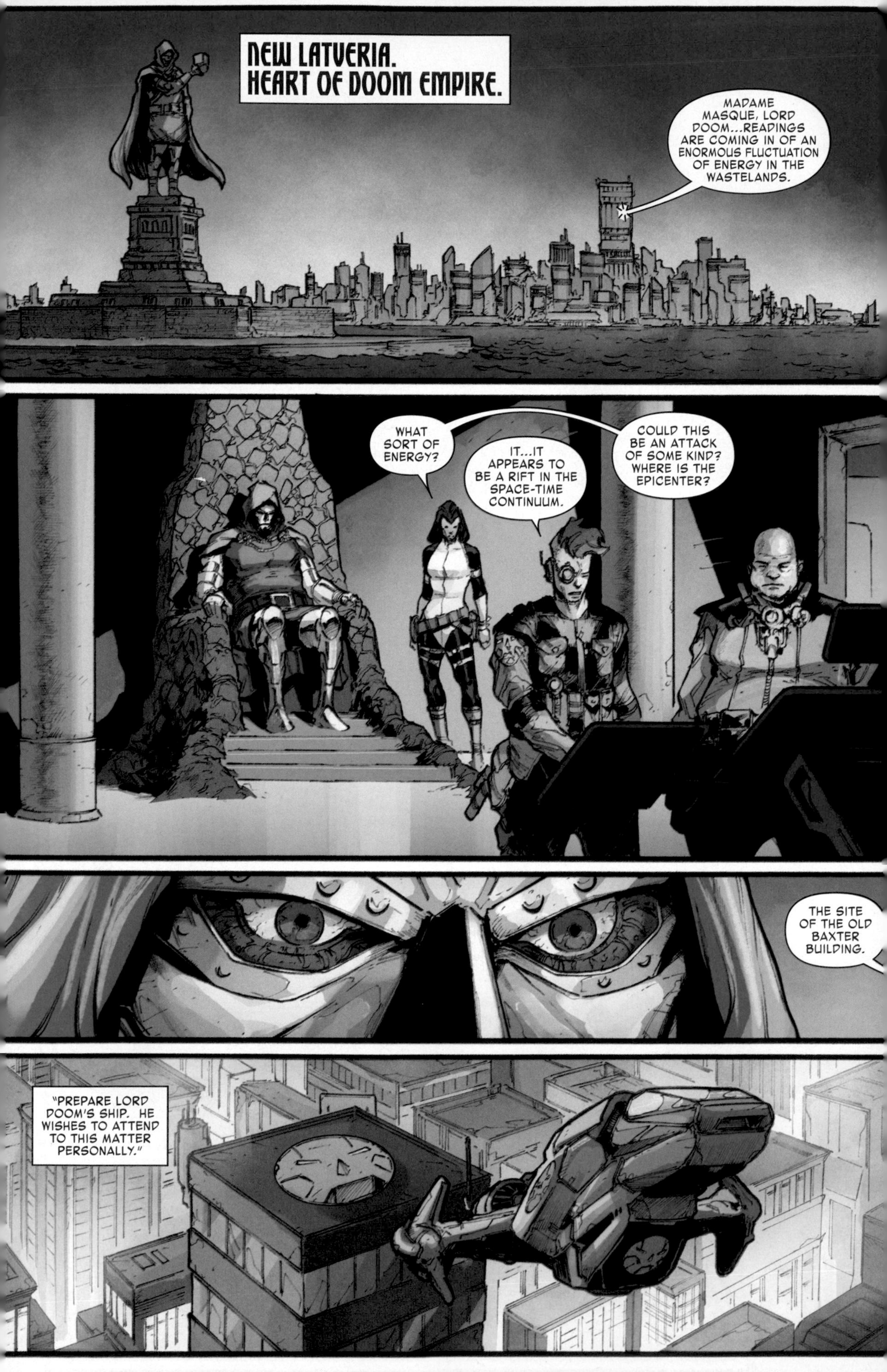
NEW LATVERIA. HEART OF DOOM EMPIRE.
MADAME MASQUE, LORD DOOM...READINGS ARE COMING IN OF AN ENORMOUS FLUCTUATION OF ENERGY IN THE WASTELANDS.
WHAT SORT OF ENERGY?
IT...IT APPEARS TO BE A RIFT IN THE SPACE-TIME CONTINUUM.
COULD THIS BE AN ATTACK OF SOME KIND? WHERE IS THE EPICENTER?
THE SITE OF THE OLD BAXTER BUILDING.
"PREPARE LORD DOOM'S SHIP. HE WISHES TO ATTEND TO THIS MATTER PERSONALLY."

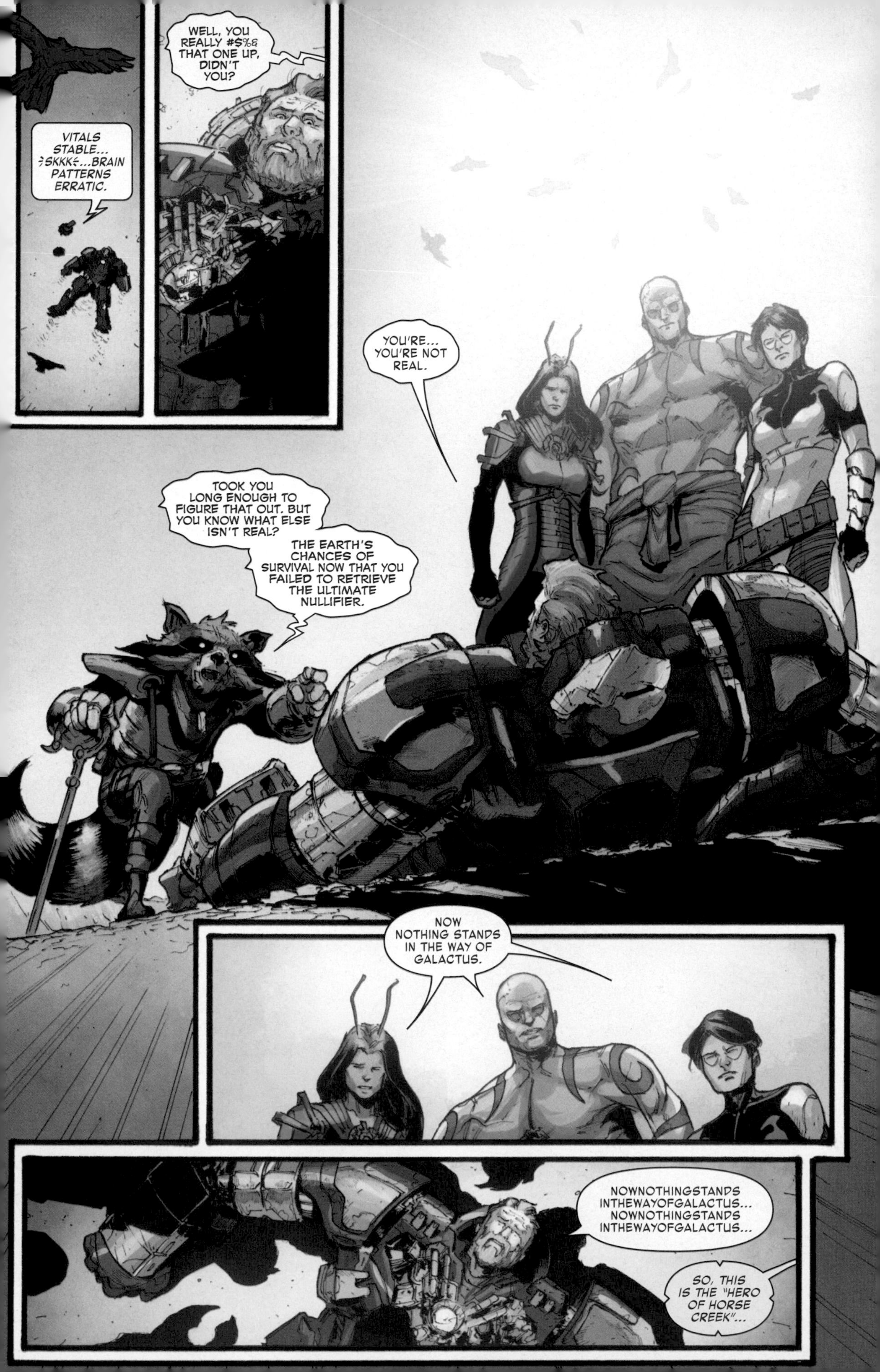
VITALS STABLE... ⚡SKKK⚡...BRAIN PATTERNS ERRATIC.
WELL, YOU REALLY #$%& THAT ONE UP, DIDN'T YOU?
YOU'RE... YOU'RE NOT REAL.
TOOK YOU LONG ENOUGH TO FIGURE THAT OUT. BUT YOU KNOW WHAT ELSE ISN'T REAL?
THE EARTH'S CHANCES OF SURVIVAL NOW THAT YOU FAILED TO RETRIEVE THE ULTIMATE NULLIFIER.
NOW NOTHING STANDS IN THE WAY OF GALACTUS.
NOWNOTHINGSTANDS INTHEWAYOFGALACTUS... NOWNOTHINGSTANDS INTHEWAYOFGALACTUS...
SO, THIS IS THE "HERO OF HORSE CREEK"...

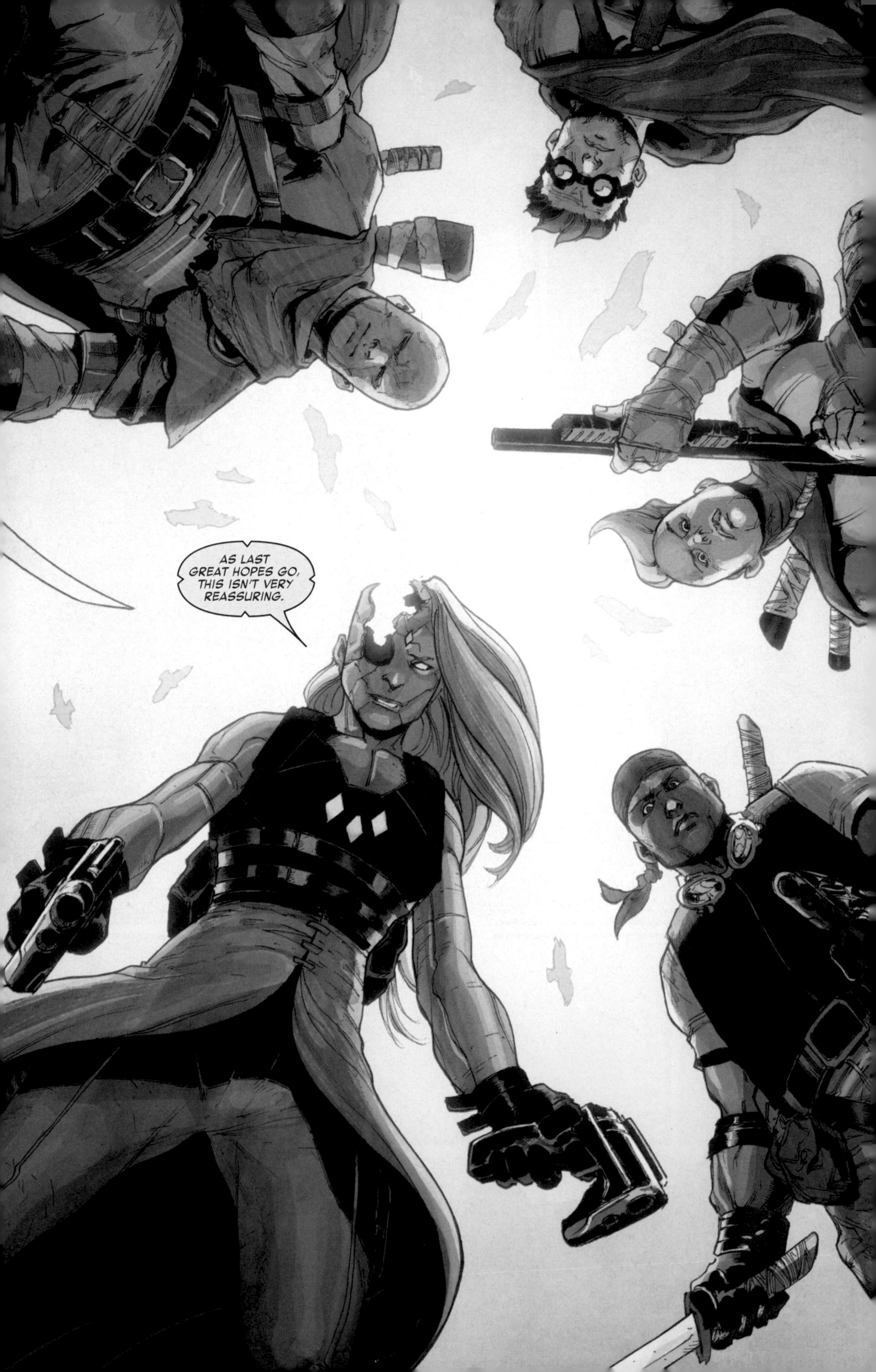
AS LAST GREAT HOPES GO, THIS ISN'T VERY REASSURING.

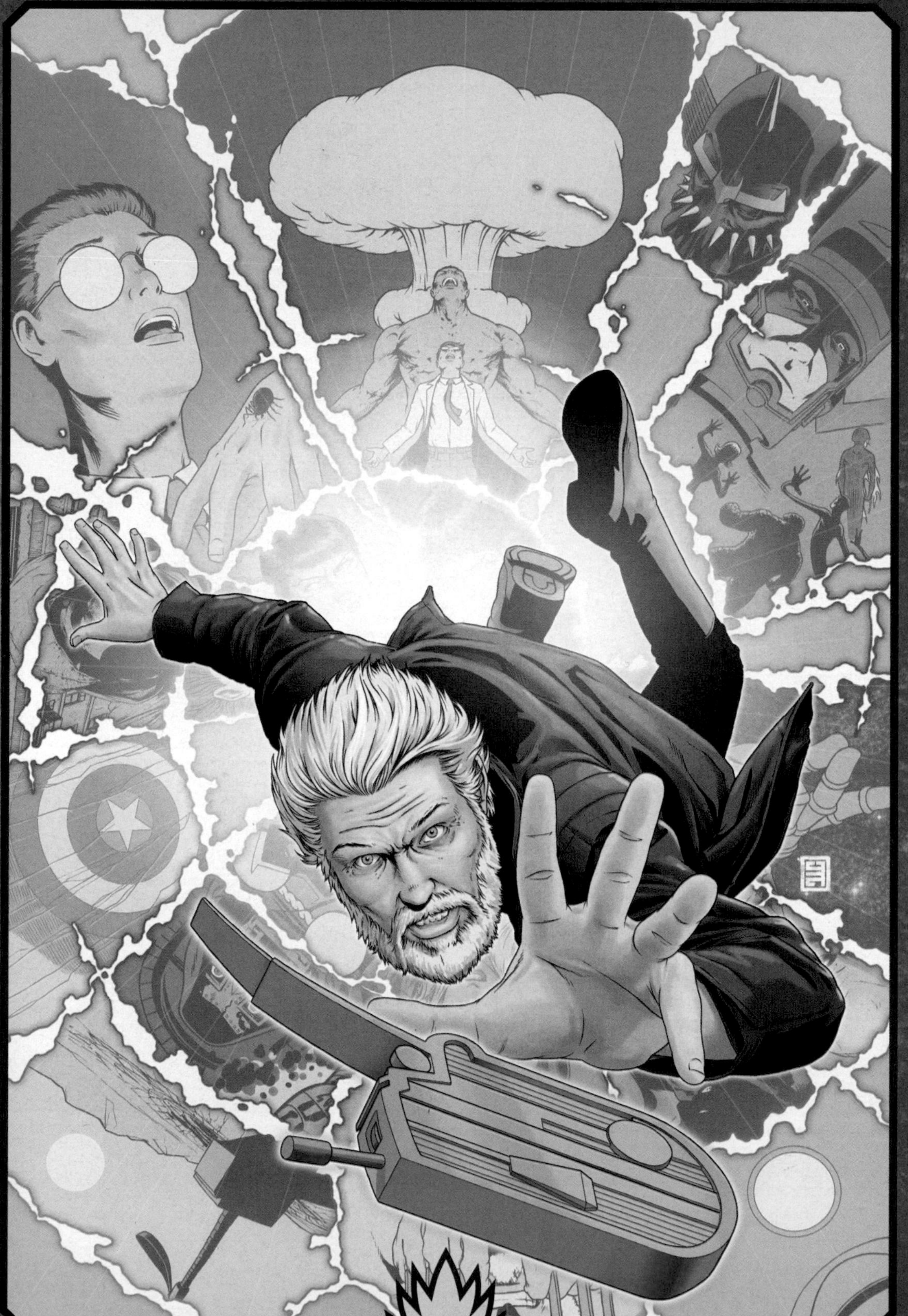

10

"TIME HAS COME TODAY"

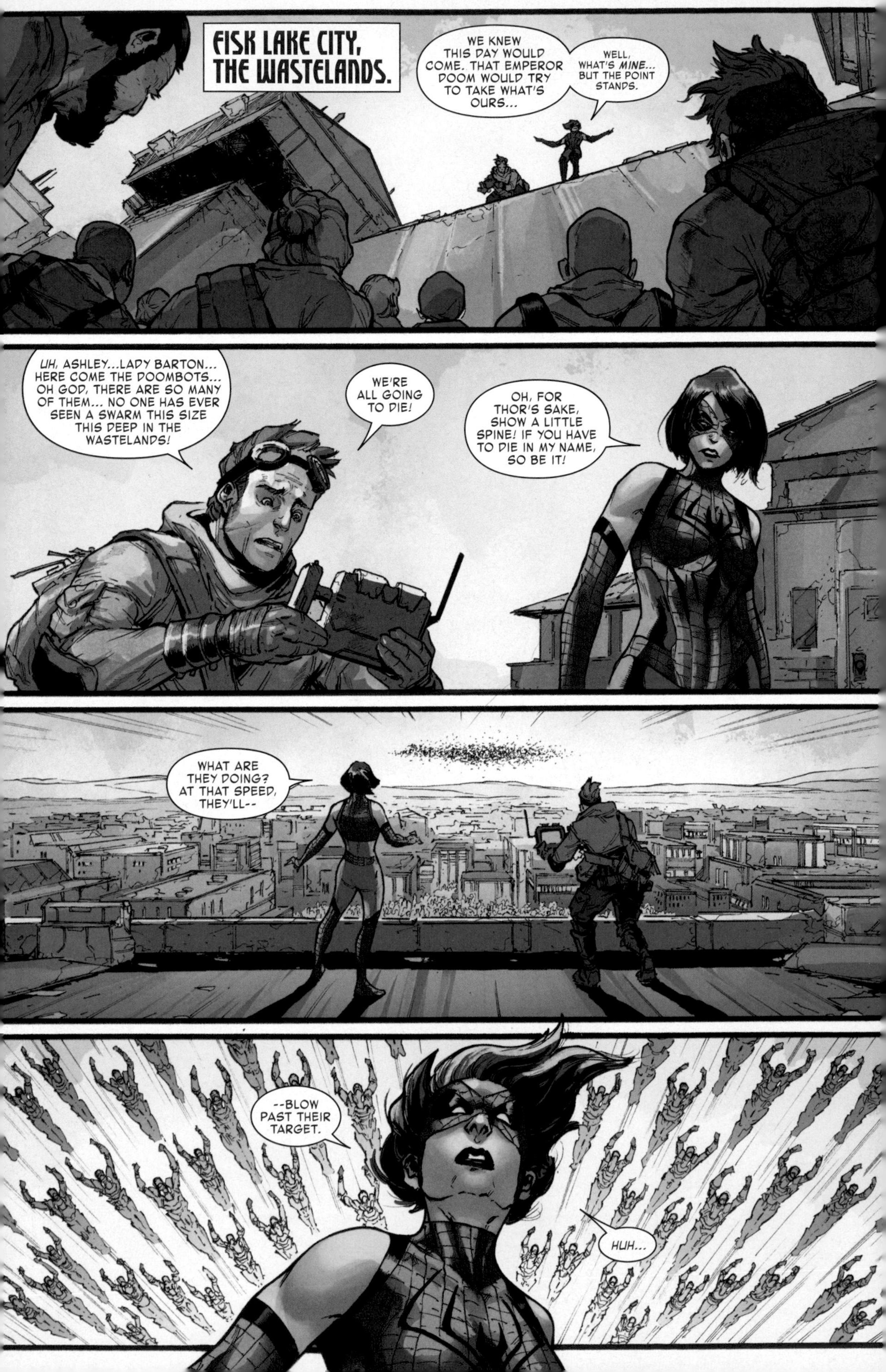
FISK LAKE CITY, THE WASTELANDS.
WE KNEW THIS DAY WOULD COME. THAT EMPEROR DOOM WOULD TRY TO TAKE WHAT'S OURS...
WELL, WHAT'S *MINE*... BUT THE POINT STANDS.
UH, ASHLEY...LADY BARTON... HERE COME THE DOOMBOTS... OH GOD, THERE ARE SO MANY OF THEM... NO ONE HAS EVER SEEN A SWARM THIS SIZE THIS DEEP IN THE WASTELANDS!
WE'RE ALL GOING TO DIE!
OH, FOR THOR'S SAKE, SHOW A LITTLE SPINE! IF YOU HAVE TO DIE IN MY NAME, SO BE IT!
WHAT ARE THEY DOING? AT THAT SPEED, THEY'LL--
--BLOW PAST THEIR TARGET.
HUH...

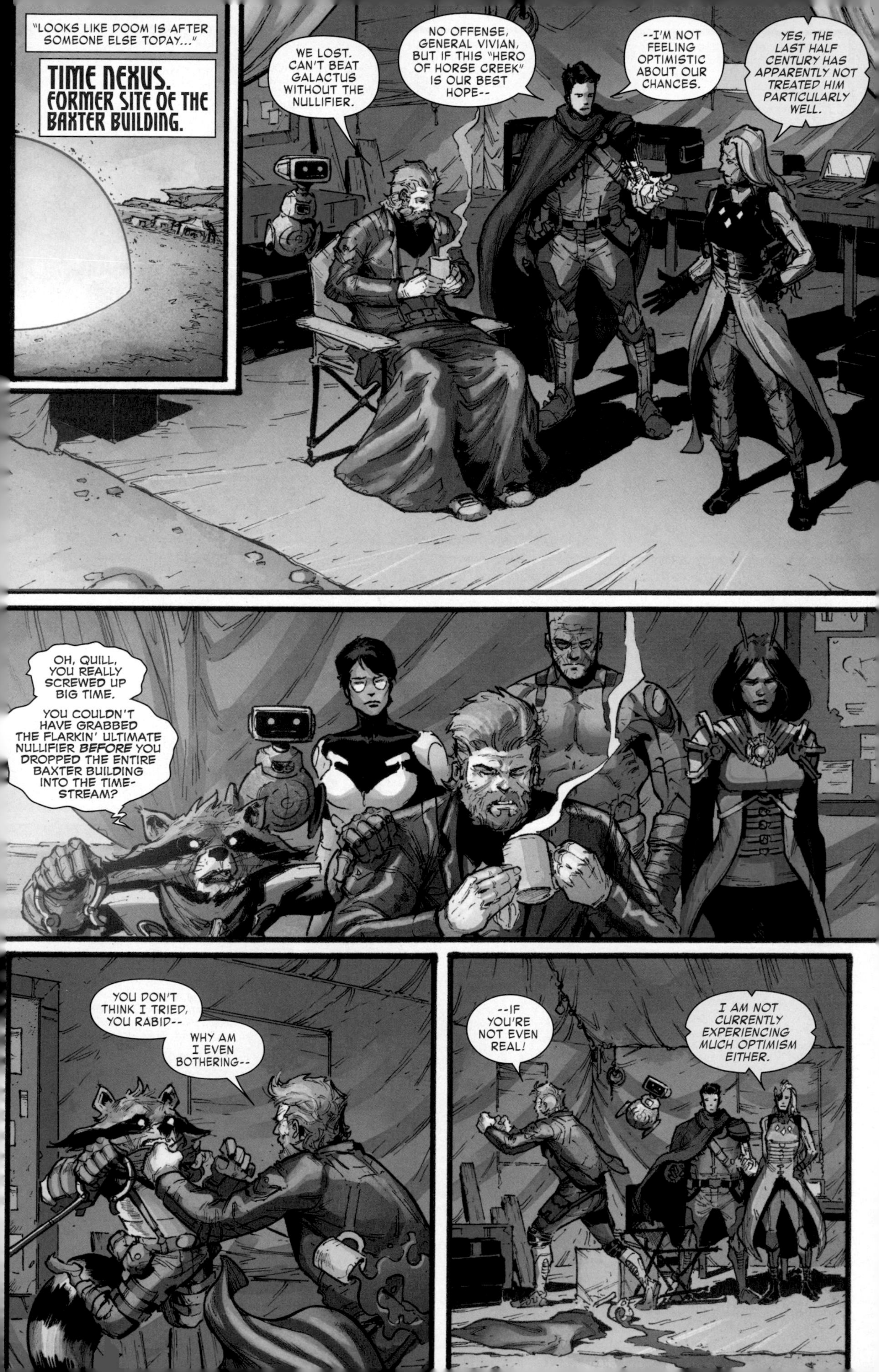
"LOOKS LIKE DOOM IS AFTER SOMEONE ELSE TODAY..."
TIME NEXUS. FORMER SITE OF THE BAXTER BUILDING.
WE LOST. CAN'T BEAT GALACTUS WITHOUT THE NULLIFIER.
NO OFFENSE, GENERAL VIVIAN, BUT IF THIS "HERO OF HORSE CREEK" IS OUR BEST HOPE--
--I'M NOT FEELING OPTIMISTIC ABOUT OUR CHANCES.
YES, THE LAST HALF CENTURY HAS APPARENTLY NOT TREATED HIM PARTICULARLY WELL.
OH, QUILL, YOU REALLY SCREWED UP BIG TIME.
YOU COULDN'T HAVE GRABBED THE FLARKIN' ULTIMATE NULLIFIER *BEFORE* YOU DROPPED THE ENTIRE BAXTER BUILDING INTO THE TIME-STREAM?
YOU DON'T THINK I TRIED, YOU RABID--
WHY AM I EVEN BOTHERING--
--IF YOU'RE NOT EVEN REAL!
I AM NOT CURRENTLY EXPERIENCING MUCH OPTIMISM EITHER.

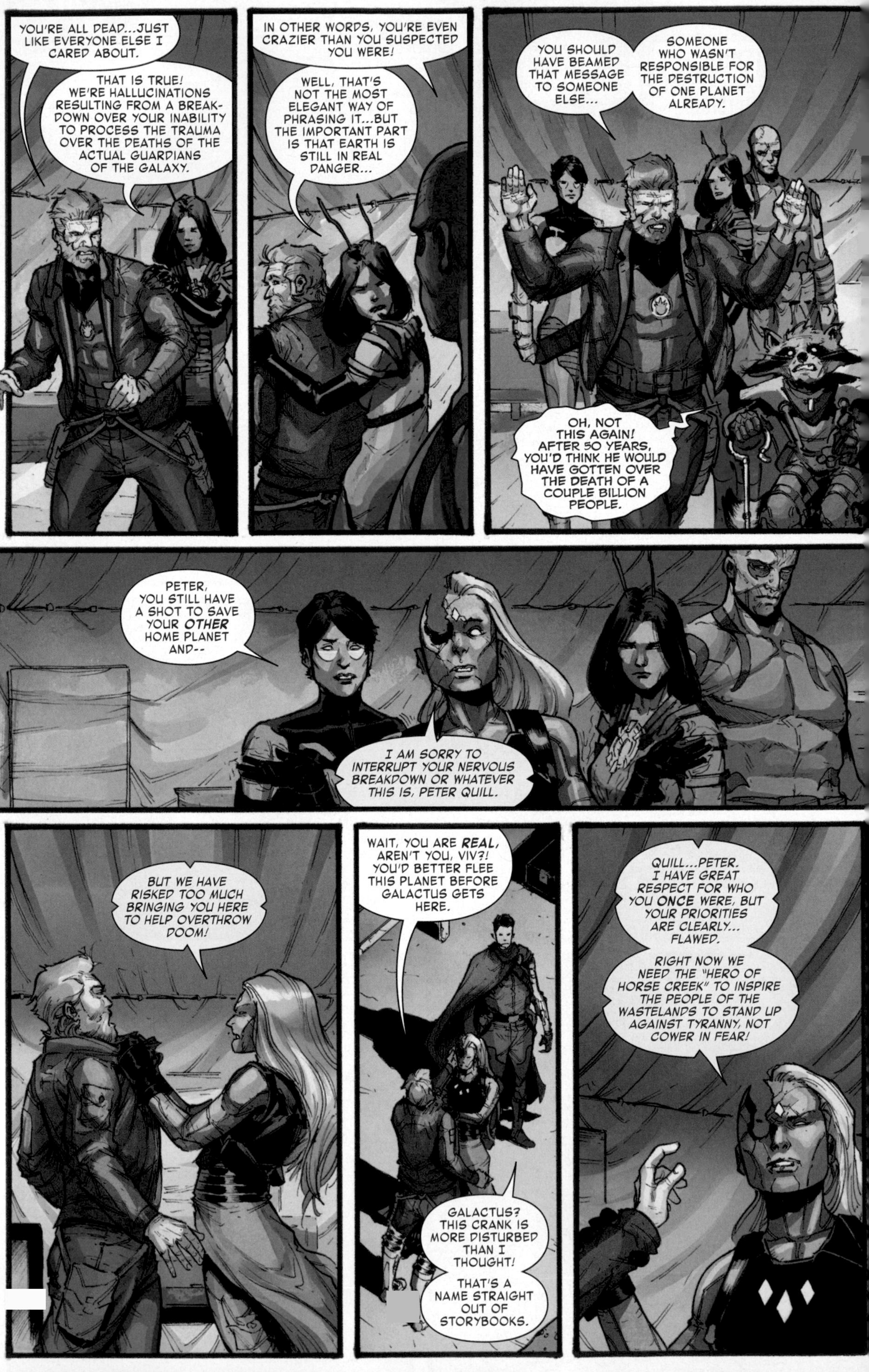
YOU'RE ALL DEAD...JUST LIKE EVERYONE ELSE I CARED ABOUT.
THAT IS TRUE! WE'RE HALLUCINATIONS RESULTING FROM A BREAK-DOWN OVER YOUR INABILITY TO PROCESS THE TRAUMA OVER THE DEATHS OF THE ACTUAL GUARDIANS OF THE GALAXY.
IN OTHER WORDS, YOU'RE EVEN CRAZIER THAN YOU SUSPECTED YOU WERE!
WELL, THAT'S NOT THE MOST ELEGANT WAY OF PHRASING IT...BUT THE IMPORTANT PART IS THAT EARTH IS STILL IN REAL DANGER...
YOU SHOULD HAVE BEAMED THAT MESSAGE TO SOMEONE ELSE...
SOMEONE WHO WASN'T RESPONSIBLE FOR THE DESTRUCTION OF ONE PLANET ALREADY.
OH, NOT THIS AGAIN! AFTER 50 YEARS, YOU'D THINK HE WOULD HAVE GOTTEN OVER THE DEATH OF A COUPLE BILLION PEOPLE.
PETER, YOU STILL HAVE A SHOT TO SAVE YOUR OTHER HOME PLANET AND--
I AM SORRY TO INTERRUPT YOUR NERVOUS BREAKDOWN OR WHATEVER THIS IS, PETER QUILL.
BUT WE HAVE RISKED TOO MUCH BRINGING YOU HERE TO HELP OVERTHROW DOOM!
WAIT, YOU ARE REAL, AREN'T YOU, VIV?! YOU'D BETTER FLEE THIS PLANET BEFORE GALACTUS GETS HERE.
GALACTUS? THIS CRANK IS MORE DISTURBED THAN I THOUGHT!
THAT'S A NAME STRAIGHT OUT OF STORYBOOKS.
QUILL...PETER. I HAVE GREAT RESPECT FOR WHO YOU ONCE WERE, BUT YOUR PRIORITIES ARE CLEARLY... FLAWED.
RIGHT NOW WE NEED THE "HERO OF HORSE CREEK" TO INSPIRE THE PEOPLE OF THE WASTELANDS TO STAND UP AGAINST TYRANNY, NOT COWER IN FEAR!

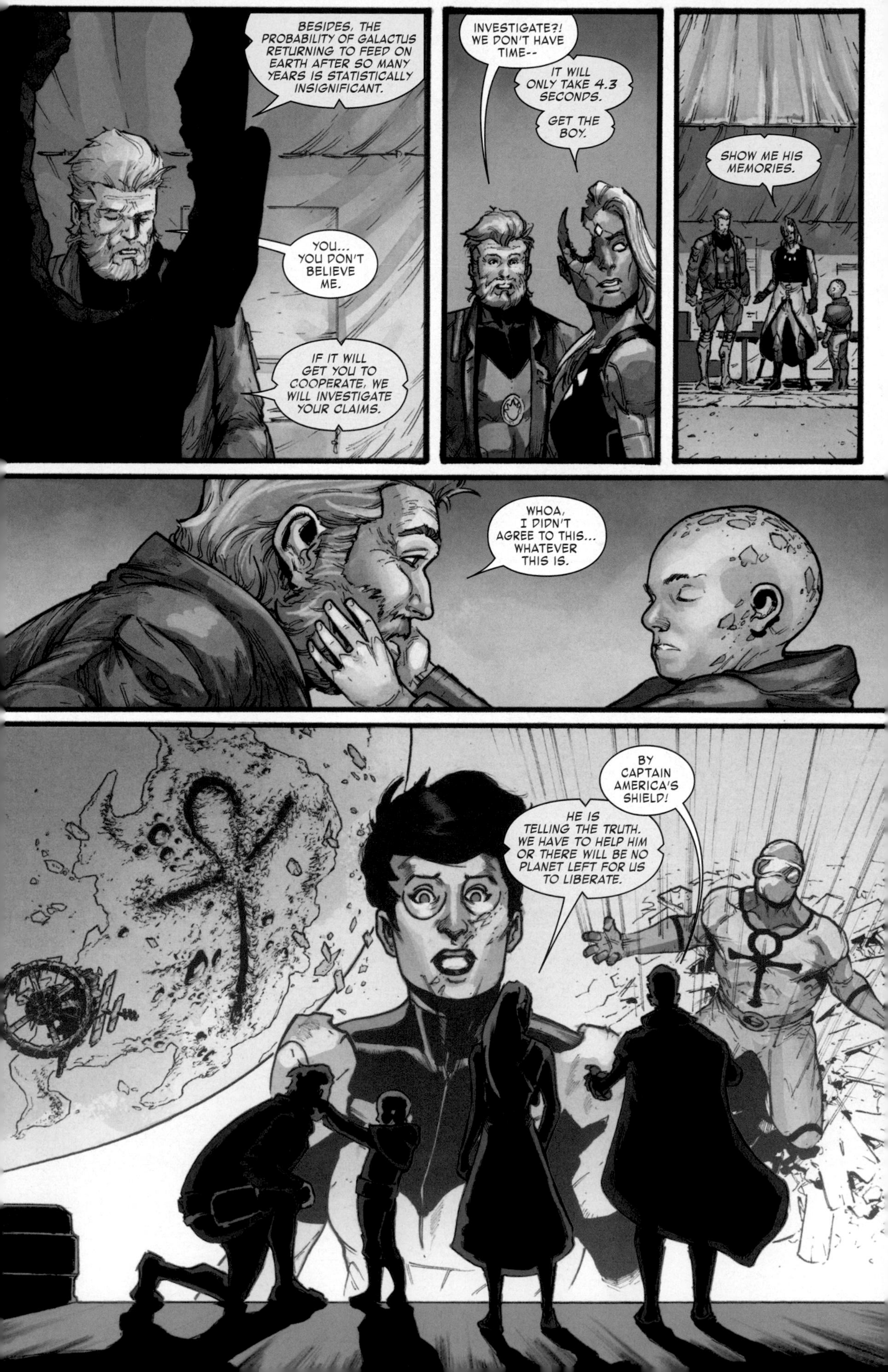
BESIDES, THE PROBABILITY OF GALACTUS RETURNING TO FEED ON EARTH AFTER SO MANY YEARS IS STATISTICALLY INSIGNIFICANT.
YOU... YOU DON'T BELIEVE ME.
IF IT WILL GET YOU TO COOPERATE, WE WILL INVESTIGATE YOUR CLAIMS.
INVESTIGATE?! WE DON'T HAVE TIME--
IT WILL ONLY TAKE 4.3 SECONDS.
GET THE BOY.
SHOW ME HIS MEMORIES.
WHOA, I DIDN'T AGREE TO THIS... WHATEVER THIS IS.
BY CAPTAIN AMERICA'S SHIELD!
HE IS TELLING THE TRUTH. WE HAVE TO HELP HIM OR THERE WILL BE NO PLANET LEFT FOR US TO LIBERATE.

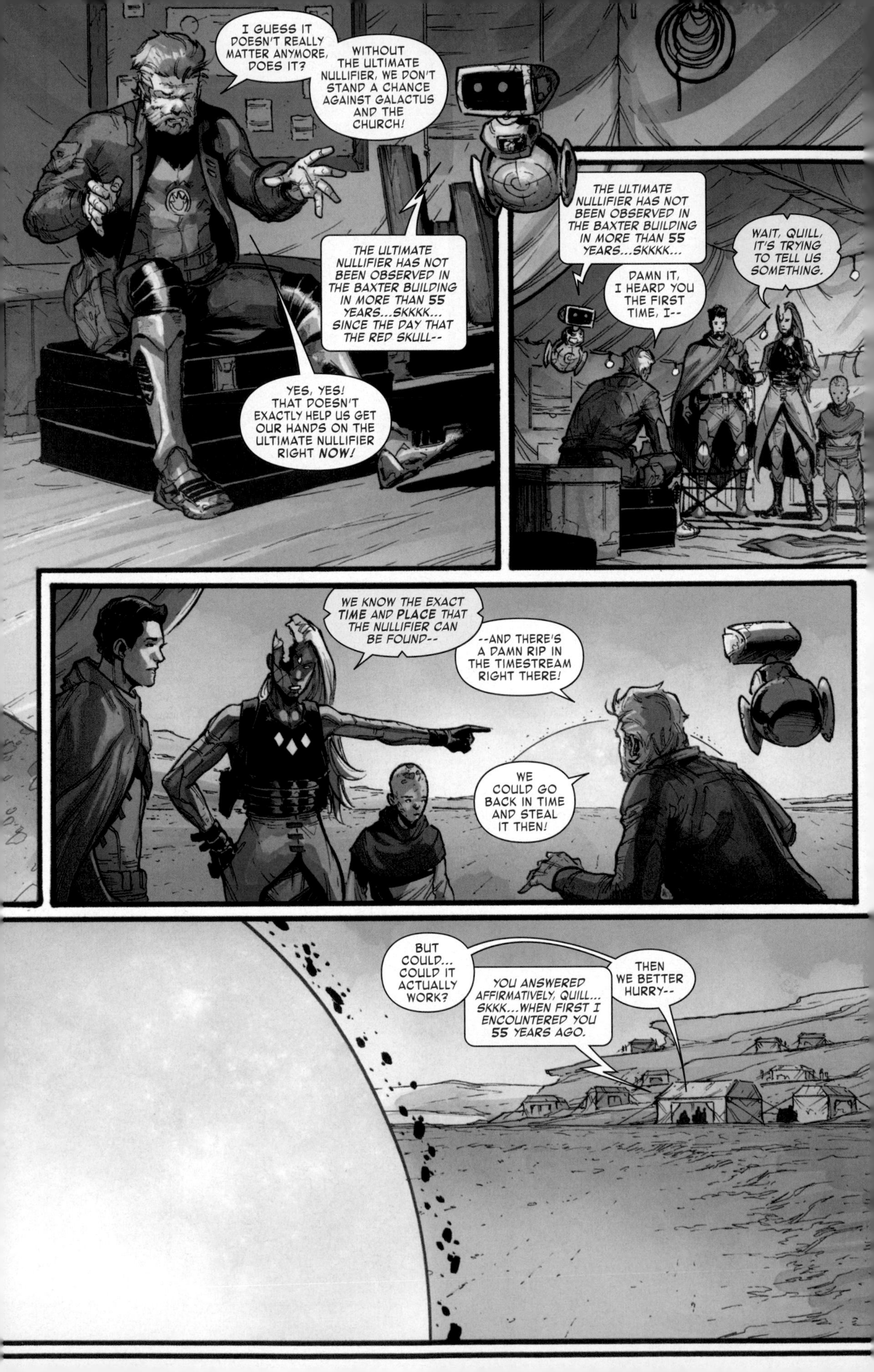
I GUESS IT DOESN'T REALLY MATTER ANYMORE, DOES IT?
WITHOUT THE ULTIMATE NULLIFIER, WE DON'T STAND A CHANCE AGAINST GALACTUS AND THE CHURCH!
THE ULTIMATE NULLIFIER HAS NOT BEEN OBSERVED IN THE BAXTER BUILDING IN MORE THAN 55 YEARS...SKKKK... SINCE THE DAY THAT THE RED SKULL--
YES, YES! THAT DOESN'T EXACTLY HELP US GET OUR HANDS ON THE ULTIMATE NULLIFIER RIGHT NOW!
THE ULTIMATE NULLIFIER HAS NOT BEEN OBSERVED IN THE BAXTER BUILDING IN MORE THAN 55 YEARS...SKKKK...
DAMN IT, I HEARD YOU THE FIRST TIME, I--
WAIT, QUILL, IT'S TRYING TO TELL US SOMETHING.
WE KNOW THE EXACT TIME AND PLACE THAT THE NULLIFIER CAN BE FOUND--
--AND THERE'S A DAMN RIP IN THE TIMESTREAM RIGHT THERE!
WE COULD GO BACK IN TIME AND STEAL IT THEN!
BUT COULD... COULD IT ACTUALLY WORK?
YOU ANSWERED AFFIRMATIVELY, QUILL... SKKK...WHEN FIRST I ENCOUNTERED YOU 55 YEARS AGO.
THEN WE BETTER HURRY--

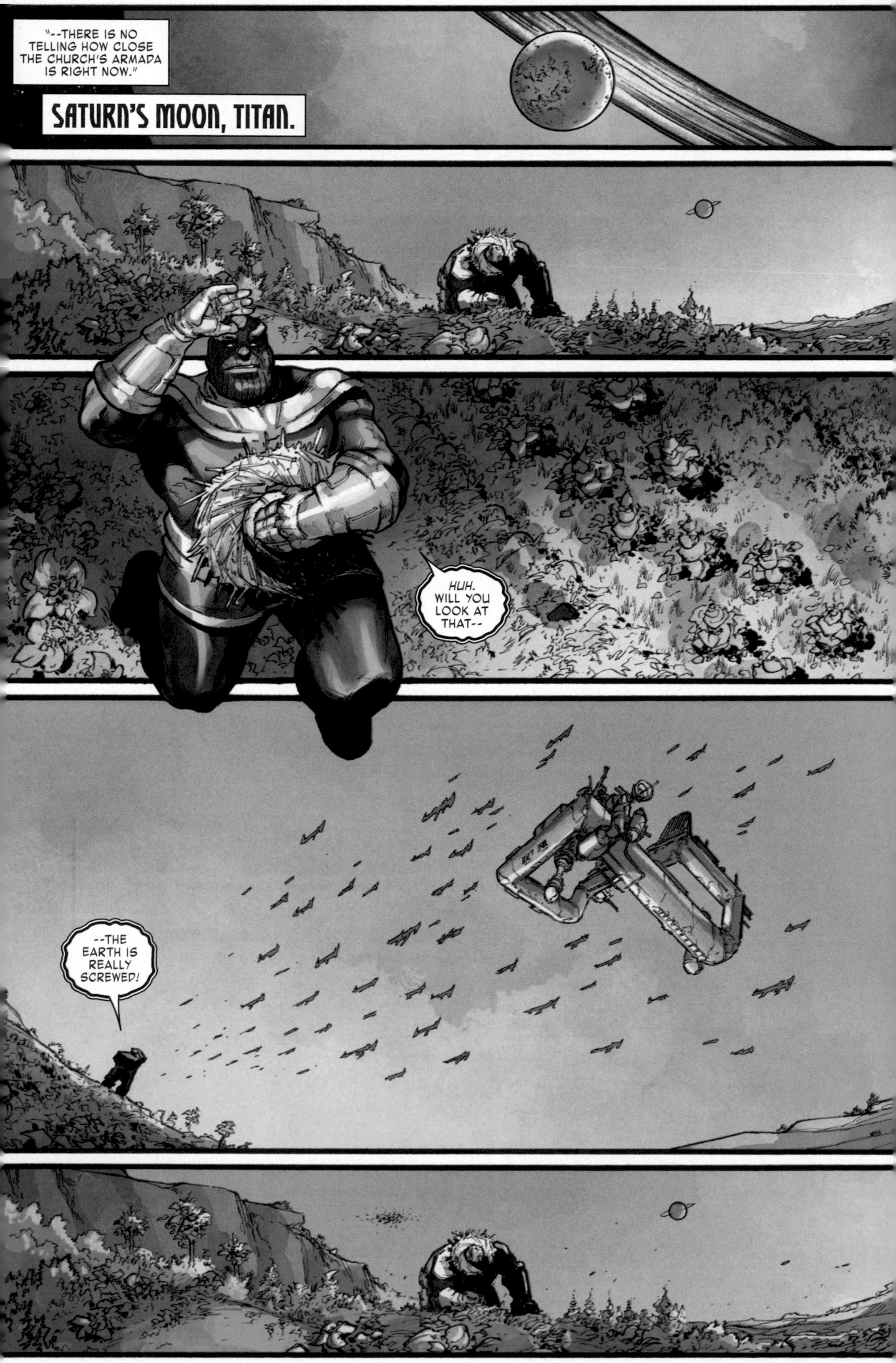
"--THERE IS NO TELLING HOW CLOSE THE CHURCH'S ARMADA IS RIGHT NOW."
SATURN'S MOON, TITAN.
HUH. WILL YOU LOOK AT THAT--
--THE EARTH IS REALLY SCREWED!

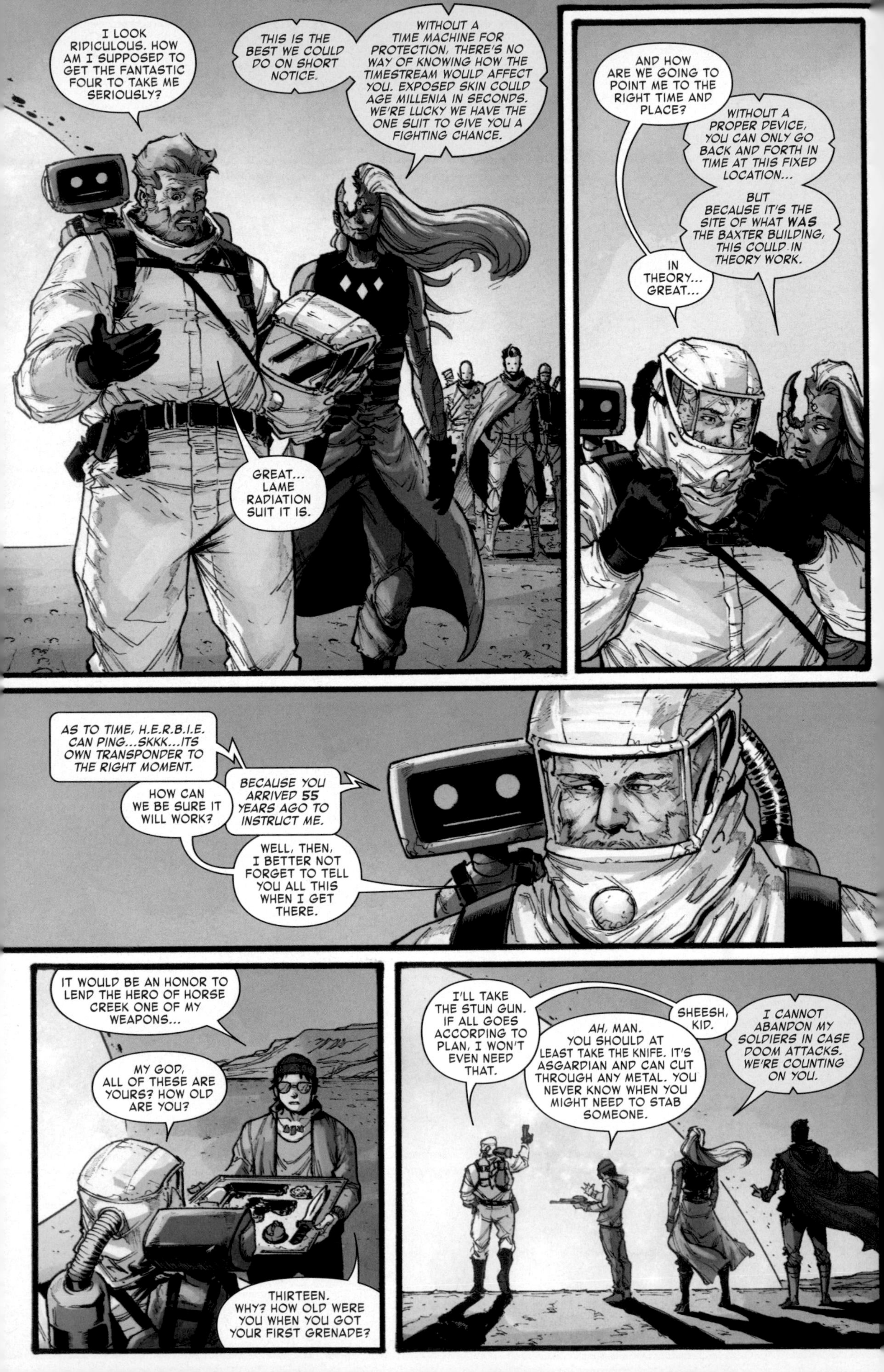
I LOOK RIDICULOUS. HOW AM I SUPPOSED TO GET THE FANTASTIC FOUR TO TAKE ME SERIOUSLY?
THIS IS THE BEST WE COULD DO ON SHORT NOTICE.
WITHOUT A TIME MACHINE FOR PROTECTION, THERE'S NO WAY OF KNOWING HOW THE TIMESTREAM WOULD AFFECT YOU. EXPOSED SKIN COULD AGE MILLENIA IN SECONDS. WE'RE LUCKY WE HAVE THE ONE SUIT TO GIVE YOU A FIGHTING CHANCE.
GREAT... LAME RADIATION SUIT IT IS.
AND HOW ARE WE GOING TO POINT ME TO THE RIGHT TIME AND PLACE?
WITHOUT A PROPER DEVICE, YOU CAN ONLY GO BACK AND FORTH IN TIME AT THIS FIXED LOCATION...
BUT BECAUSE IT'S THE SITE OF WHAT WAS THE BAXTER BUILDING, THIS COULD IN THEORY WORK.
IN THEORY... GREAT...
AS TO TIME, H.E.R.B.I.E. CAN PING...SKKK...ITS OWN TRANSPONDER TO THE RIGHT MOMENT.
HOW CAN WE BE SURE IT WILL WORK?
BECAUSE YOU ARRIVED 55 YEARS AGO TO INSTRUCT ME.
WELL, THEN, I BETTER NOT FORGET TO TELL YOU ALL THIS WHEN I GET THERE.
IT WOULD BE AN HONOR TO LEND THE HERO OF HORSE CREEK ONE OF MY WEAPONS...
MY GOD, ALL OF THESE ARE YOURS? HOW OLD ARE YOU?
THIRTEEN. WHY? HOW OLD WERE YOU WHEN YOU GOT YOUR FIRST GRENADE?
I'LL TAKE THE STUN GUN. IF ALL GOES ACCORDING TO PLAN, I WON'T EVEN NEED THAT.
SHEESH, KID.
AH, MAN. YOU SHOULD AT LEAST TAKE THE KNIFE. IT'S ASGARDIAN AND CAN CUT THROUGH ANY METAL. YOU NEVER KNOW WHEN YOU MIGHT NEED TO STAB SOMEONE.
I CANNOT ABANDON MY SOLDIERS IN CASE DOOM ATTACKS. WE'RE COUNTING ON YOU.

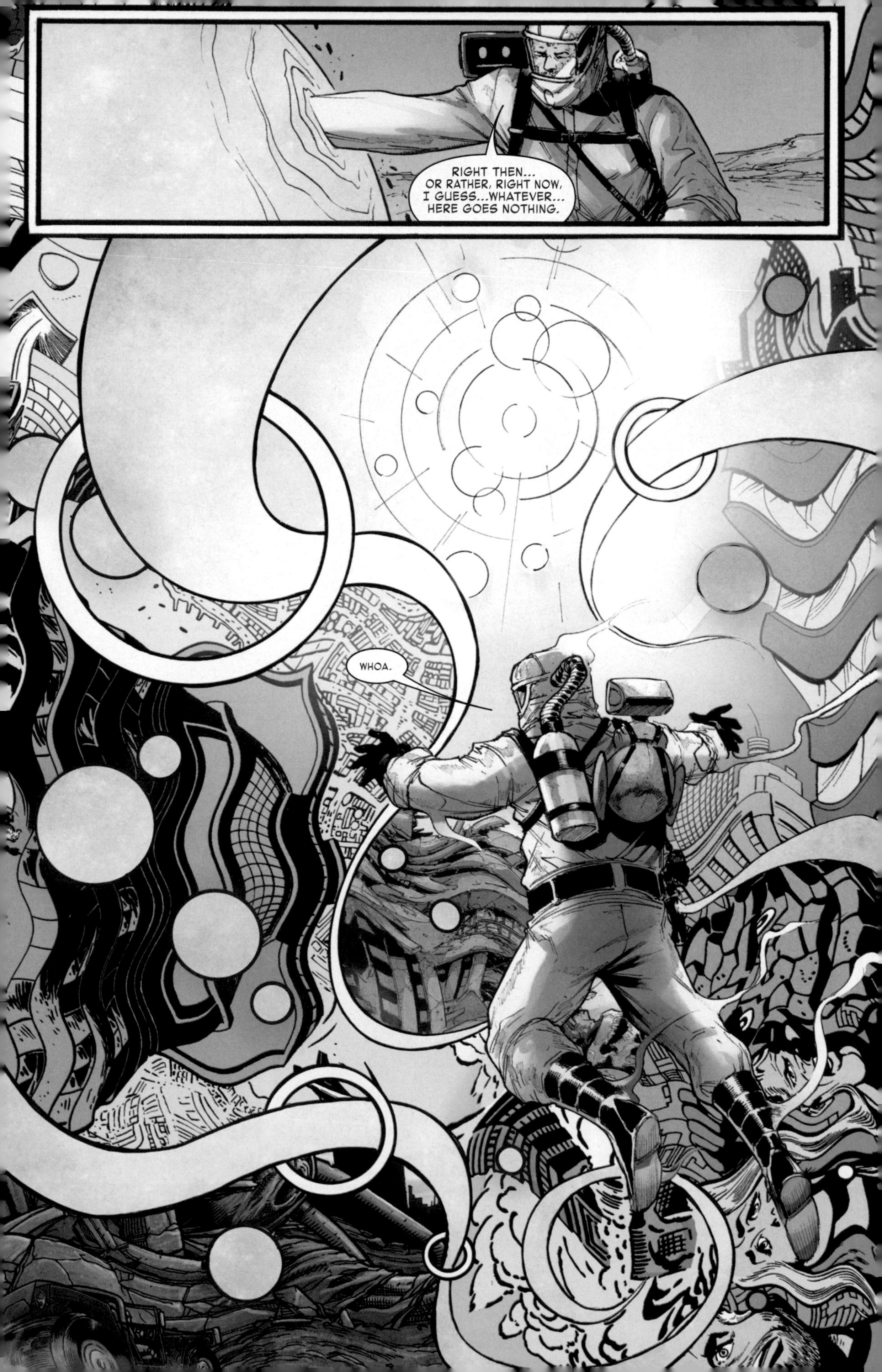
RIGHT THEN... OR RATHER, RIGHT NOW, I GUESS...WHATEVER... HERE GOES NOTHING.
WHOA.

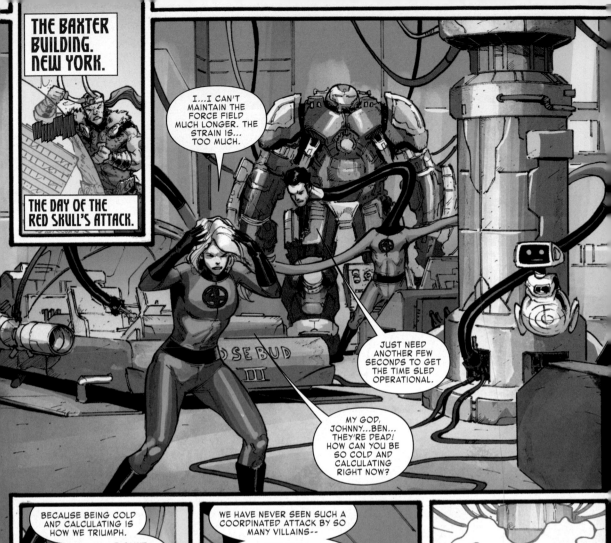

THE BAXTER BUILDING. NEW YORK.

THE DAY OF THE RED SKULL'S ATTACK.

I...I CAN'T MAINTAIN THE FORCE FIELD MUCH LONGER. THE STRAIN IS...TOO MUCH.

JUST NEED ANOTHER FEW SECONDS TO GET THE TIME SLED OPERATIONAL.

MY GOD, JOHNNY...BEN...THEY'RE DEAD! HOW CAN YOU BE SO COLD AND CALCULATING RIGHT NOW?

BECAUSE BEING COLD AND CALCULATING IS HOW WE TRIUMPH.

I CAN'T RAISE THE X-MEN OR THE AVENGERS.

SO THEN LET'S GET ON WITH IT AND SAVE THE WORLD...YET AGAIN.

WE HAVE NEVER SEEN SUCH A COORDINATED ATTACK BY SO MANY VILLAINS--

AND IT'S A MATTER OF TIME BEFORE THEY BREACH THE BAXTER BUILDING, SO WE MUST KEEP THE DANGEROUS WEAPONS WE STORE HERE OUT OF THEIR HANDS UNTIL WE CAN FORMULATE A COUNTERATTACK!

AND WHAT BETTER PLACE TO HIDE THEM THAN IN THE TIMESTREAM--

WAIT, WHAT'S THAT?

ALERT...ALERT...RECEIVING A TRANSMISSION FROM THE TIME PORTAL.

THE TIME PORTAL? BUT HOW? SOMEONE MUST HAVE ACTIVATED IT REMOTELY!

WHOEVER COULD NAVIGATE THE TIMESTREAM SO ADEPTLY COULD BE A DIRE THREAT!

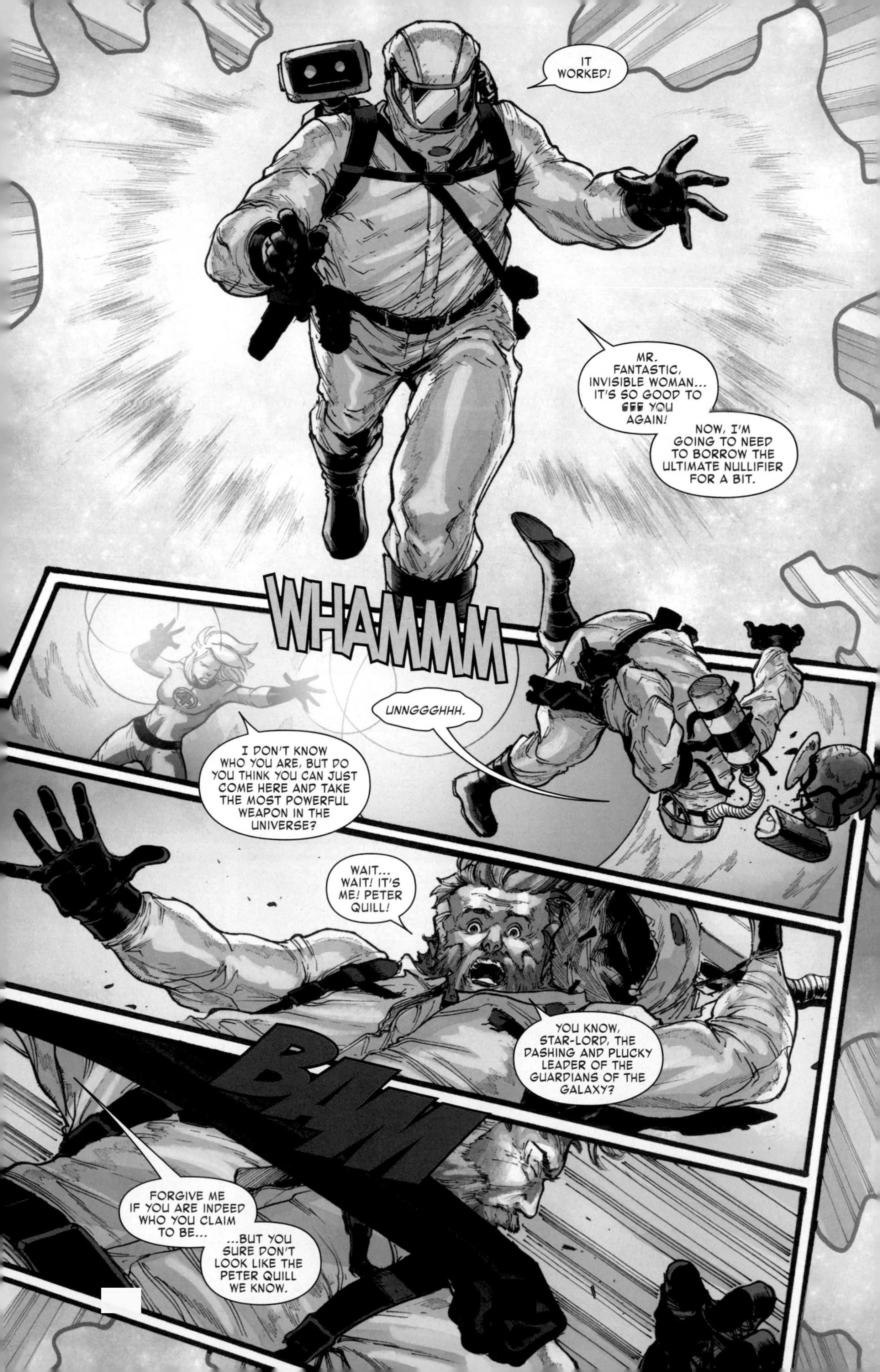
IT WORKED!
MR. FANTASTIC, INVISIBLE WOMAN... IT'S SO GOOD TO SEE YOU AGAIN!
NOW, I'M GOING TO NEED TO BORROW THE ULTIMATE NULLIFIER FOR A BIT.
WHAMMM
UNNGGGHHH.
I DON'T KNOW WHO YOU ARE, BUT DO YOU THINK YOU CAN JUST COME HERE AND TAKE THE MOST POWERFUL WEAPON IN THE UNIVERSE?
WAIT... WAIT! IT'S ME! PETER QUILL!
YOU KNOW, STAR-LORD, THE DASHING AND PLUCKY LEADER OF THE GUARDIANS OF THE GALAXY?
BAM
FORGIVE ME IF YOU ARE INDEED WHO YOU CLAIM TO BE...
...BUT YOU SURE DON'T LOOK LIKE THE PETER QUILL WE KNOW.

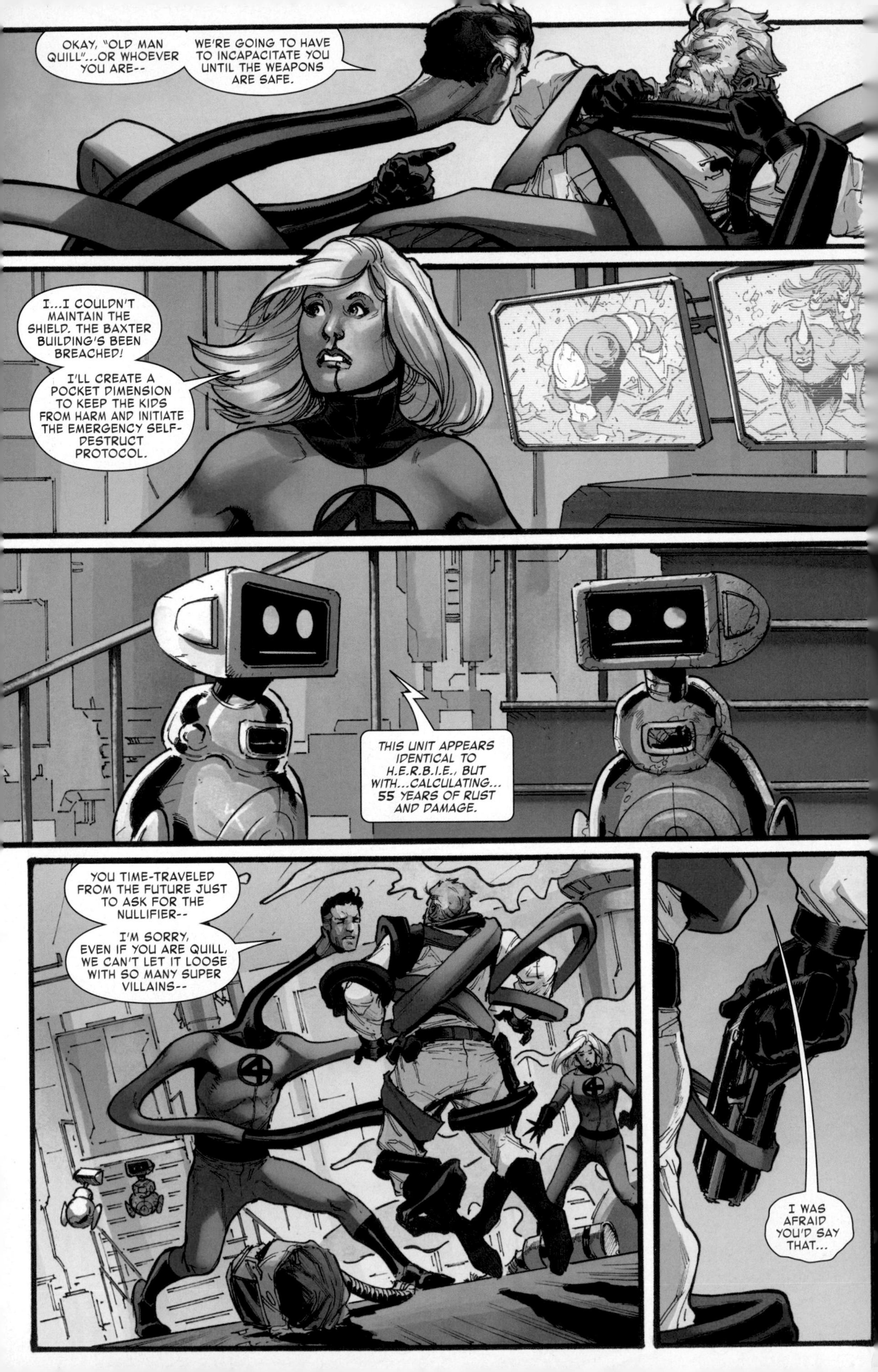

OKAY, "OLD MAN QUILL"...OR WHOEVER YOU ARE--
WE'RE GOING TO HAVE TO INCAPACITATE YOU UNTIL THE WEAPONS ARE SAFE.
I...I COULDN'T MAINTAIN THE SHIELD. THE BAXTER BUILDING'S BEEN BREACHED!
I'LL CREATE A POCKET DIMENSION TO KEEP THE KIDS FROM HARM AND INITIATE THE EMERGENCY SELF-DESTRUCT PROTOCOL.
THIS UNIT APPEARS IDENTICAL TO H.E.R.B.I.E., BUT WITH...CALCULATING... 55 YEARS OF RUST AND DAMAGE.
YOU TIME-TRAVELED FROM THE FUTURE JUST TO ASK FOR THE NULLIFIER--
I'M SORRY, EVEN IF YOU ARE QUILL, WE CAN'T LET IT LOOSE WITH SO MANY SUPER VILLAINS--
I WAS AFRAID YOU'D SAY THAT...

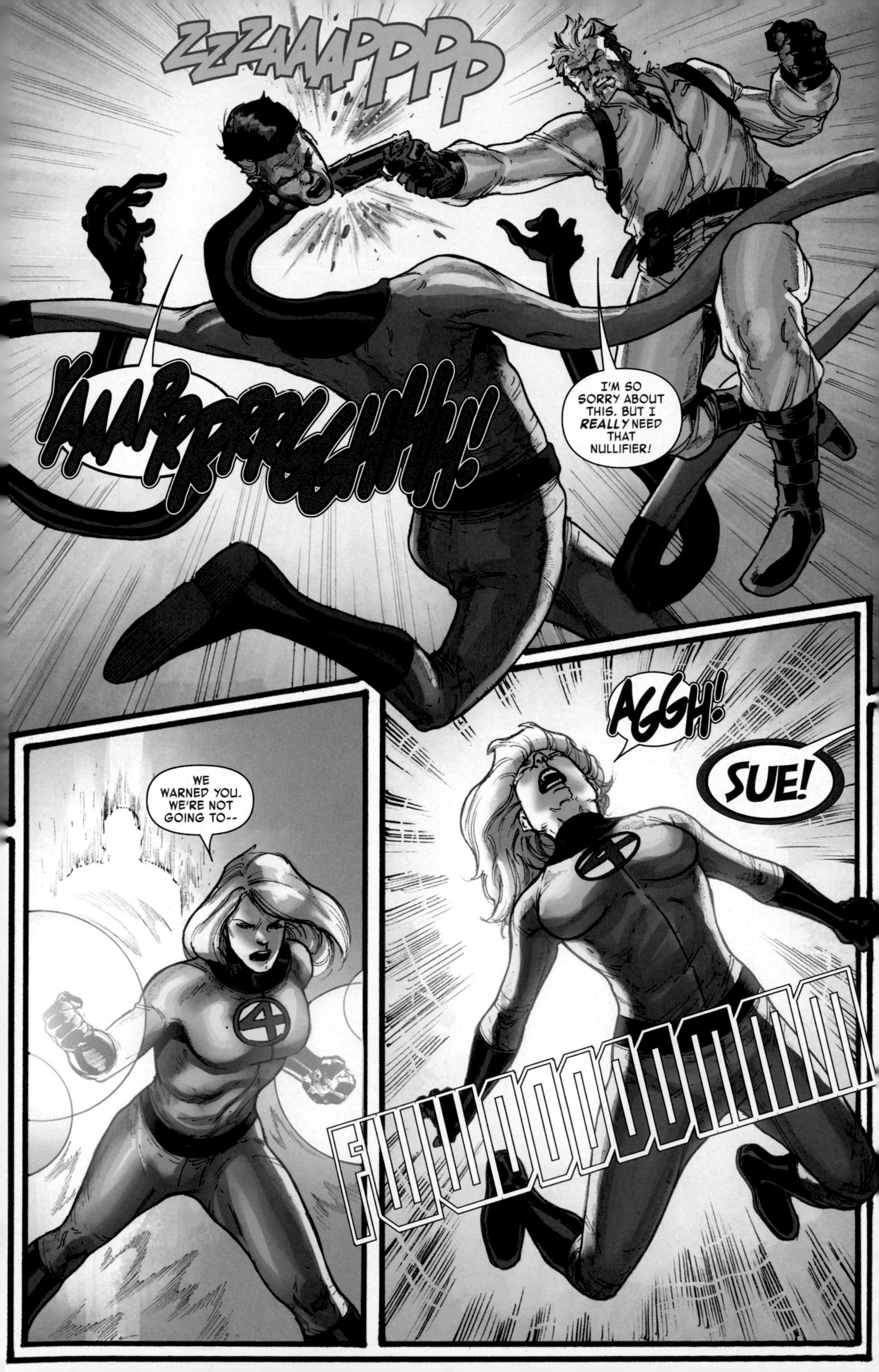
ZZZAAAPPPP
YAAARRRRGHHHH!
I'M SO SORRY ABOUT THIS. BUT I REALLY NEED THAT NULLIFIER!
WE WARNED YOU. WE'RE NOT GOING TO--
AGGH!
SUE!
FWOOOOOMM

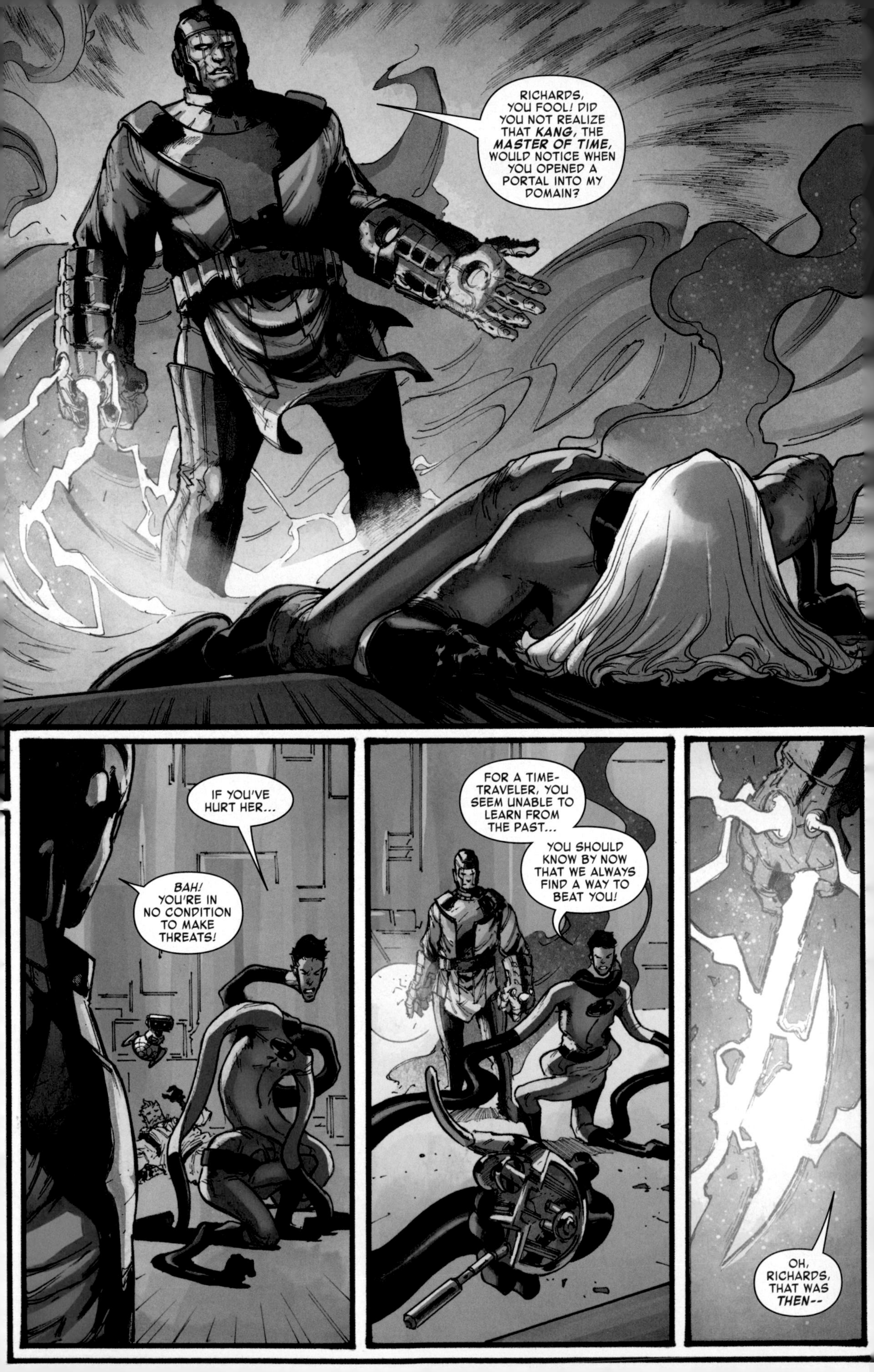
RICHARDS, YOU FOOL! DID YOU NOT REALIZE THAT KANG, THE MASTER OF TIME, WOULD NOTICE WHEN YOU OPENED A PORTAL INTO MY DOMAIN?
IF YOU'VE HURT HER...
BAH! YOU'RE IN NO CONDITION TO MAKE THREATS!
FOR A TIME-TRAVELER, YOU SEEM UNABLE TO LEARN FROM THE PAST...
YOU SHOULD KNOW BY NOW THAT WE ALWAYS FIND A WAY TO BEAT YOU!
OH, RICHARDS, THAT WAS THEN--

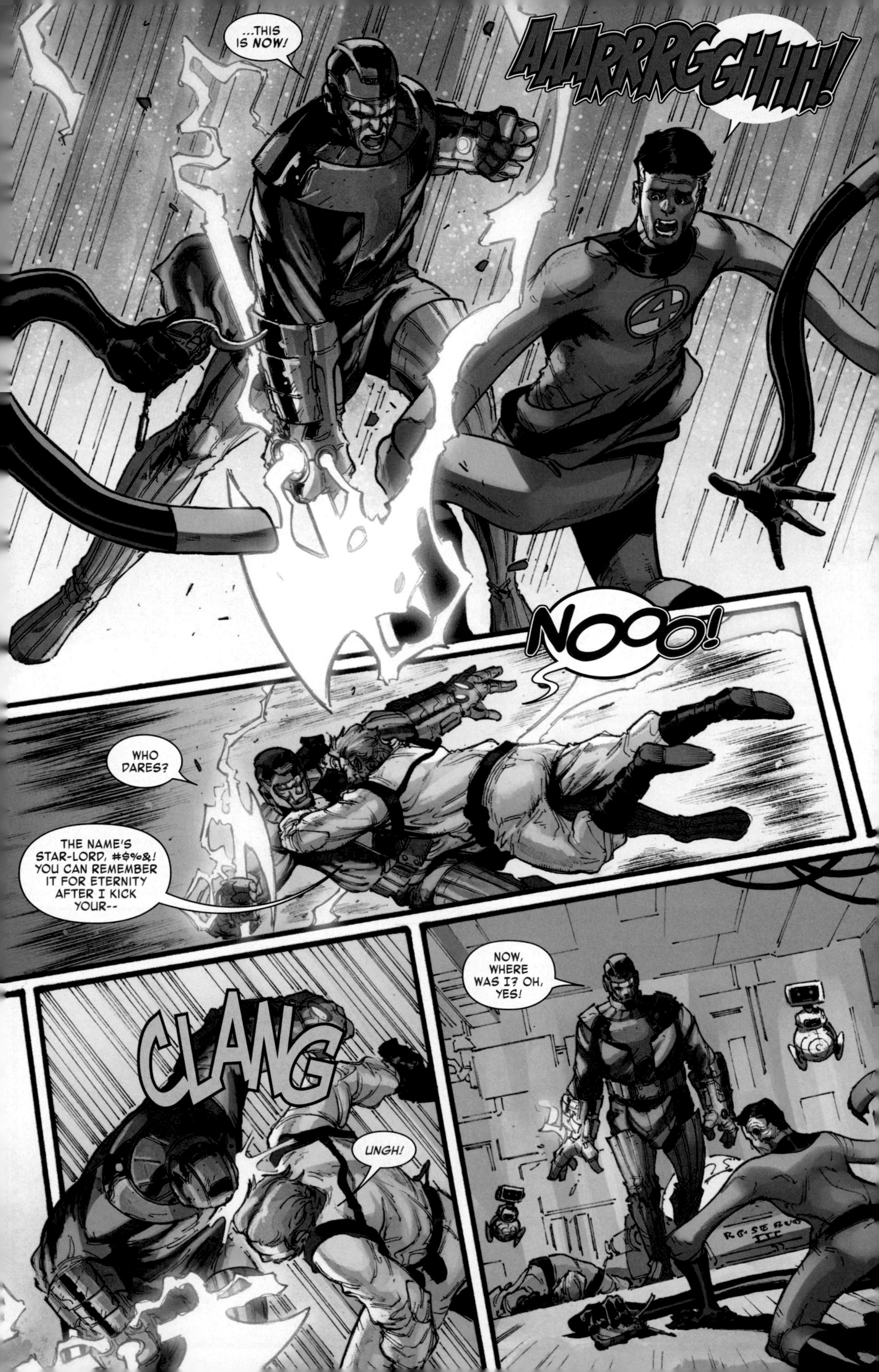
...THIS IS NOW!
AAARRRGGHHH!
NOOO!
WHO DARES?
THE NAME'S STAR-LORD, #$%&! YOU CAN REMEMBER IT FOR ETERNITY AFTER I KICK YOUR--
CLANG
UNGH!
NOW, WHERE WAS I? OH, YES!

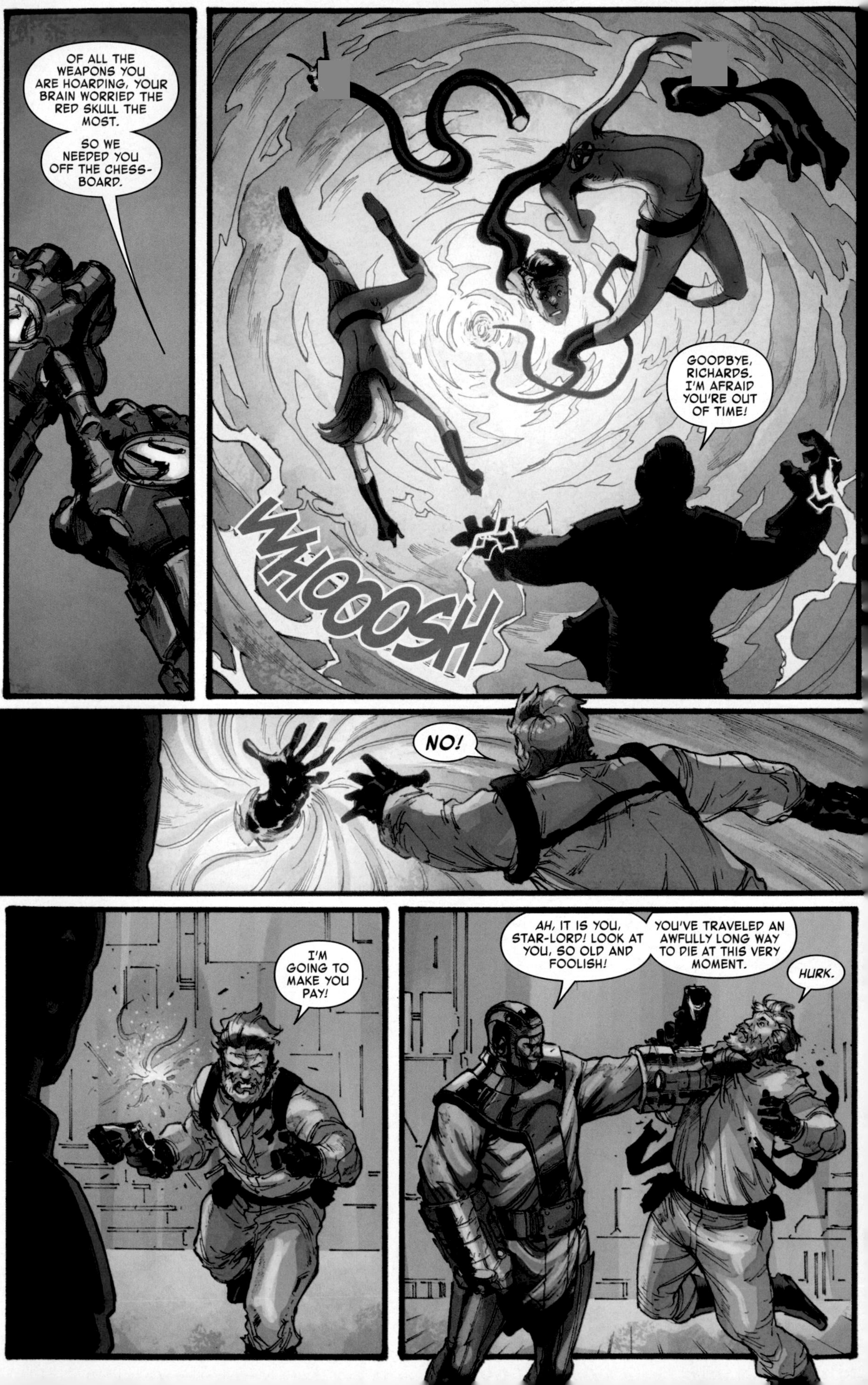
OF ALL THE WEAPONS YOU ARE HOARDING, YOUR BRAIN WORRIED THE RED SKULL THE MOST.
SO WE NEEDED YOU OFF THE CHESS-BOARD.
GOODBYE, RICHARDS. I'M AFRAID YOU'RE OUT OF TIME!
WHOOOSH
NO!
I'M GOING TO MAKE YOU PAY!
AH, IT IS YOU, STAR-LORD! LOOK AT YOU, SO OLD AND FOOLISH!
YOU'VE TRAVELED AN AWFULLY LONG WAY TO DIE AT THIS VERY MOMENT.
HURK.

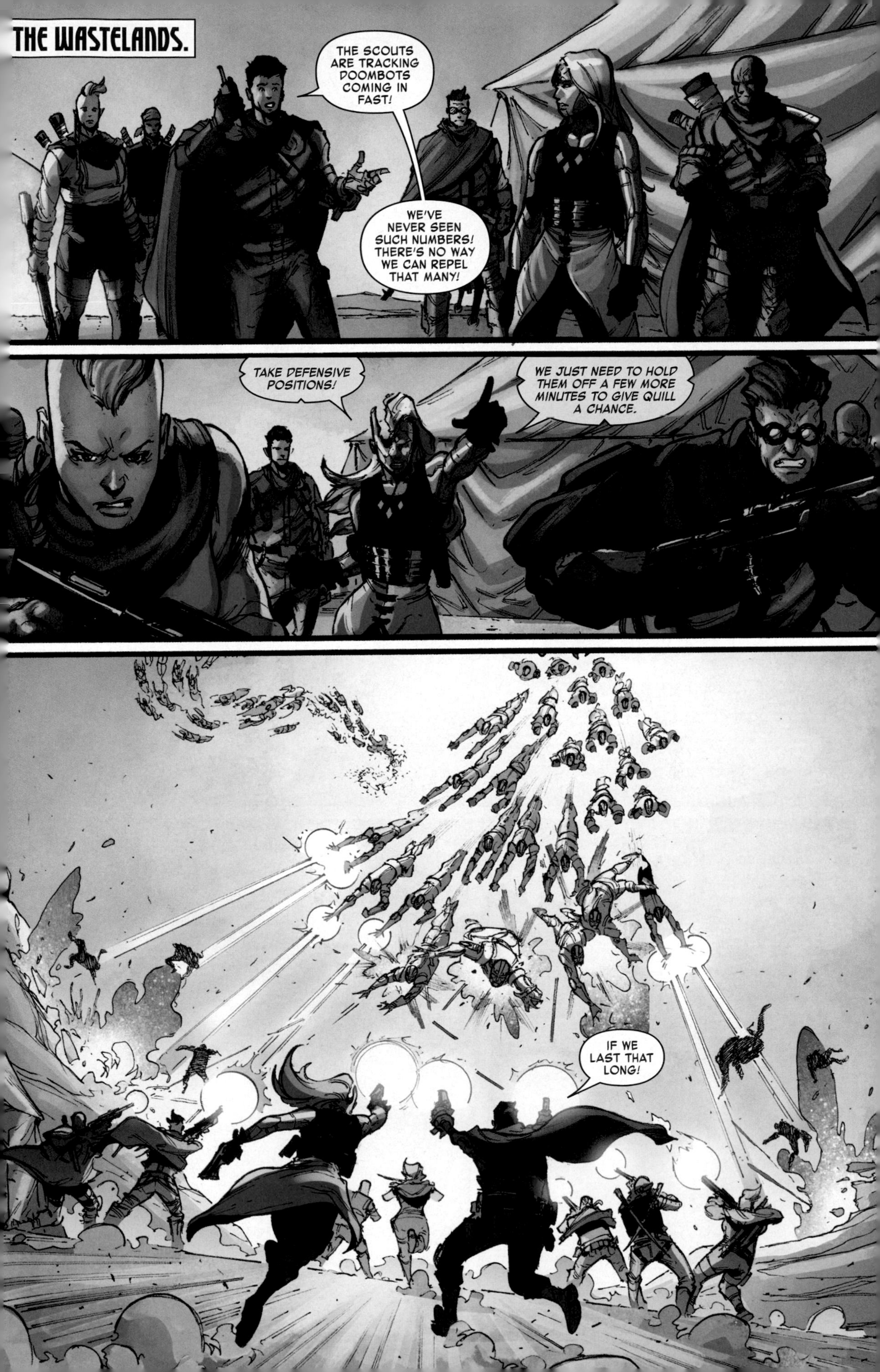
THE WASTELANDS.
THE SCOUTS ARE TRACKING DOOMBOTS COMING IN FAST!
WE'VE NEVER SEEN SUCH NUMBERS! THERE'S NO WAY WE CAN REPEL THAT MANY!
TAKE DEFENSIVE POSITIONS!
WE JUST NEED TO HOLD THEM OFF A FEW MORE MINUTES TO GIVE QUILL A CHANCE.
IF WE LAST THAT LONG!

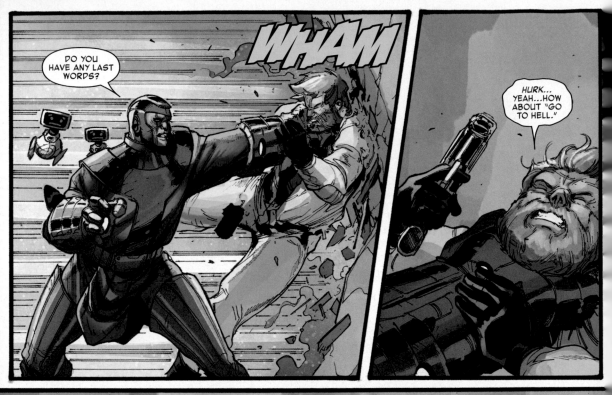

DO YOU HAVE ANY LAST WORDS?

WHAM

HURK... YEAH...HOW ABOUT "GO TO HELL."

CRUNCH

OKAY THEN, HOW ABOUT... ⸘CHOKE⸘...THESE LAST WORDS... ⸘CHOKE⸘... H.E.R.B.I.E.?

VOICE RECOGNITION UNABLE TO PROVIDE MATCH. QUERY DENIED.

UPDATE DATABASE TO: PETER QUILL... SKKK...STAR-LORD, FRIEND TO FANTASTIC FOUR.

UPDATE COMPLETE. WHAT IS YOUR QUERY?

⸘CHOKE⸘... REMIND PAST ME... ⸘CHOKE⸘...

...TO BORROW THAT KID'S KNIFE...

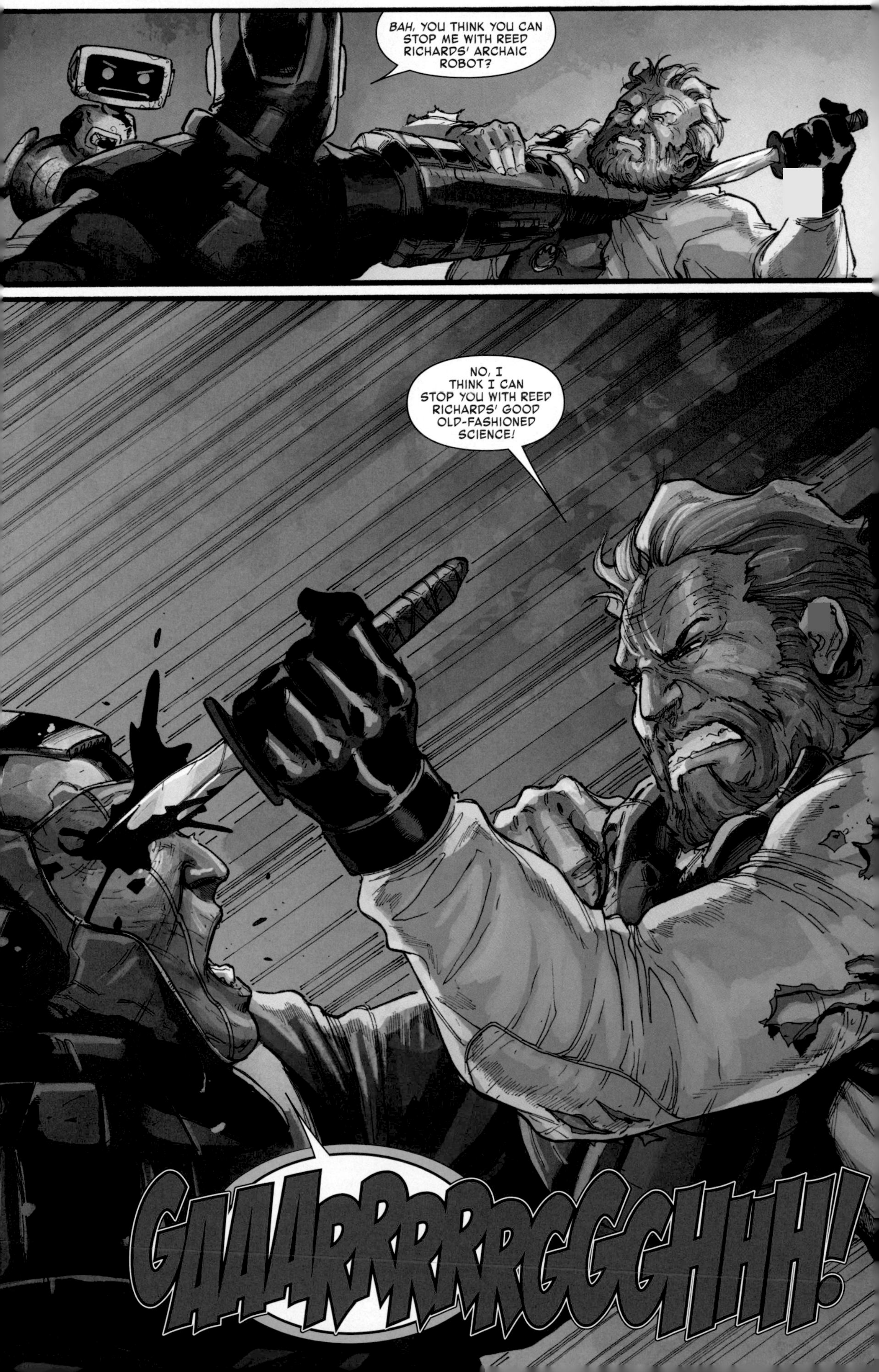
BAH, YOU THINK YOU CAN STOP ME WITH REED RICHARDS' ARCHAIC ROBOT?
NO, I THINK I CAN STOP YOU WITH REED RICHARDS' GOOD OLD-FASHIONED SCIENCE!
GAAARRRRRRGGGHHH!

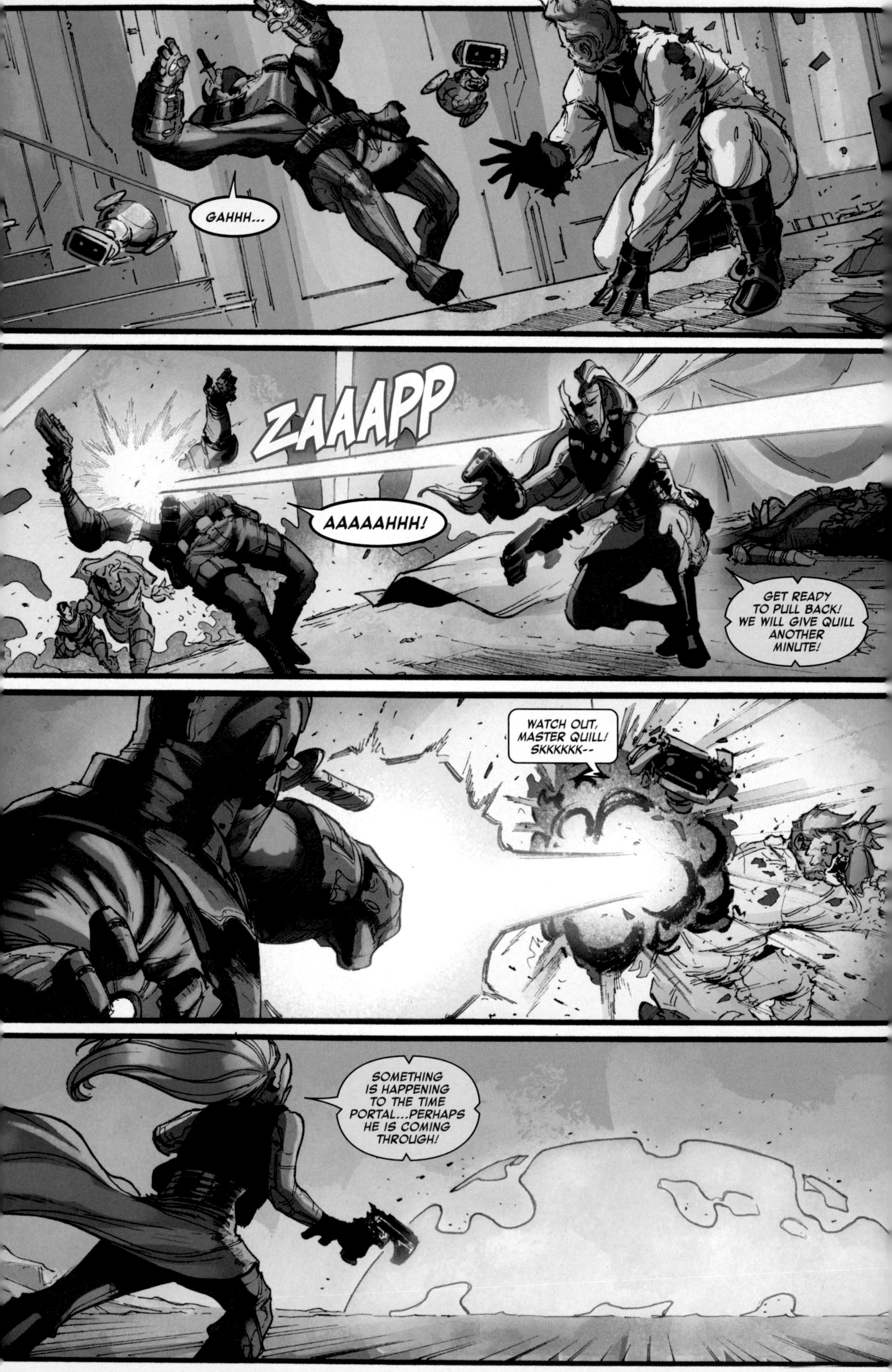
GAHHH...
ZAAAPP
AAAAAHHH!
GET READY TO PULL BACK! WE WILL GIVE QUILL ANOTHER MINUTE!
WATCH OUT, MASTER QUILL! SKKKKKK--
SOMETHING IS HAPPENING TO THE TIME PORTAL...PERHAPS HE IS COMING THROUGH!

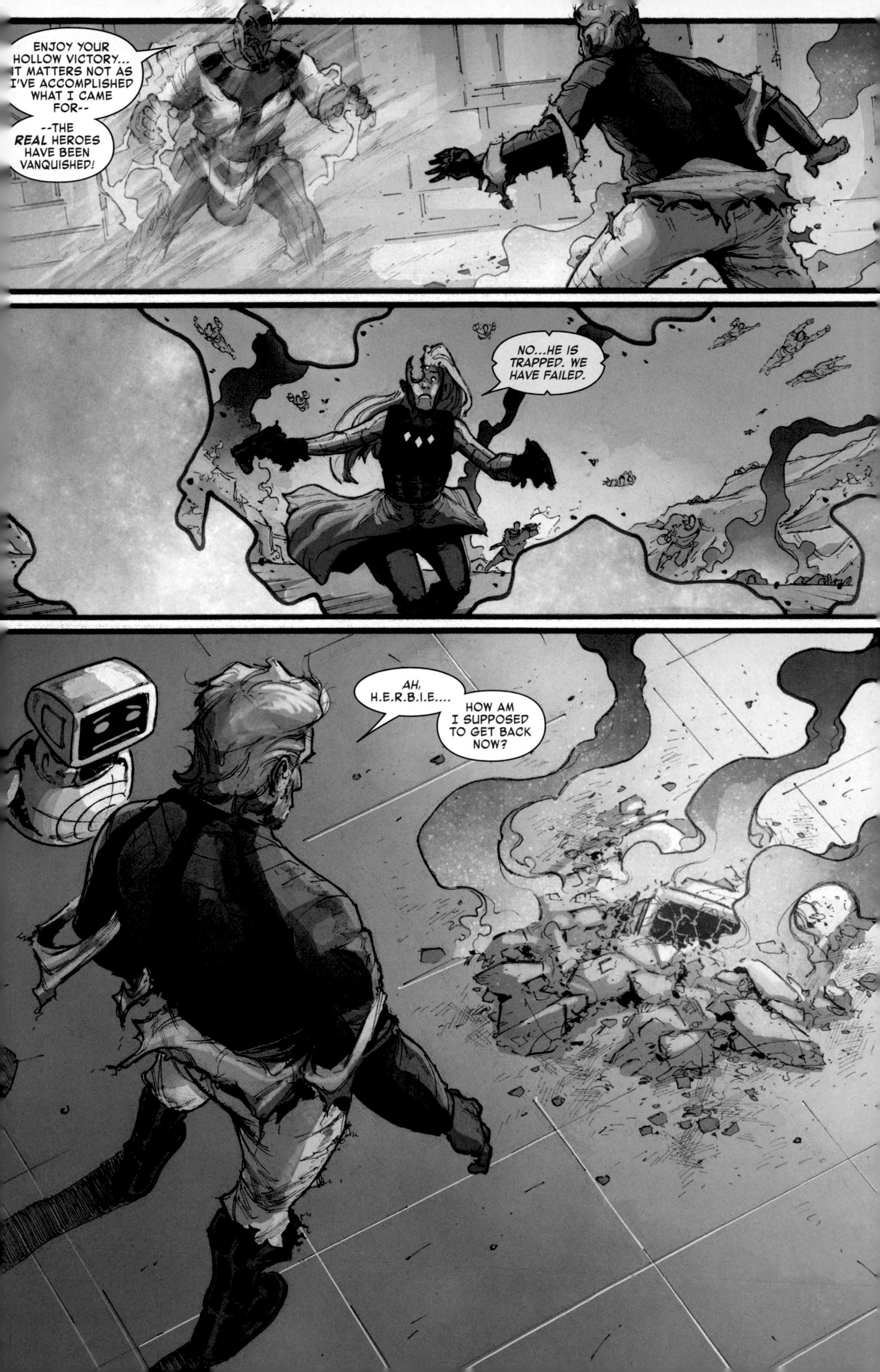
ENJOY YOUR HOLLOW VICTORY... IT MATTERS NOT AS I'VE ACCOMPLISHED WHAT I CAME FOR--
--THE *REAL* HEROES HAVE BEEN VANQUISHED!
NO...HE IS TRAPPED. WE HAVE FAILED.
AH, H.E.R.B.I.E....
HOW AM I SUPPOSED TO GET BACK NOW?

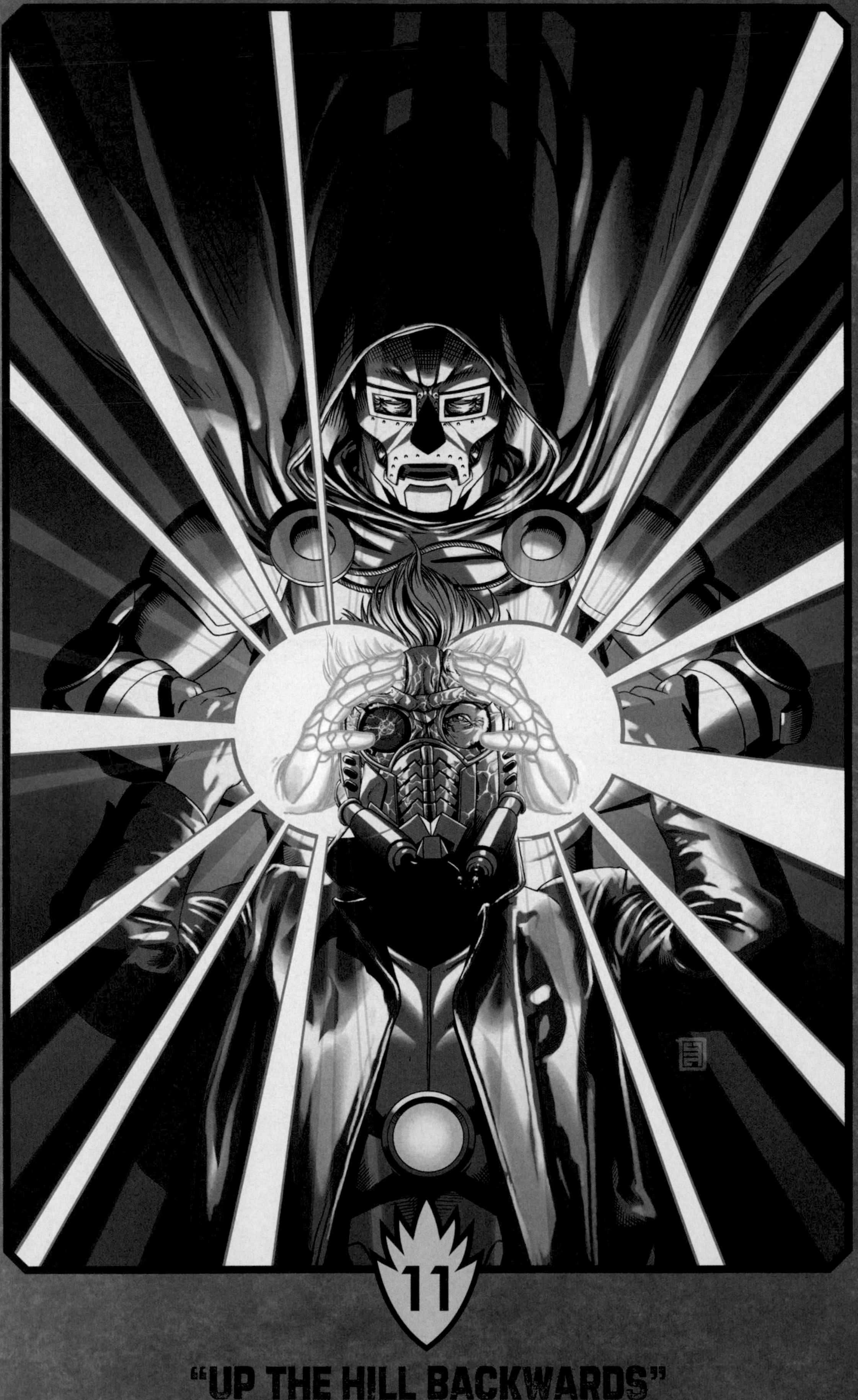
11

"UP THE HILL BACKWARDS"

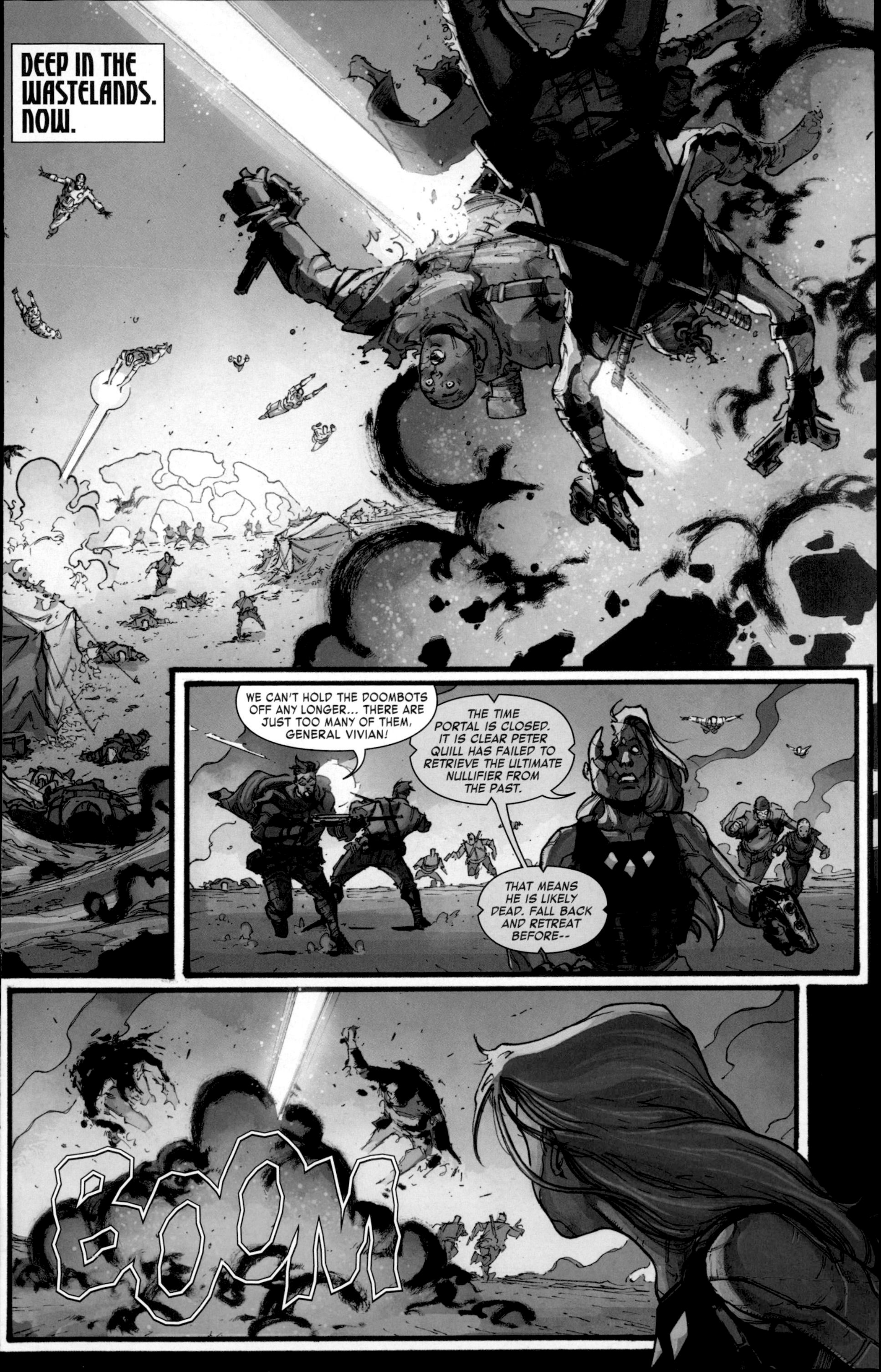
DEEP IN THE WASTELANDS. NOW.
WE CAN'T HOLD THE DOOMBOTS OFF ANY LONGER... THERE ARE JUST TOO MANY OF THEM, GENERAL VIVIAN!
THE TIME PORTAL IS CLOSED. IT IS CLEAR PETER QUILL HAS FAILED TO RETRIEVE THE ULTIMATE NULLIFIER FROM THE PAST.
THAT MEANS HE IS LIKELY DEAD. FALL BACK AND RETREAT BEFORE--
BOOM

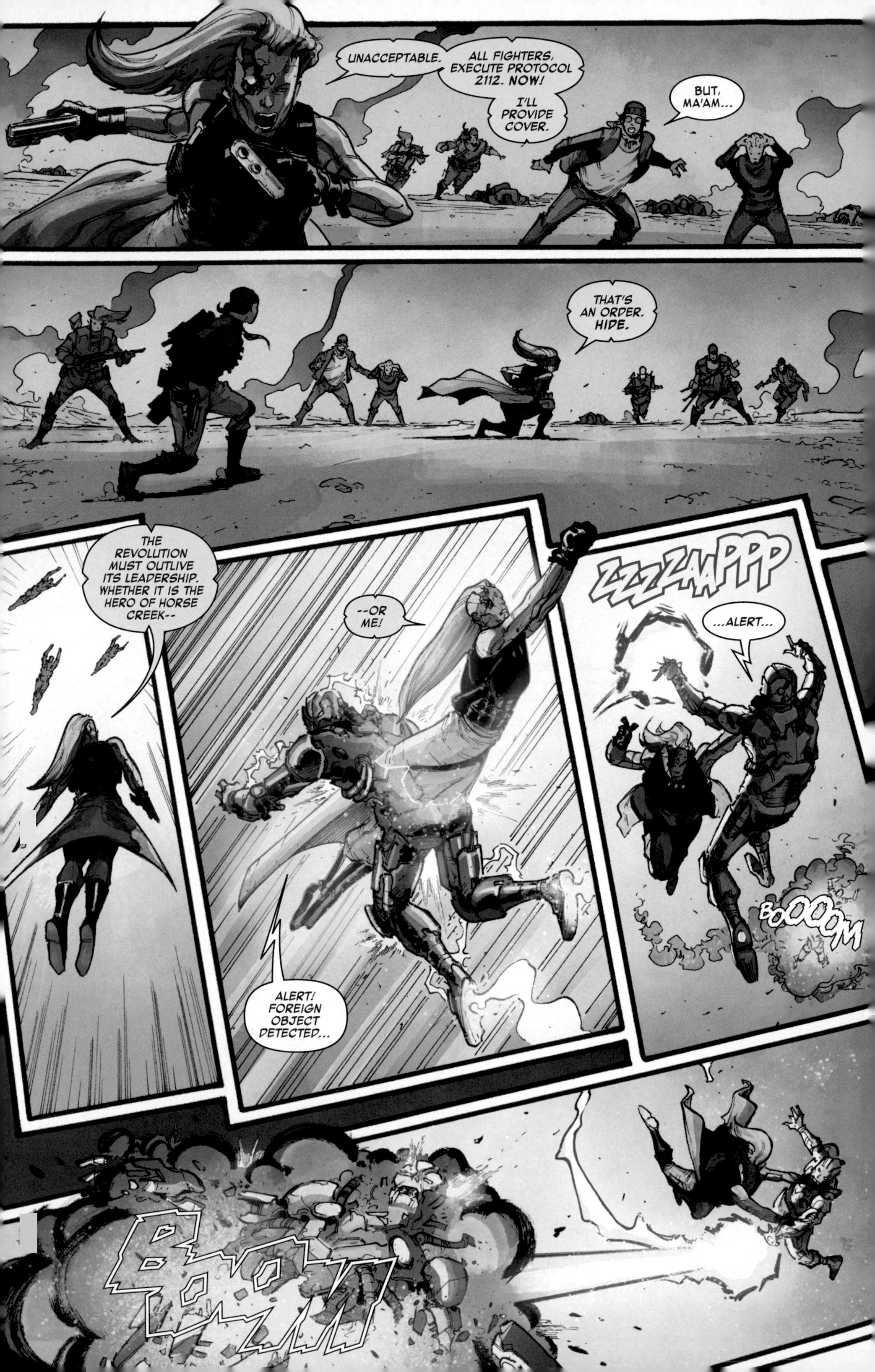
UNACCEPTABLE.
ALL FIGHTERS, EXECUTE PROTOCOL 2112. NOW!
I'LL PROVIDE COVER.
BUT, MA'AM...
THAT'S AN ORDER. HIDE.
THE REVOLUTION MUST OUTLIVE ITS LEADERSHIP. WHETHER IT IS THE HERO OF HORSE CREEK--
--OR ME!
ALERT! FOREIGN OBJECT DETECTED...
ZZZZAAPPP
...ALERT...
BOOOOM

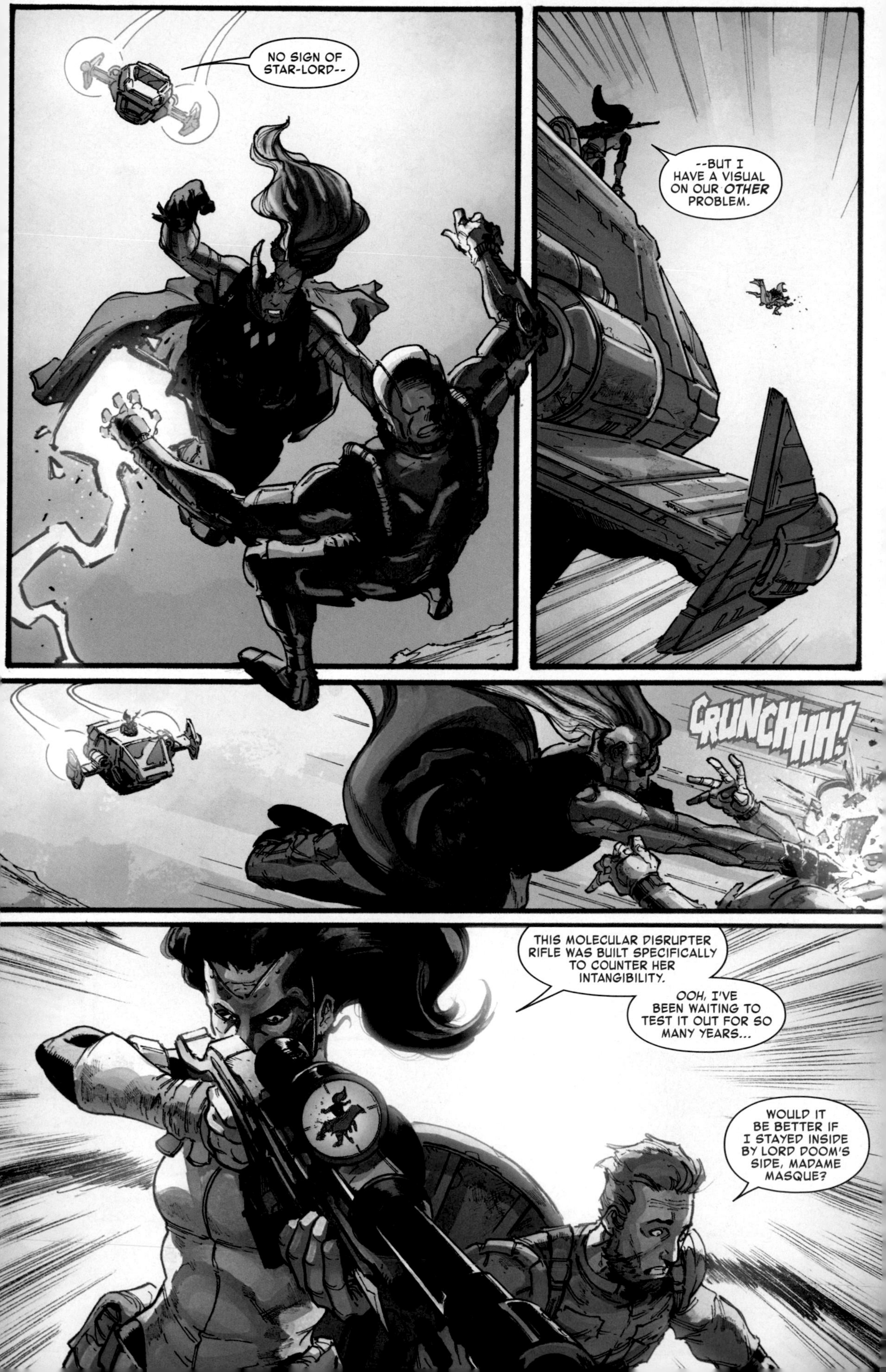
NO SIGN OF STAR-LORD--
--BUT I HAVE A VISUAL ON OUR *OTHER* PROBLEM.
CRUNCHHH!
THIS MOLECULAR DISRUPTER RIFLE WAS BUILT SPECIFICALLY TO COUNTER HER INTANGIBILITY.
OOH, I'VE BEEN WAITING TO TEST IT OUT FOR SO MANY YEARS...
WOULD IT BE BETTER IF I STAYED INSIDE BY LORD DOOM'S SIDE, MADAME MASQUE?

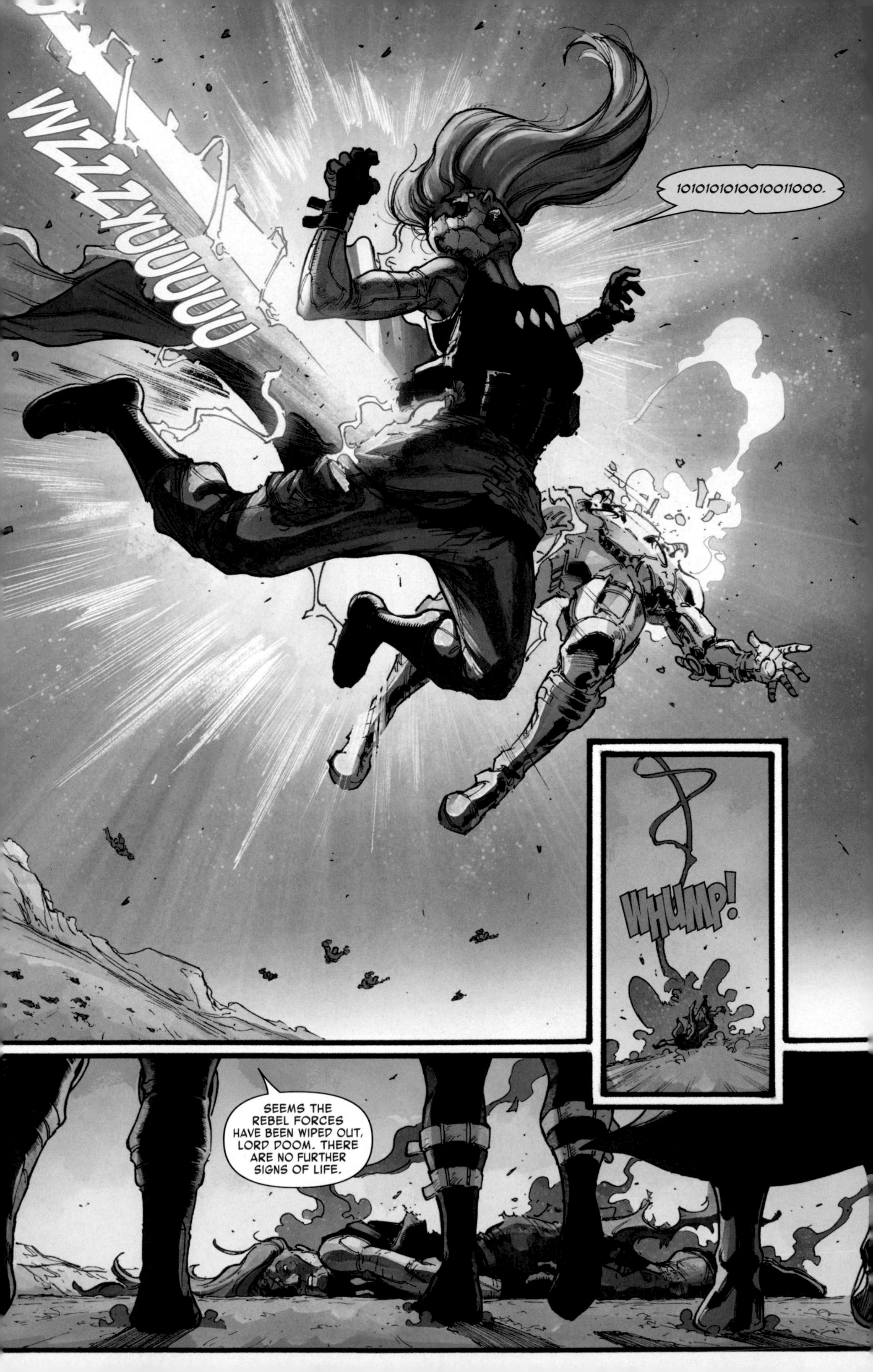

WZZZUUUUUU
1010101010010011000.
WHUMP!
SEEMS THE REBEL FORCES HAVE BEEN WIPED OUT, LORD DOOM. THERE ARE NO FURTHER SIGNS OF LIFE.

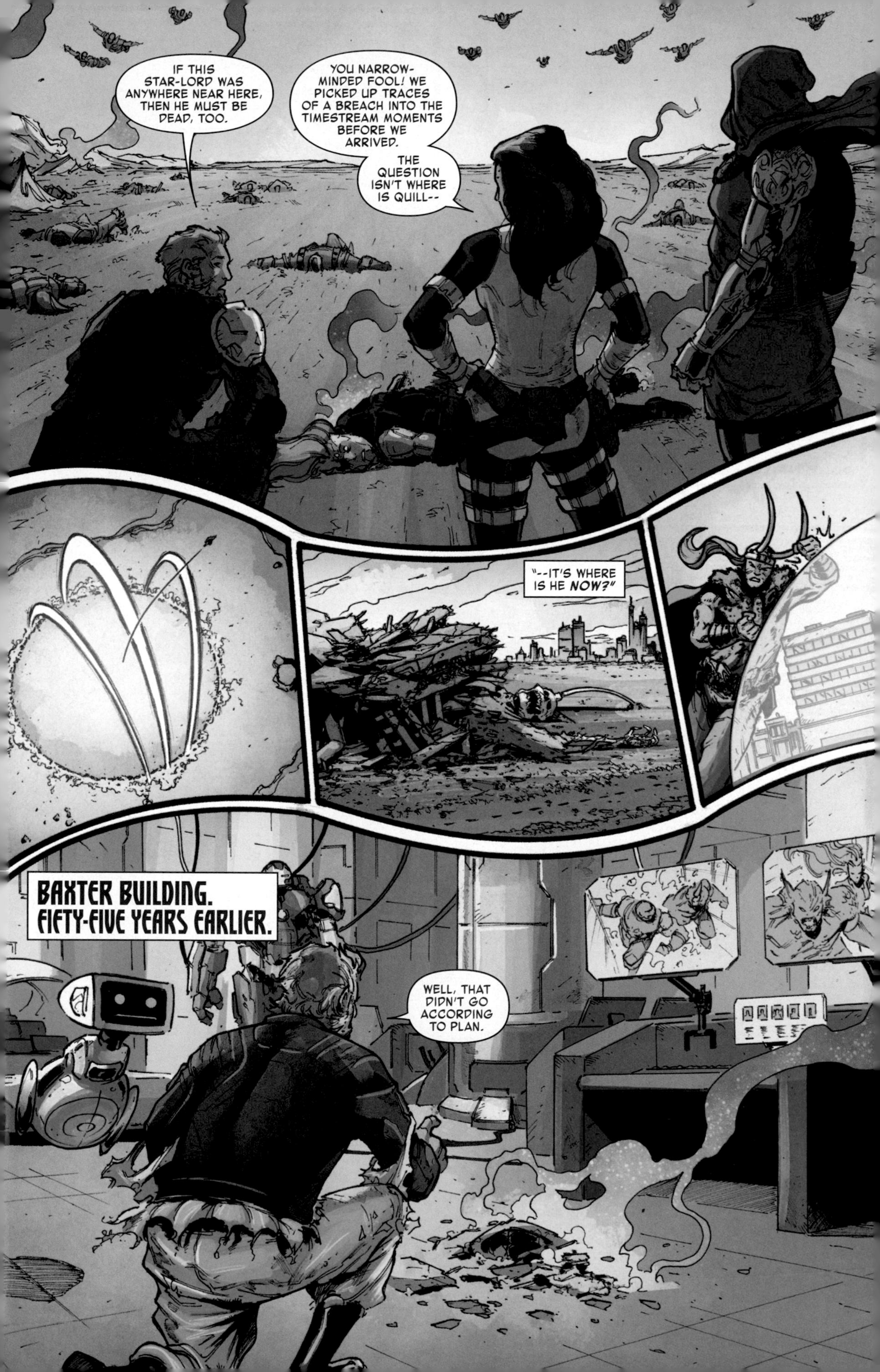
IF THIS STAR-LORD WAS ANYWHERE NEAR HERE, THEN HE MUST BE DEAD, TOO.
YOU NARROW-MINDED FOOL! WE PICKED UP TRACES OF A BREACH INTO THE TIMESTREAM MOMENTS BEFORE WE ARRIVED.
THE QUESTION ISN'T WHERE IS QUILL--
"--IT'S WHERE IS HE *NOW?*"
BAXTER BUILDING. FIFTY-FIVE YEARS EARLIER.
WELL, THAT DIDN'T GO ACCORDING TO PLAN.

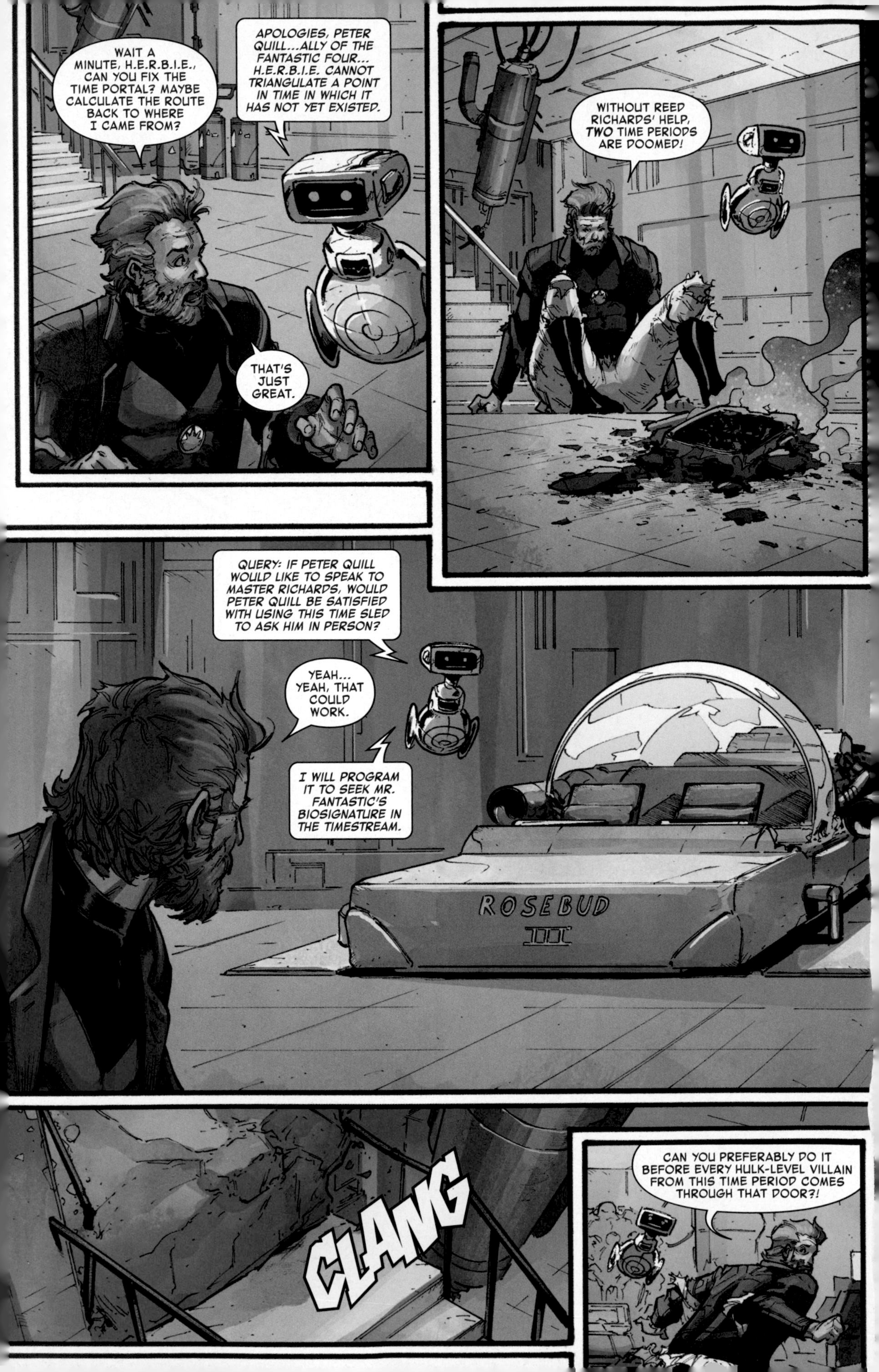
WAIT A MINUTE, H.E.R.B.I.E., CAN YOU FIX THE TIME PORTAL? MAYBE CALCULATE THE ROUTE BACK TO WHERE I CAME FROM?
APOLOGIES, PETER QUILL...ALLY OF THE FANTASTIC FOUR... H.E.R.B.I.E. CANNOT TRIANGULATE A POINT IN TIME IN WHICH IT HAS NOT YET EXISTED.
THAT'S JUST GREAT.
WITHOUT REED RICHARDS' HELP, TWO TIME PERIODS ARE DOOMED!
QUERY: IF PETER QUILL WOULD LIKE TO SPEAK TO MASTER RICHARDS, WOULD PETER QUILL BE SATISFIED WITH USING THIS TIME SLED TO ASK HIM IN PERSON?
YEAH... YEAH, THAT COULD WORK.
I WILL PROGRAM IT TO SEEK MR. FANTASTIC'S BIOSIGNATURE IN THE TIMESTREAM.
ROSEBUD
III
CLANG
CAN YOU PREFERABLY DO IT BEFORE EVERY HULK-LEVEL VILLAIN FROM THIS TIME PERIOD COMES THROUGH THAT DOOR?!

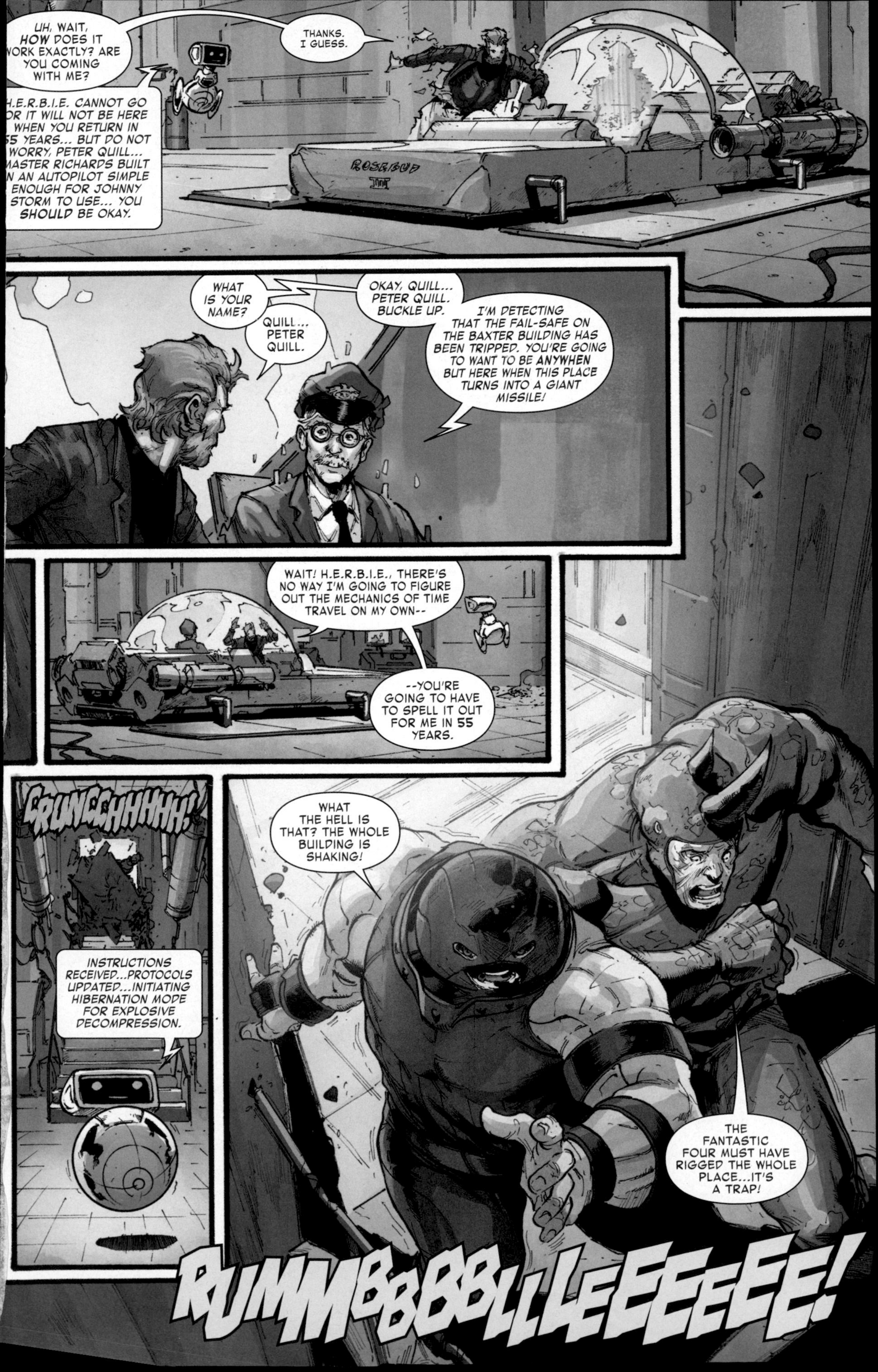

UH, WAIT, HOW DOES IT WORK EXACTLY? ARE YOU COMING WITH ME?
THANKS. I GUESS.
H.E.R.B.I.E. CANNOT GO OR IT WILL NOT BE HERE WHEN YOU RETURN IN 55 YEARS... BUT DO NOT WORRY, PETER QUILL... MASTER RICHARDS BUILT IN AN AUTOPILOT SIMPLE ENOUGH FOR JOHNNY STORM TO USE... YOU SHOULD BE OKAY.
ROSEBUD III
WHAT IS YOUR NAME?
QUILL... PETER QUILL.
OKAY, QUILL... PETER QUILL. BUCKLE UP.
I'M DETECTING THAT THE FAIL-SAFE ON THE BAXTER BUILDING HAS BEEN TRIPPED. YOU'RE GOING TO WANT TO BE ANYWHEN BUT HERE WHEN THIS PLACE TURNS INTO A GIANT MISSILE!
WAIT! H.E.R.B.I.E., THERE'S NO WAY I'M GOING TO FIGURE OUT THE MECHANICS OF TIME TRAVEL ON MY OWN--
--YOU'RE GOING TO HAVE TO SPELL IT OUT FOR ME IN 55 YEARS.
CRUNCCHHHHH!
INSTRUCTIONS RECEIVED...PROTOCOLS UPDATED...INITIATING HIBERNATION MODE FOR EXPLOSIVE DECOMPRESSION.
WHAT THE HELL IS THAT? THE WHOLE BUILDING IS SHAKING!
THE FANTASTIC FOUR MUST HAVE RIGGED THE WHOLE PLACE...IT'S A TRAP!
RUMMBBBBLLLEEEEEEE!

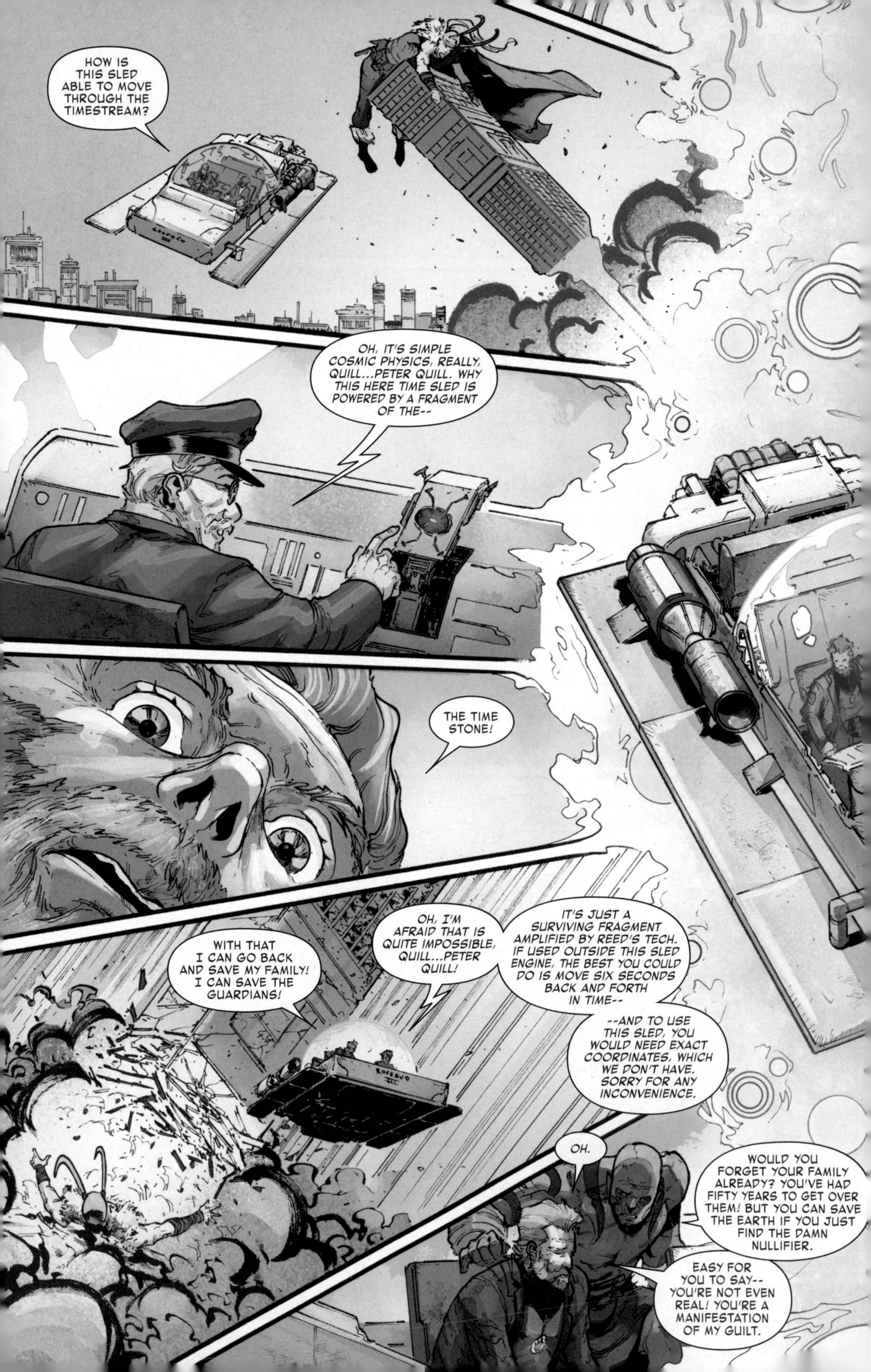
HOW IS THIS SLED ABLE TO MOVE THROUGH THE TIMESTREAM?
OH, IT'S SIMPLE COSMIC PHYSICS, REALLY, QUILL...PETER QUILL. WHY THIS HERE TIME SLED IS POWERED BY A FRAGMENT OF THE--
THE TIME STONE!
WITH THAT I CAN GO BACK AND SAVE MY FAMILY! I CAN SAVE THE GUARDIANS!
OH, I'M AFRAID THAT IS QUITE IMPOSSIBLE, QUILL...PETER QUILL!
IT'S JUST A SURVIVING FRAGMENT AMPLIFIED BY REED'S TECH. IF USED OUTSIDE THIS SLED ENGINE, THE BEST YOU COULD DO IS MOVE SIX SECONDS BACK AND FORTH IN TIME--
--AND TO USE THIS SLED, YOU WOULD NEED EXACT COORDINATES, WHICH WE DON'T HAVE. SORRY FOR ANY INCONVENIENCE.
OH.
WOULD YOU FORGET YOUR FAMILY ALREADY? YOU'VE HAD FIFTY YEARS TO GET OVER THEM! BUT YOU CAN SAVE THE EARTH IF YOU JUST FIND THE DAMN NULLIFIER.
EASY FOR YOU TO SAY-- YOU'RE NOT EVEN REAL! YOU'RE A MANIFESTATION OF MY GUILT.

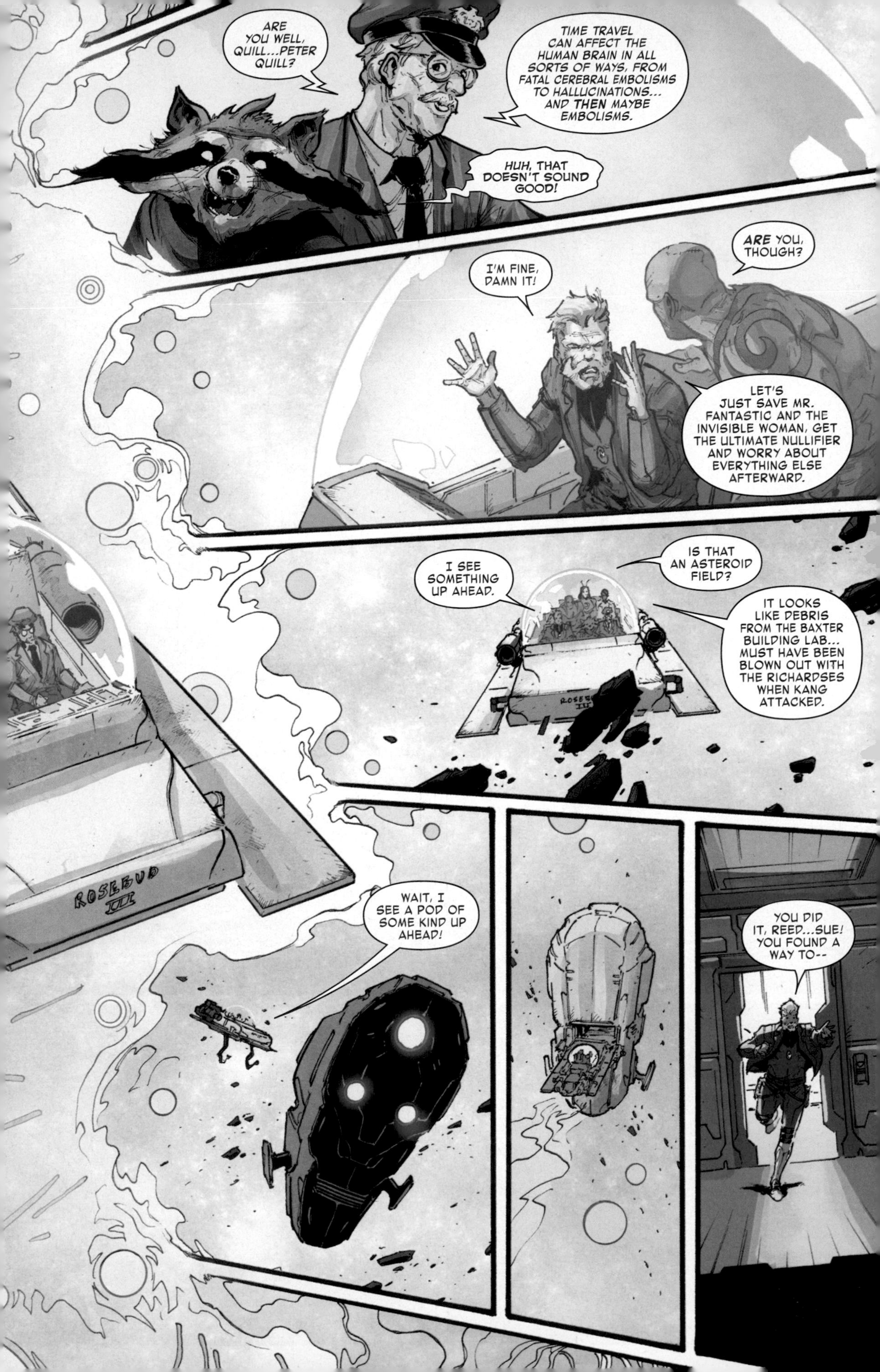
ARE YOU WELL, QUILL...PETER QUILL?
TIME TRAVEL CAN AFFECT THE HUMAN BRAIN IN ALL SORTS OF WAYS, FROM FATAL CEREBRAL EMBOLISMS TO HALLUCINATIONS... AND THEN MAYBE EMBOLISMS.
HUH, THAT DOESN'T SOUND GOOD!
I'M FINE, DAMN IT!
ARE YOU, THOUGH?
LET'S JUST SAVE MR. FANTASTIC AND THE INVISIBLE WOMAN, GET THE ULTIMATE NULLIFIER AND WORRY ABOUT EVERYTHING ELSE AFTERWARD.
I SEE SOMETHING UP AHEAD.
IS THAT AN ASTEROID FIELD?
IT LOOKS LIKE DEBRIS FROM THE BAXTER BUILDING LAB... MUST HAVE BEEN BLOWN OUT WITH THE RICHARDSES WHEN KANG ATTACKED.
ROSEBUD III
WAIT, I SEE A POD OF SOME KIND UP AHEAD!
YOU DID IT, REED...SUE! YOU FOUND A WAY TO--

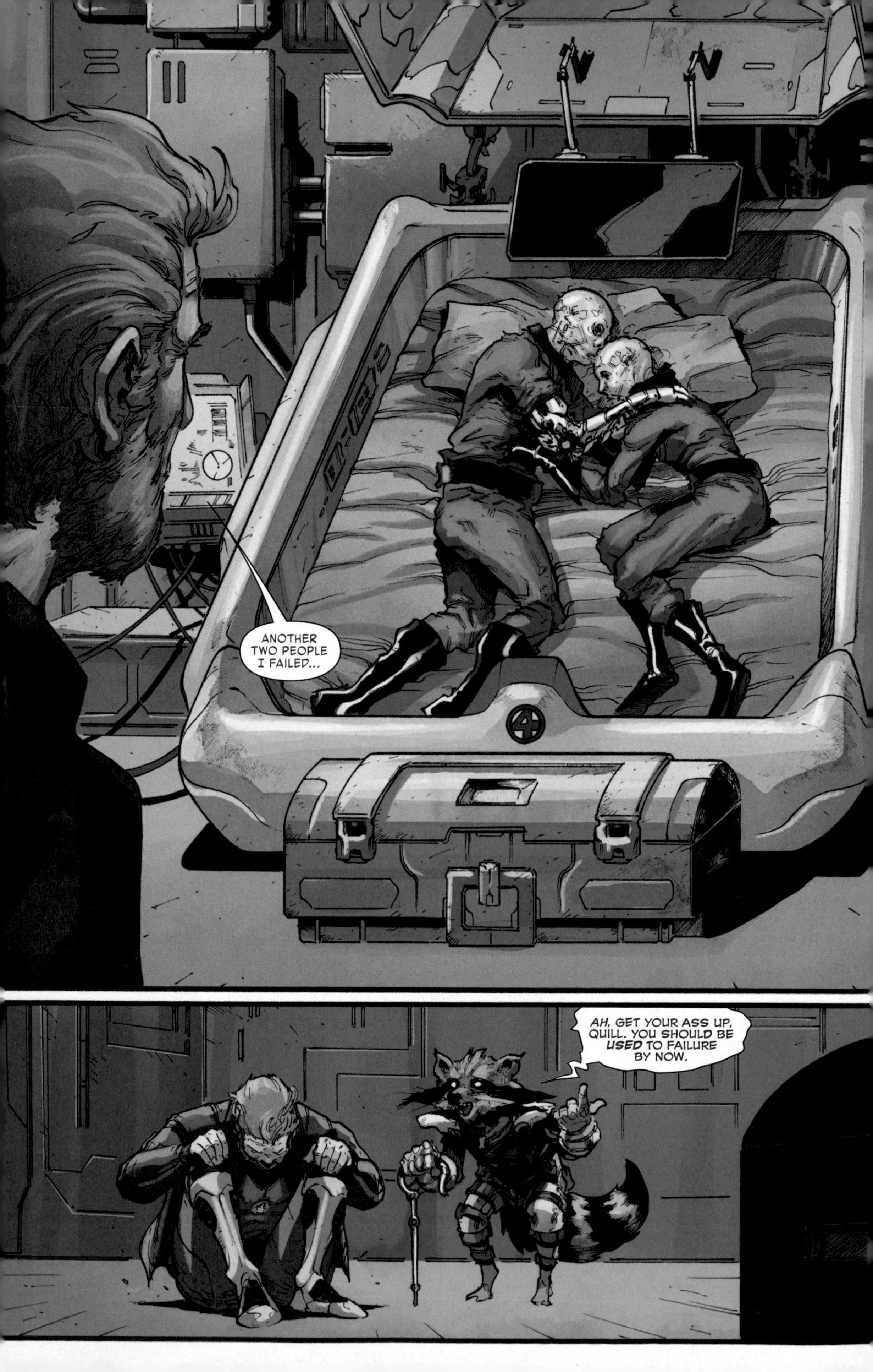
ANOTHER TWO PEOPLE I FAILED...
AH, GET YOUR ASS UP, QUILL. YOU SHOULD BE USED TO FAILURE BY NOW.

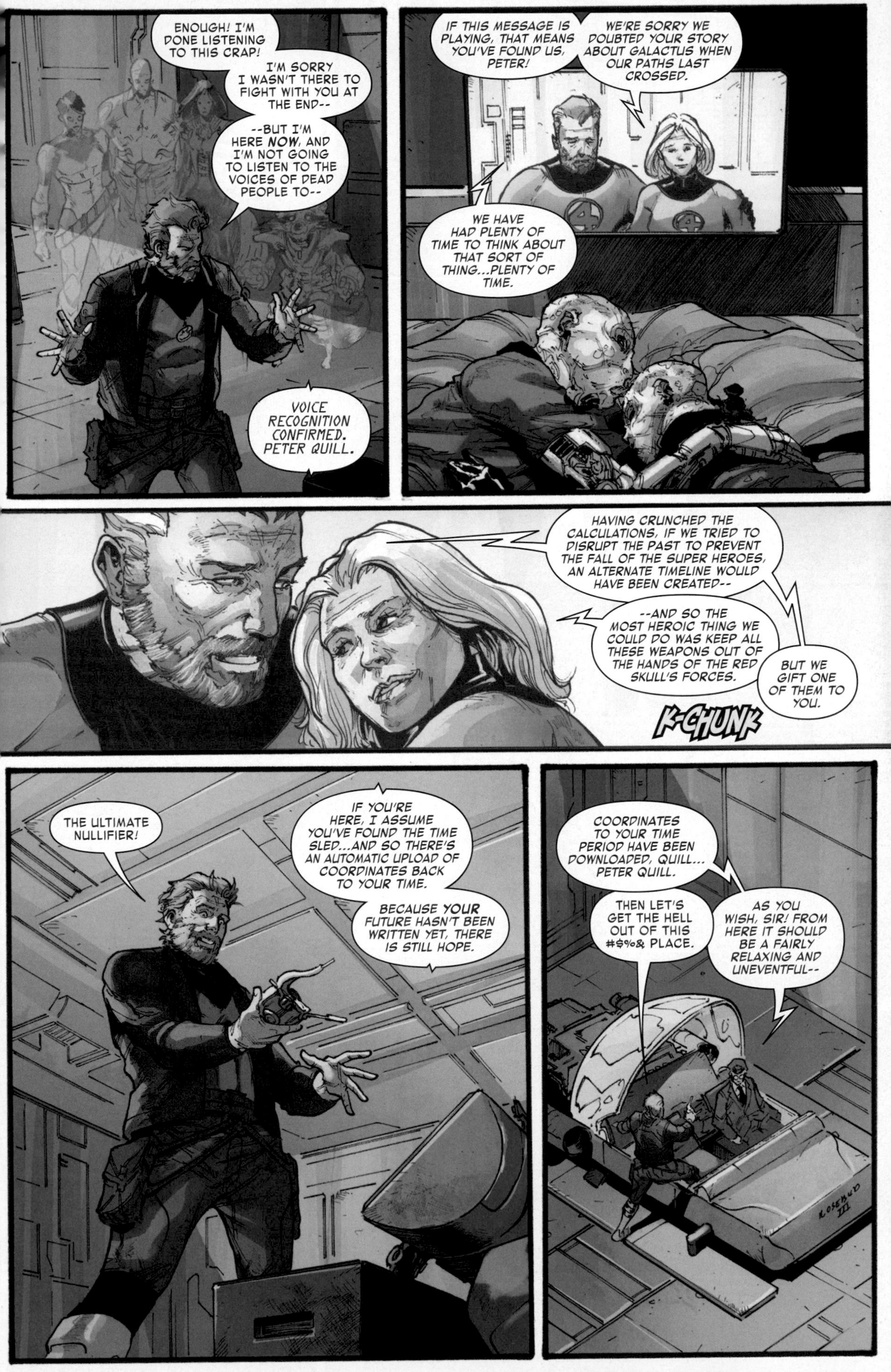
ENOUGH! I'M DONE LISTENING TO THIS CRAP!
I'M SORRY I WASN'T THERE TO FIGHT WITH YOU AT THE END--
--BUT I'M HERE NOW, AND I'M NOT GOING TO LISTEN TO THE VOICES OF DEAD PEOPLE TO--
VOICE RECOGNITION CONFIRMED. PETER QUILL.
IF THIS MESSAGE IS PLAYING, THAT MEANS YOU'VE FOUND US, PETER!
WE'RE SORRY WE DOUBTED YOUR STORY ABOUT GALACTUS WHEN OUR PATHS LAST CROSSED.
WE HAVE HAD PLENTY OF TIME TO THINK ABOUT THAT SORT OF THING...PLENTY OF TIME.
HAVING CRUNCHED THE CALCULATIONS, IF WE TRIED TO DISRUPT THE PAST TO PREVENT THE FALL OF THE SUPER HEROES, AN ALTERNATE TIMELINE WOULD HAVE BEEN CREATED--
--AND SO THE MOST HEROIC THING WE COULD DO WAS KEEP ALL THESE WEAPONS OUT OF THE HANDS OF THE RED SKULL'S FORCES.
BUT WE GIFT ONE OF THEM TO YOU.
K-CHUNK
THE ULTIMATE NULLIFIER!
IF YOU'RE HERE, I ASSUME YOU'VE FOUND THE TIME SLED...AND SO THERE'S AN AUTOMATIC UPLOAD OF COORDINATES BACK TO YOUR TIME.
BECAUSE YOUR FUTURE HASN'T BEEN WRITTEN YET, THERE IS STILL HOPE.
COORDINATES TO YOUR TIME PERIOD HAVE BEEN DOWNLOADED, QUILL... PETER QUILL.
THEN LET'S GET THE HELL OUT OF THIS #$%& PLACE.
AS YOU WISH, SIR! FROM HERE IT SHOULD BE A FAIRLY RELAXING AND UNEVENTFUL--

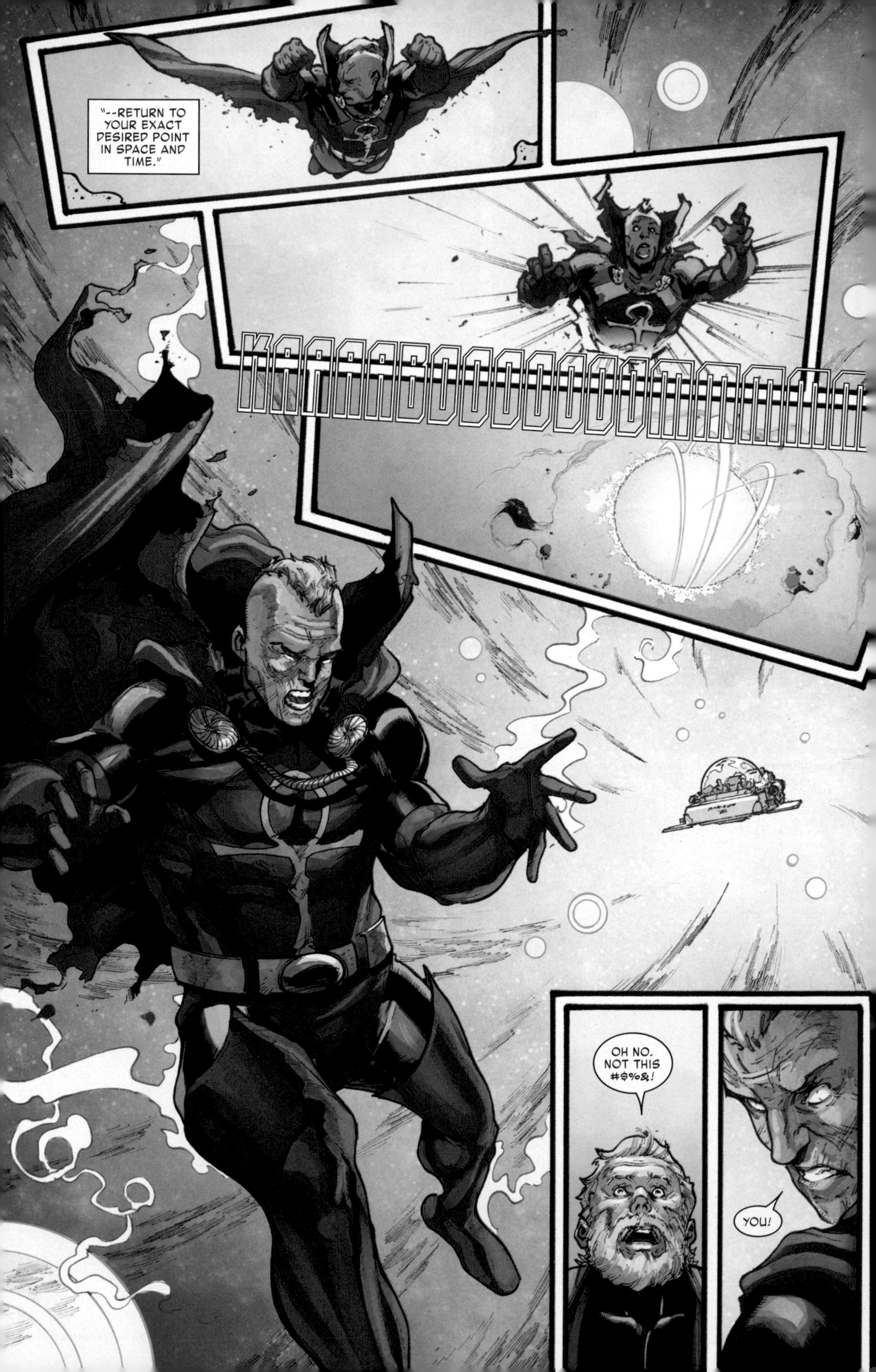
"--RETURN TO YOUR EXACT DESIRED POINT IN SPACE AND TIME."
KRAAAABOOOOOOOOOMMMMMM
OH NO. NOT THIS #$%&!
YOU!

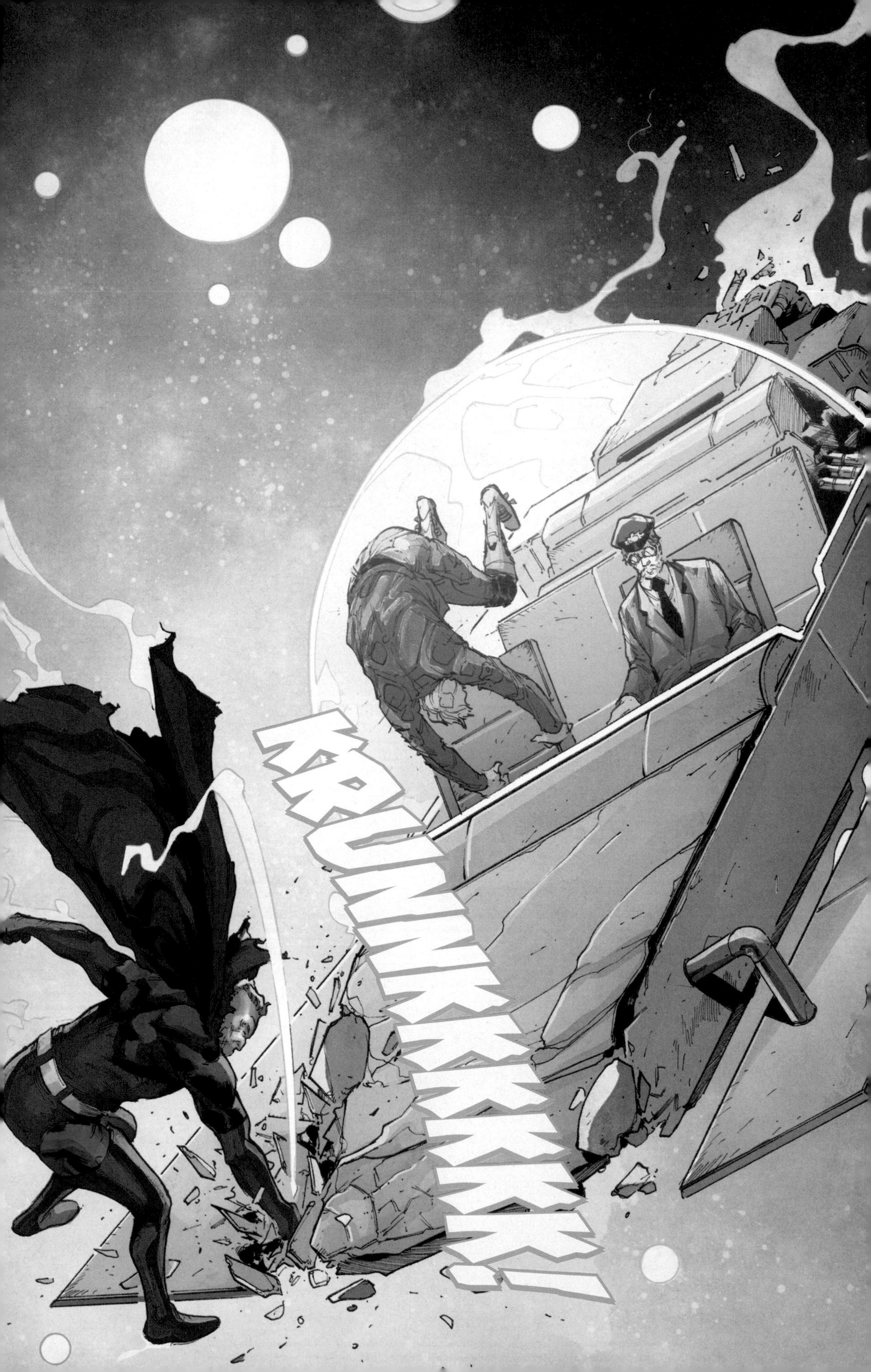
KRUNKKKKK!!

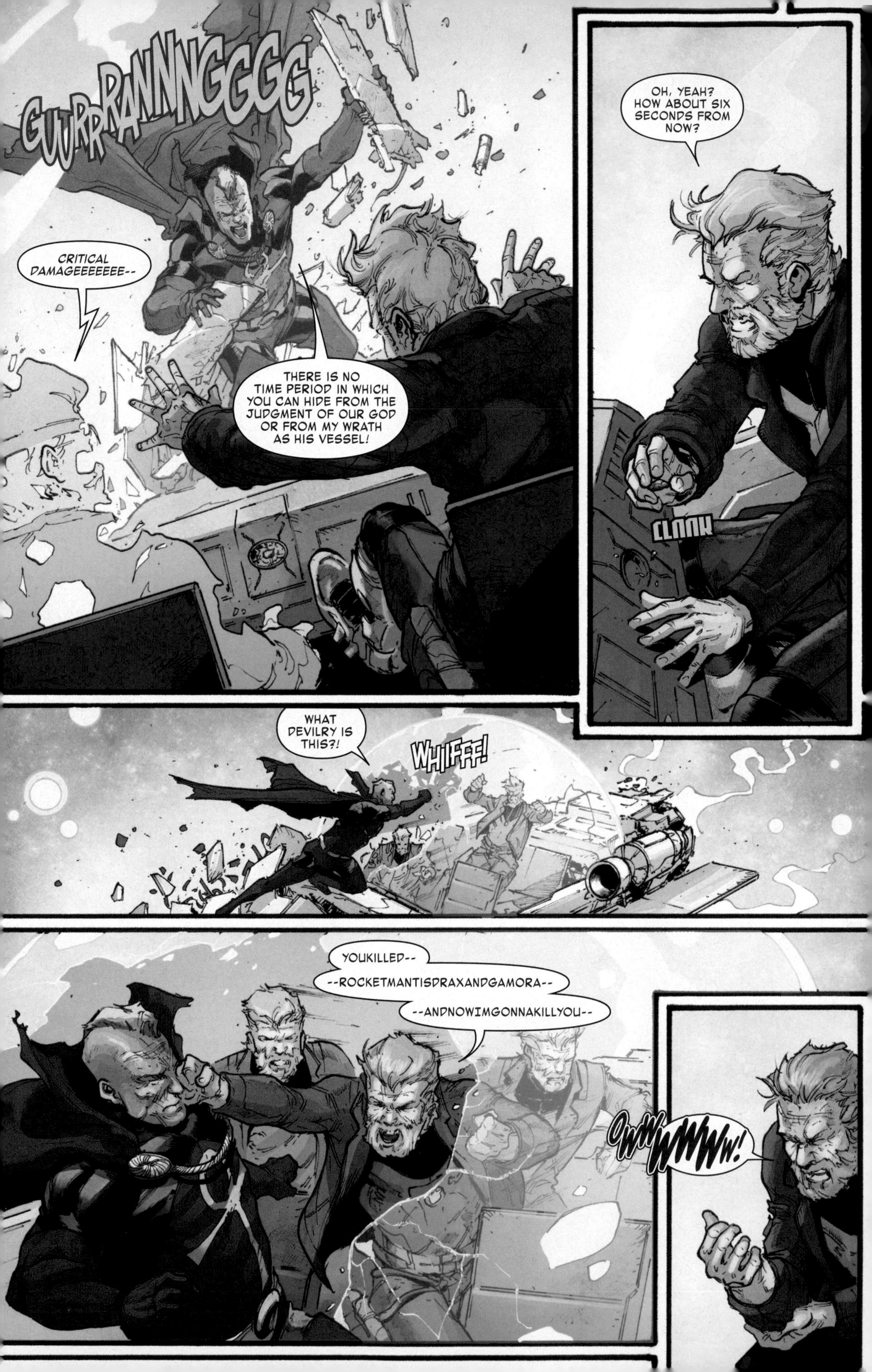
GUURRRANNNGGGG
CRITICAL DAMAGEEEEEEE--
THERE IS NO TIME PERIOD IN WHICH YOU CAN HIDE FROM THE JUDGMENT OF OUR GOD OR FROM MY WRATH AS HIS VESSEL!
OH, YEAH? HOW ABOUT SIX SECONDS FROM NOW?
CLNNK
WHAT DEVILRY IS THIS?!
WHIIFFF!
YOUKILLED--
--ROCKETMANTISDRAXANDGAMORA--
--ANDNOWIMGONNAKILLYOU--
OWWWWWW!

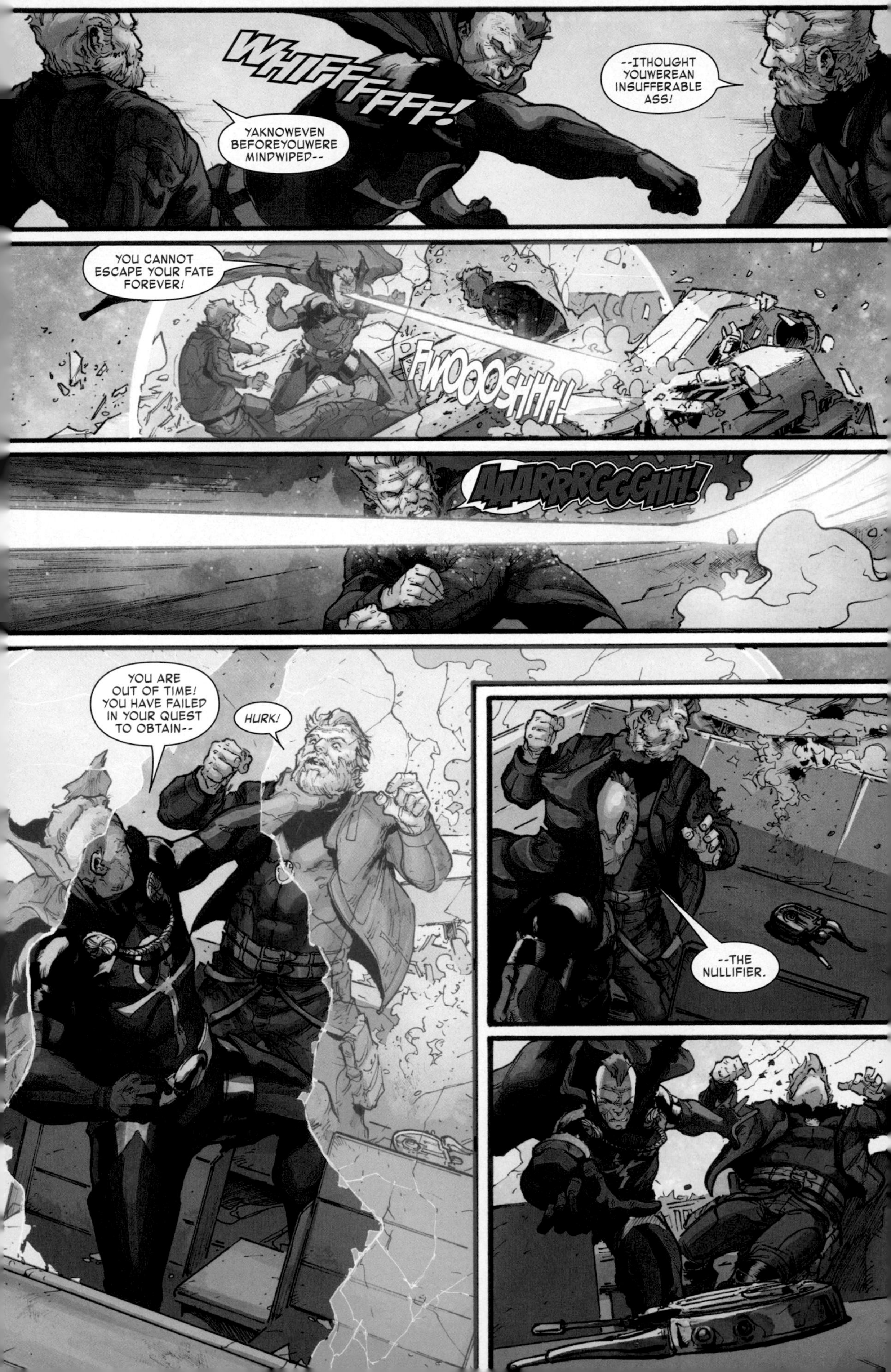
WHIFFFFFF!
YAKNOWEVEN BEFOREYOUWERE MINDWIPED--
--ITHOUGHT YOUWEREAN INSUFFERABLE ASS!
YOU CANNOT ESCAPE YOUR FATE FOREVER!
FWOOOSHHH!
AAARRRGGGHH!
YOU ARE OUT OF TIME! YOU HAVE FAILED IN YOUR QUEST TO OBTAIN--
HURK!
--THE NULLIFIER.

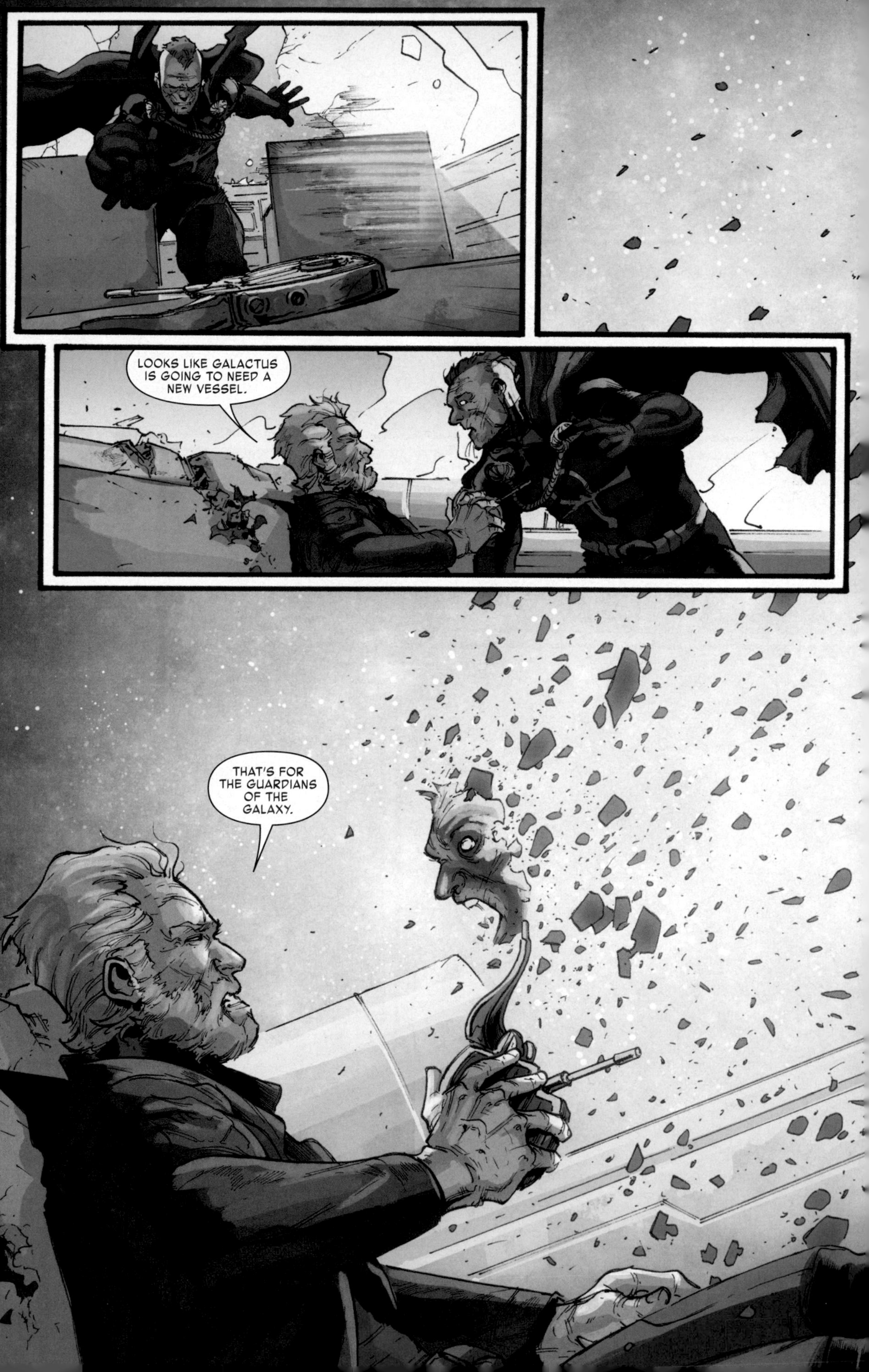
LOOKS LIKE GALACTUS IS GOING TO NEED A NEW VESSEL.
THAT'S FOR THE GUARDIANS OF THE GALAXY.

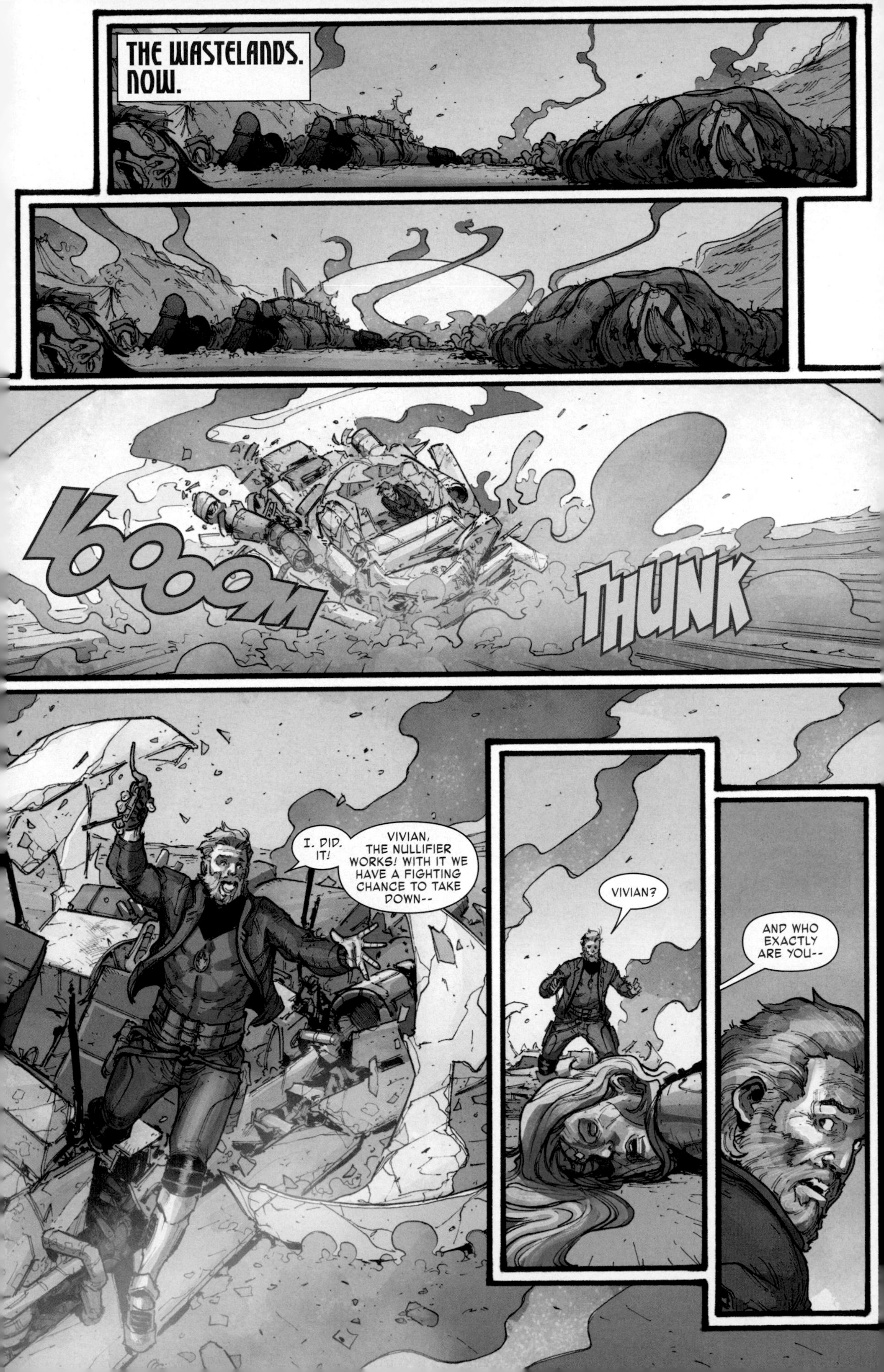
THE WASTELANDS. NOW.
VOOOOOM
THUNK
I. DID. IT!
VIVIAN, THE NULLIFIER WORKS! WITH IT WE HAVE A FIGHTING CHANCE TO TAKE DOWN--
VIVIAN?
AND WHO EXACTLY ARE YOU--

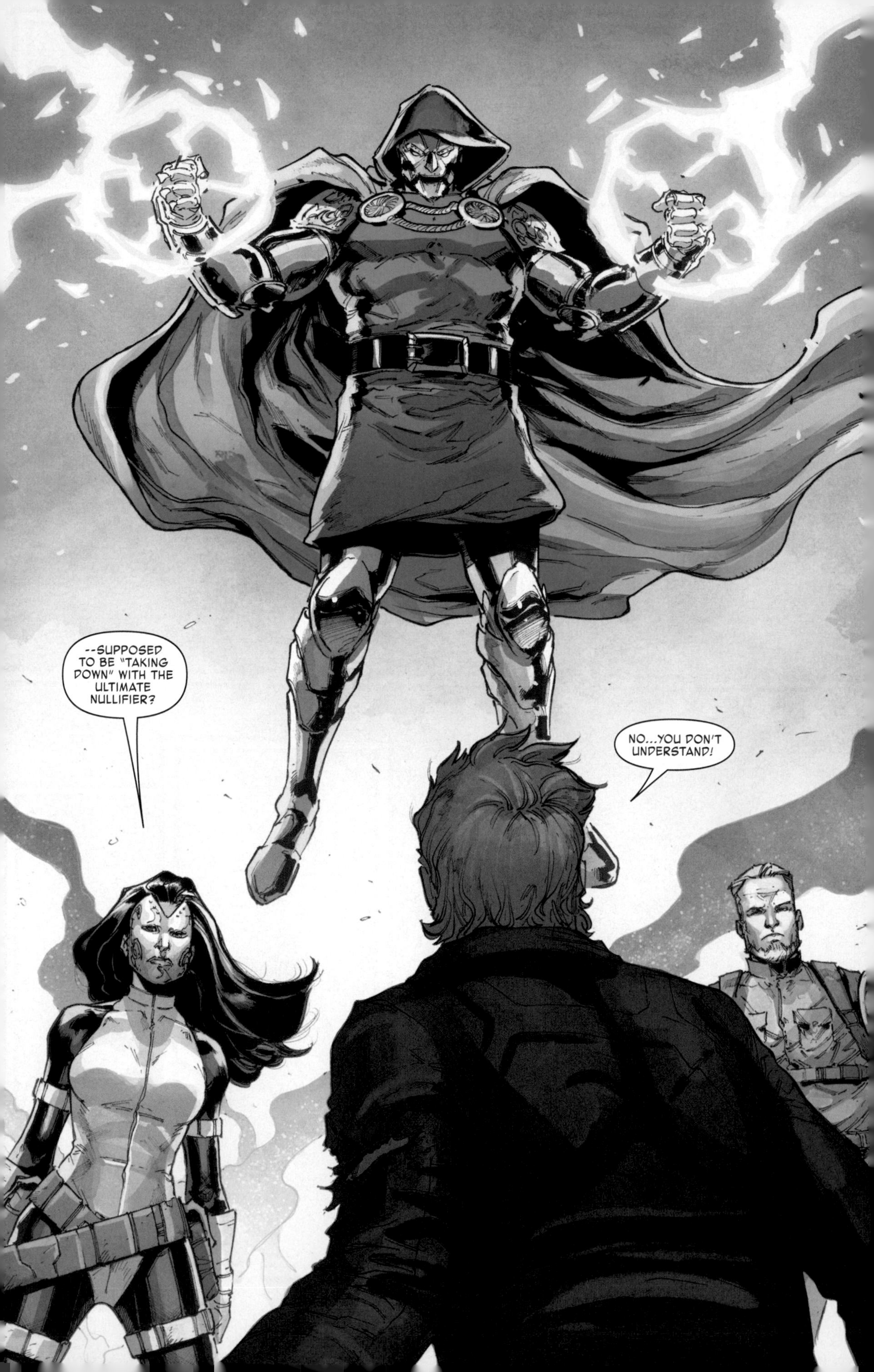
--SUPPOSED TO BE "TAKING DOWN" WITH THE ULTIMATE NULLIFIER?
NO...YOU DON'T UNDERSTAND!

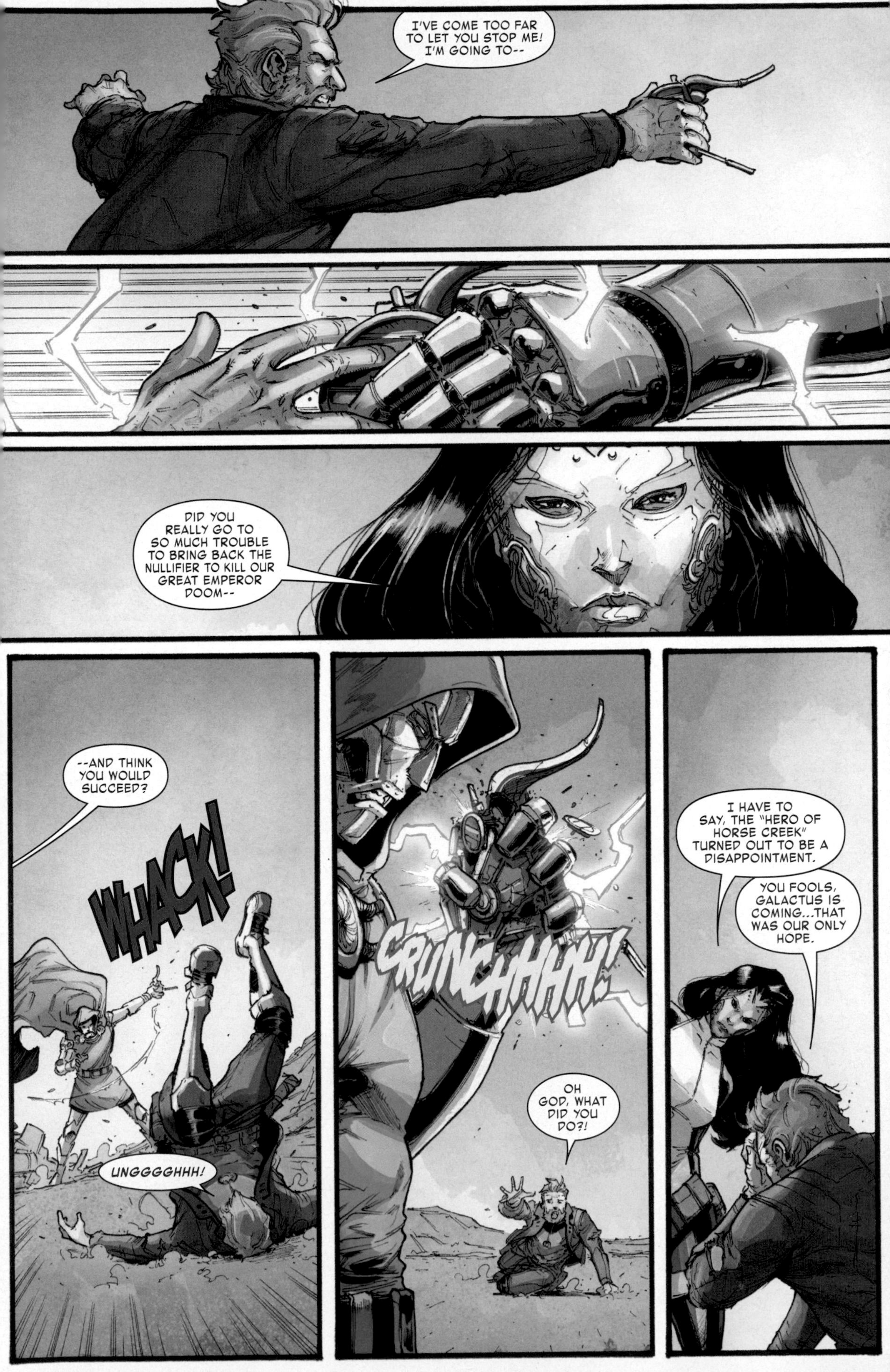

I'VE COME TOO FAR TO LET YOU STOP ME! I'M GOING TO--
DID YOU REALLY GO TO SO MUCH TROUBLE TO BRING BACK THE NULLIFIER TO KILL OUR GREAT EMPEROR DOOM--
--AND THINK YOU WOULD SUCCEED?
WHACK!
UNGGGGHHH!
CRUNCHHHH!
OH GOD, WHAT DID YOU DO?!
I HAVE TO SAY, THE "HERO OF HORSE CREEK" TURNED OUT TO BE A DISAPPOINTMENT.
YOU FOOLS, GALACTUS IS COMING...THAT WAS OUR ONLY HOPE.

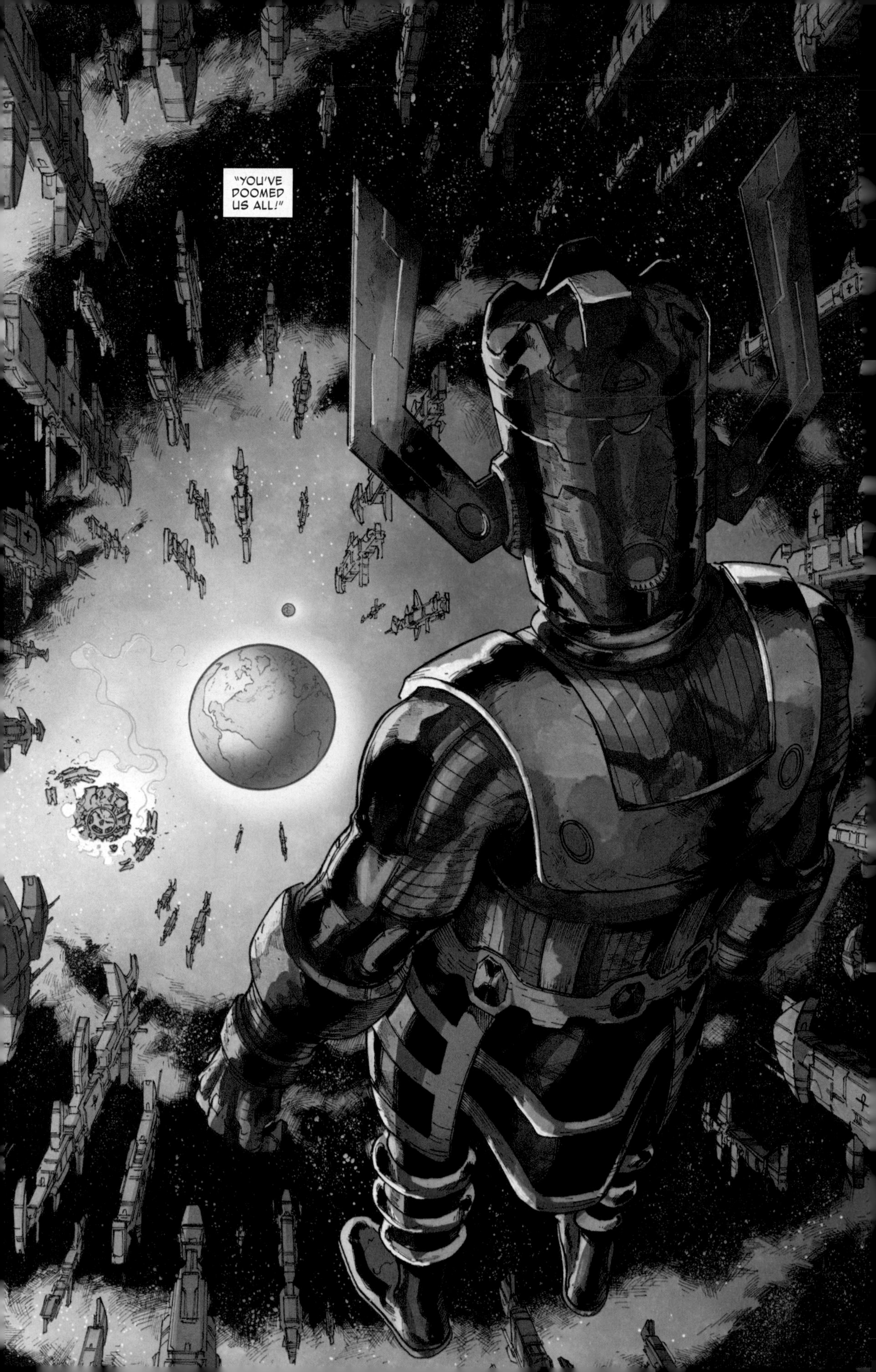
"YOU'VE DOOMED US ALL!"

"SPIRIT IN THE SKY"

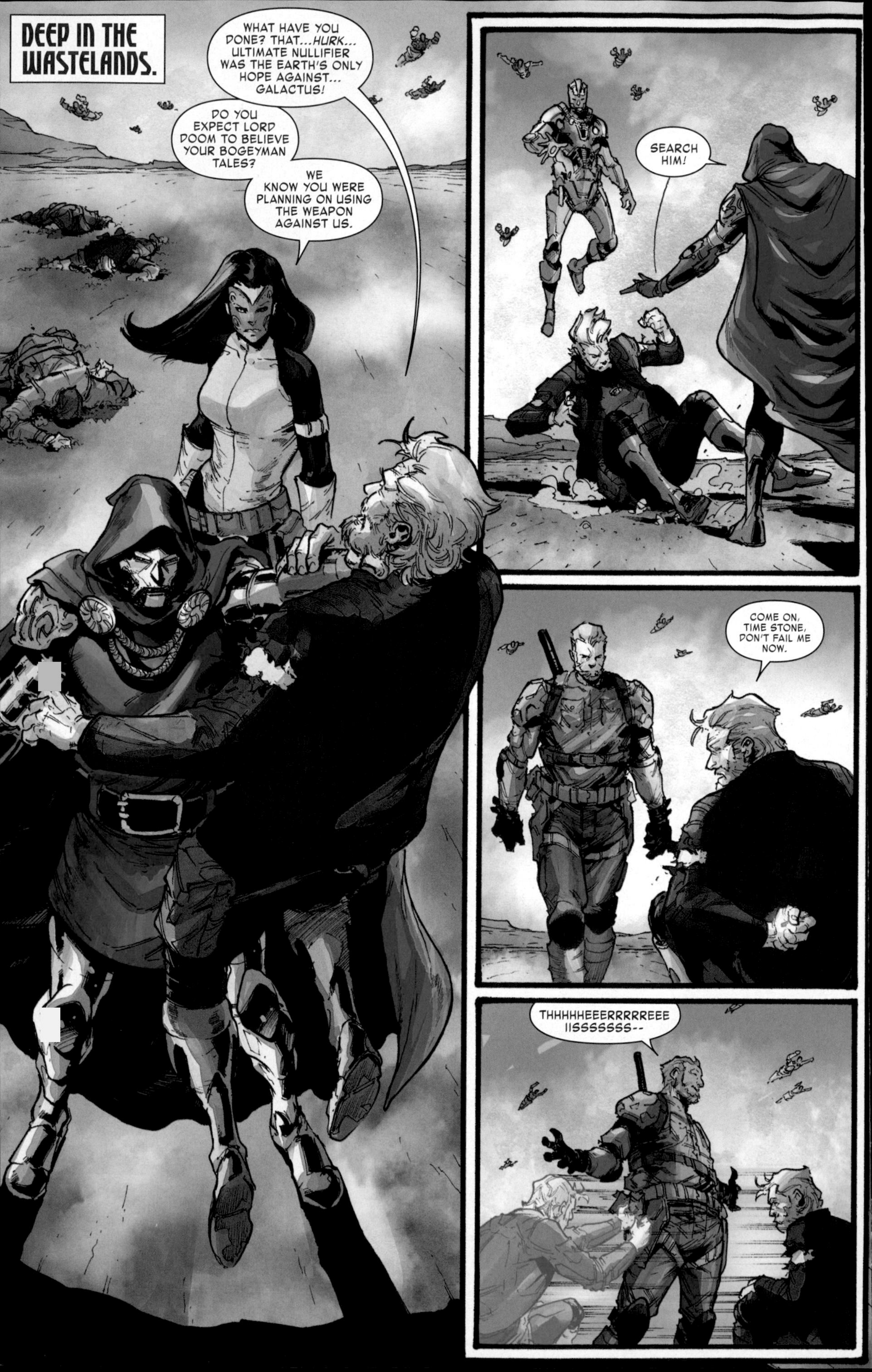
DEEP IN THE WASTELANDS.
WHAT HAVE YOU DONE? THAT...HURK... ULTIMATE NULLIFIER WAS THE EARTH'S ONLY HOPE AGAINST... GALACTUS!
DO YOU EXPECT LORD DOOM TO BELIEVE YOUR BOGEYMAN TALES?
WE KNOW YOU WERE PLANNING ON USING THE WEAPON AGAINST US.
SEARCH HIM!
COME ON, TIME STONE, DON'T FAIL ME NOW.
THHHHHEEERRRRREEE IISSSSSS--

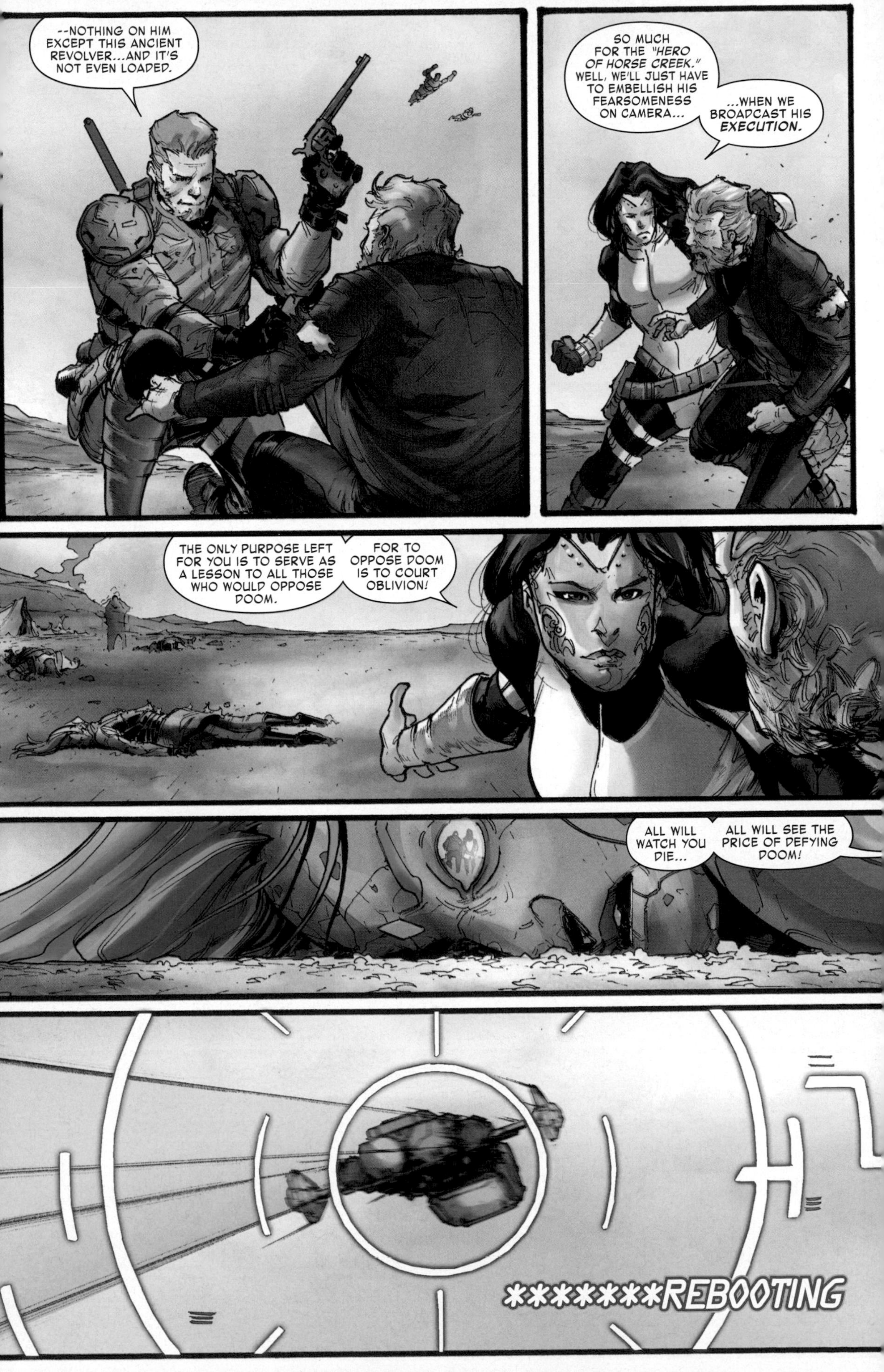
--NOTHING ON HIM EXCEPT THIS ANCIENT REVOLVER...AND IT'S NOT EVEN LOADED.
SO MUCH FOR THE "HERO OF HORSE CREEK." WELL, WE'LL JUST HAVE TO EMBELLISH HIS FEARSOMENESS ON CAMERA...
...WHEN WE BROADCAST HIS EXECUTION.
THE ONLY PURPOSE LEFT FOR YOU IS TO SERVE AS A LESSON TO ALL THOSE WHO WOULD OPPOSE DOOM.
FOR TO OPPOSE DOOM IS TO COURT OBLIVION!
ALL WILL WATCH YOU DIE...
ALL WILL SEE THE PRICE OF DEFYING DOOM!
*******REBOOTING

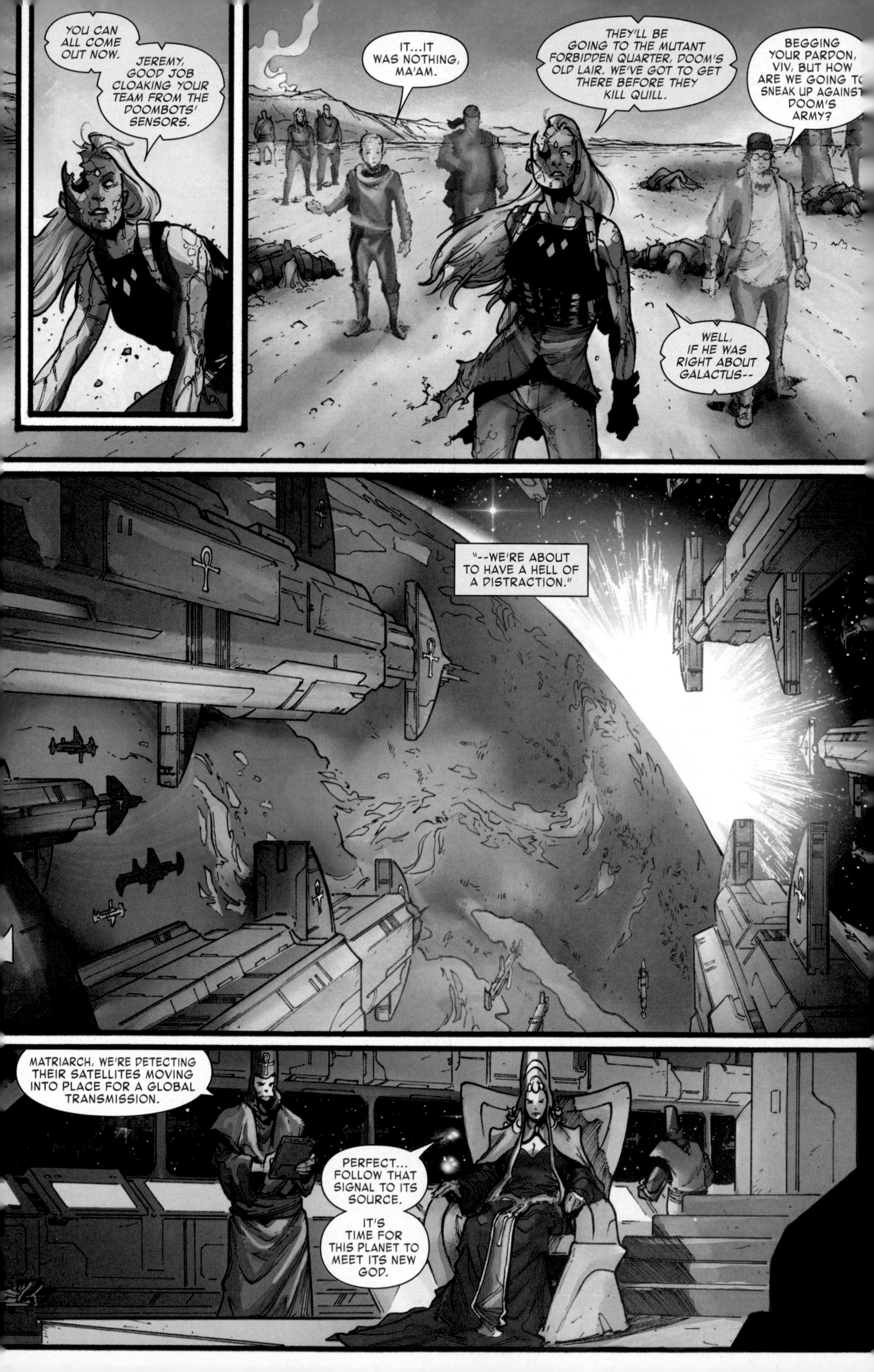
YOU CAN ALL COME OUT NOW.
JEREMY, GOOD JOB CLOAKING YOUR TEAM FROM THE DOOMBOTS' SENSORS.
IT...IT WAS NOTHING, MA'AM.
THEY'LL BE GOING TO THE MUTANT FORBIDDEN QUARTER, DOOM'S OLD LAIR. WE'VE GOT TO GET THERE BEFORE THEY KILL QUILL.
BEGGING YOUR PARDON, VIV, BUT HOW ARE WE GOING TO SNEAK UP AGAINST DOOM'S ARMY?
WELL, IF HE WAS RIGHT ABOUT GALACTUS--
"--WE'RE ABOUT TO HAVE A HELL OF A DISTRACTION."
MATRIARCH, WE'RE DETECTING THEIR SATELLITES MOVING INTO PLACE FOR A GLOBAL TRANSMISSION.
PERFECT... FOLLOW THAT SIGNAL TO ITS SOURCE.
IT'S TIME FOR THIS PLANET TO MEET ITS NEW GOD.

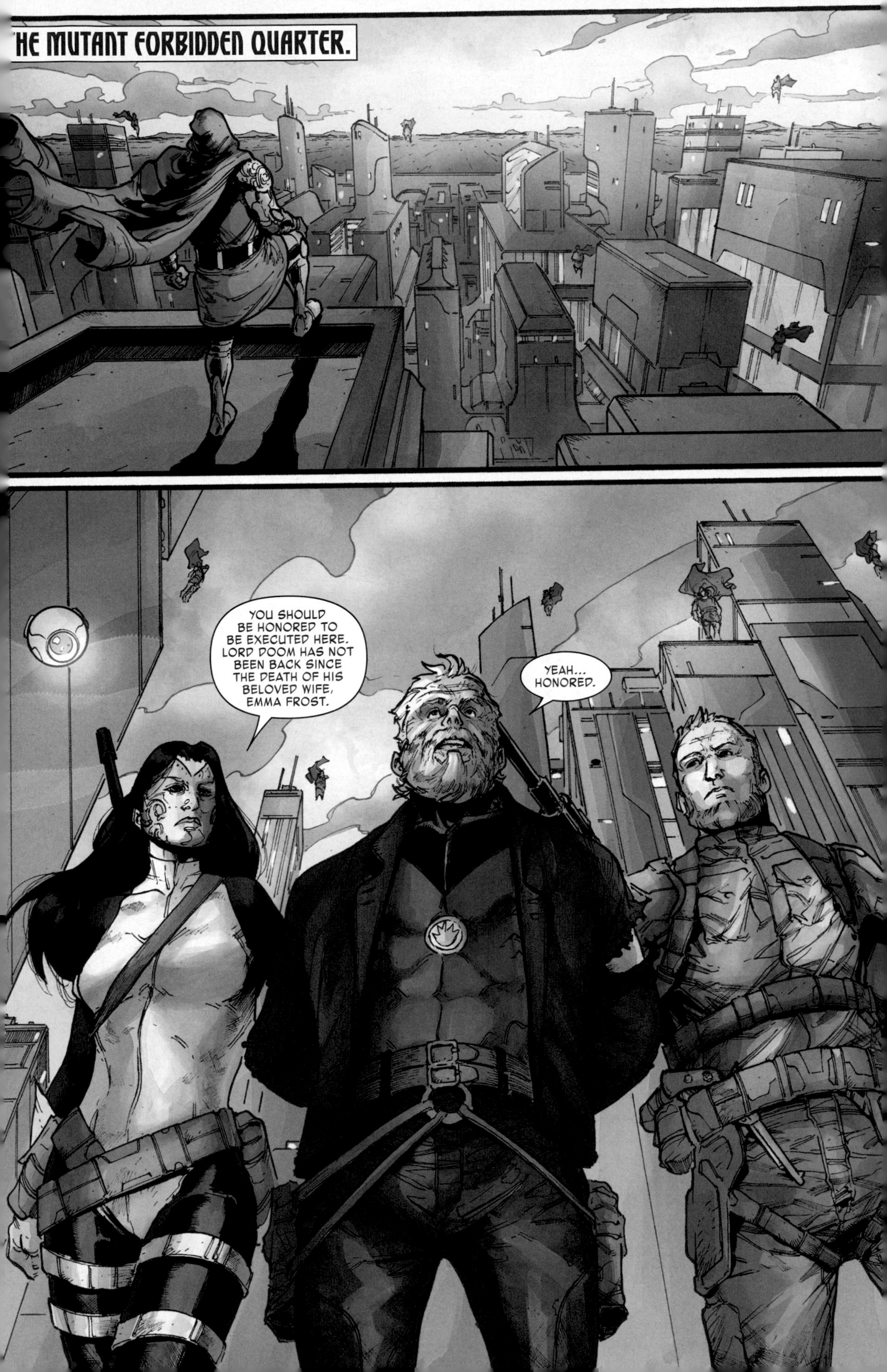
THE MUTANT FORBIDDEN QUARTER.
YOU SHOULD BE HONORED TO BE EXECUTED HERE. LORD DOOM HAS NOT BEEN BACK SINCE THE DEATH OF HIS BELOVED WIFE, EMMA FROST.
YEAH... HONORED.

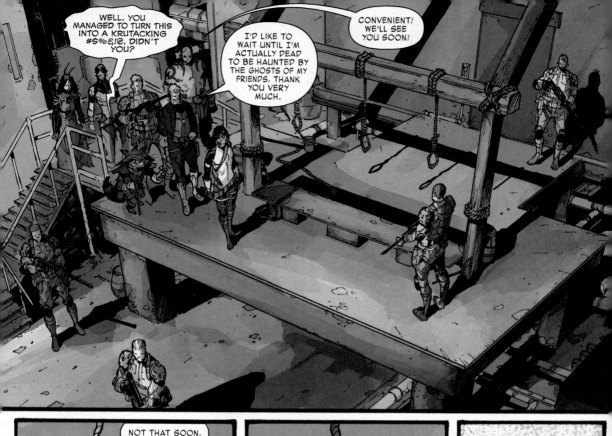

WELL, YOU MANAGED TO TURN THIS INTO A KRUTACKING #$%&!@, DIDN'T YOU?

I'D LIKE TO WAIT UNTIL I'M ACTUALLY DEAD TO BE HAUNTED BY THE GHOSTS OF MY FRIENDS, THANK YOU VERY MUCH.

CONVENIENT! WE'LL SEE YOU SOON!

NOT THAT SOON, RIGHT, PETER?

YOU HAVE ONE LAST TRICK UP YOUR SLEEVE?

SOMETHING LIKE THAT.

HE'S... UH...TALKING TO HIMSELF AGAIN.

LET'S JUST HURRY UP. HOPEFULLY THE AUDIENCE WILL ASSUME HE WAS A ONCE-FEARSOME WARRIOR BROUGHT LOW BY DOOM AND NOT A SENILE FOOL.

START THE BROADCAST.

GREETINGS, CITIZENS OF DOOM'S DOMAIN!

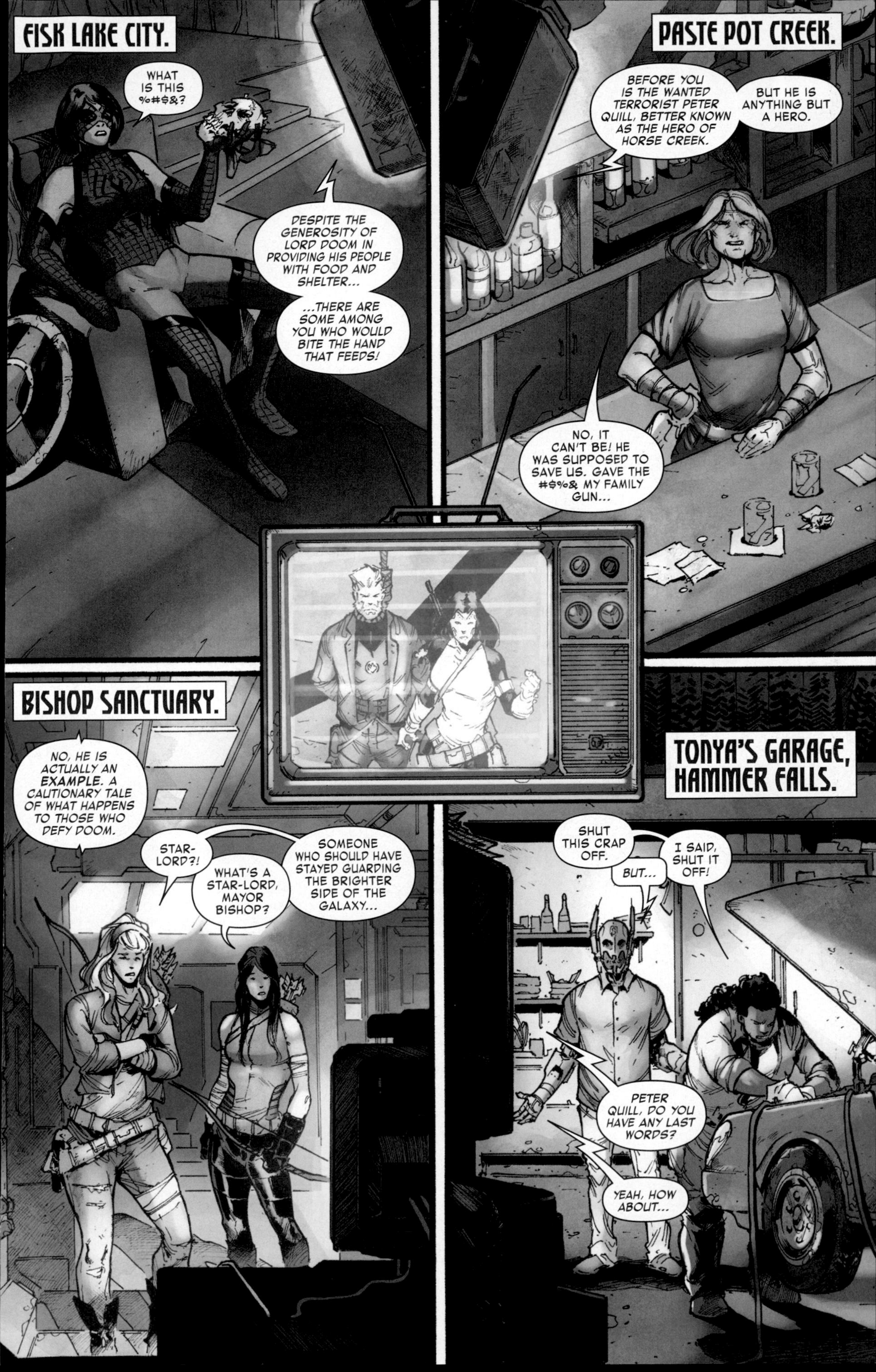

FISK LAKE CITY.
WHAT IS THIS %#$&?
DESPITE THE GENEROSITY OF LORD DOOM IN PROVIDING HIS PEOPLE WITH FOOD AND SHELTER...
...THERE ARE SOME AMONG YOU WHO WOULD BITE THE HAND THAT FEEDS!
PASTE POT CREEK.
BEFORE YOU IS THE WANTED TERRORIST PETER QUILL, BETTER KNOWN AS THE HERO OF HORSE CREEK.
BUT HE IS ANYTHING BUT A HERO.
NO, IT CAN'T BE! HE WAS SUPPOSED TO SAVE US. GAVE THE #$%& MY FAMILY GUN...
BISHOP SANCTUARY.
NO, HE IS ACTUALLY AN EXAMPLE. A CAUTIONARY TALE OF WHAT HAPPENS TO THOSE WHO DEFY DOOM.
STAR-LORD?!
WHAT'S A STAR-LORD, MAYOR BISHOP?
SOMEONE WHO SHOULD HAVE STAYED GUARDING THE BRIGHTER SIDE OF THE GALAXY...
TONYA'S GARAGE, HAMMER FALLS.
SHUT THIS CRAP OFF.
BUT...
I SAID, SHUT IT OFF!
PETER QUILL, DO YOU HAVE ANY LAST WORDS?
YEAH, HOW ABOUT...

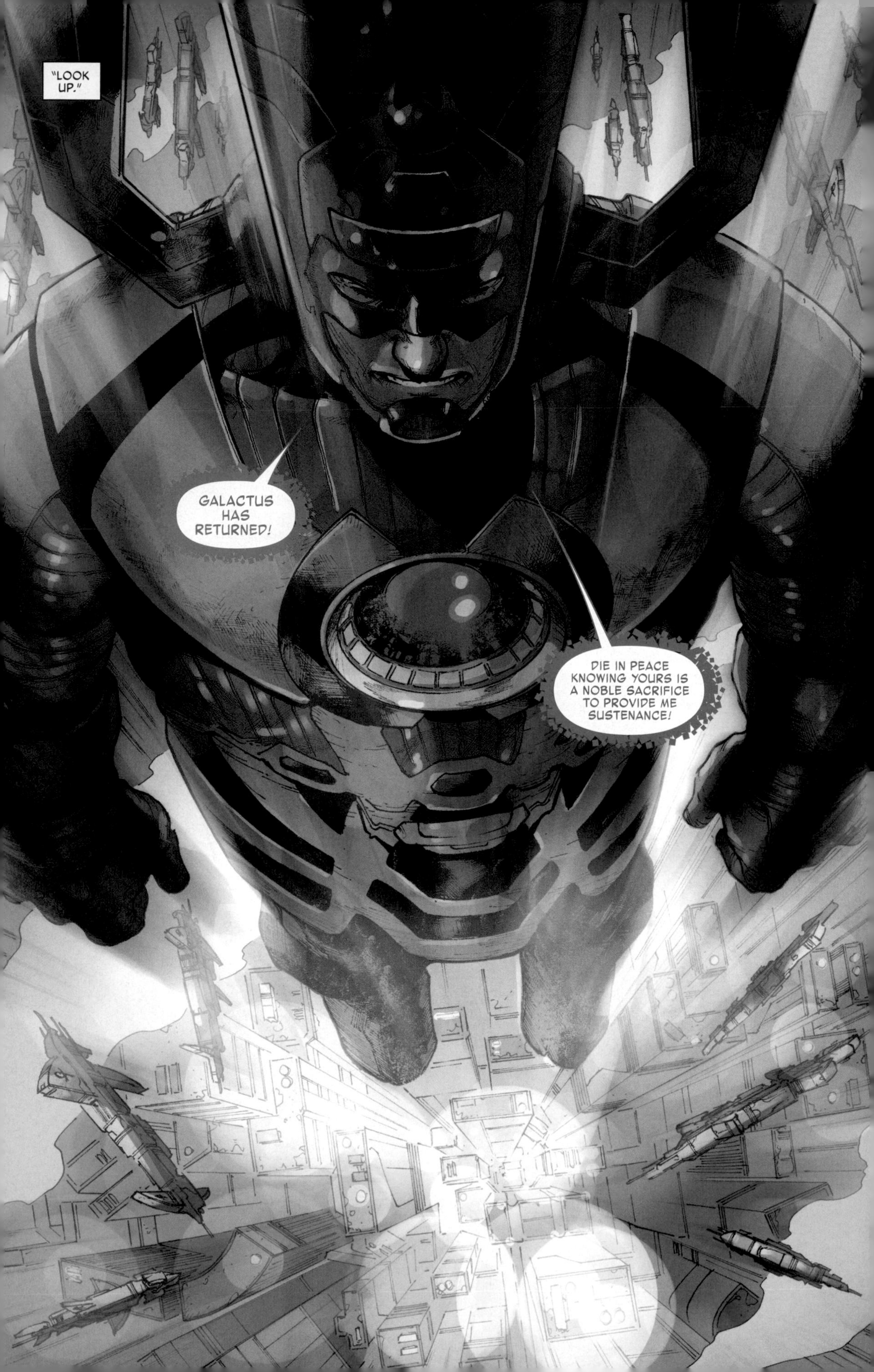
"LOOK UP."
GALACTUS HAS RETURNED!
DIE IN PEACE KNOWING YOURS IS A NOBLE SACRIFICE TO PROVIDE ME SUSTENANCE!

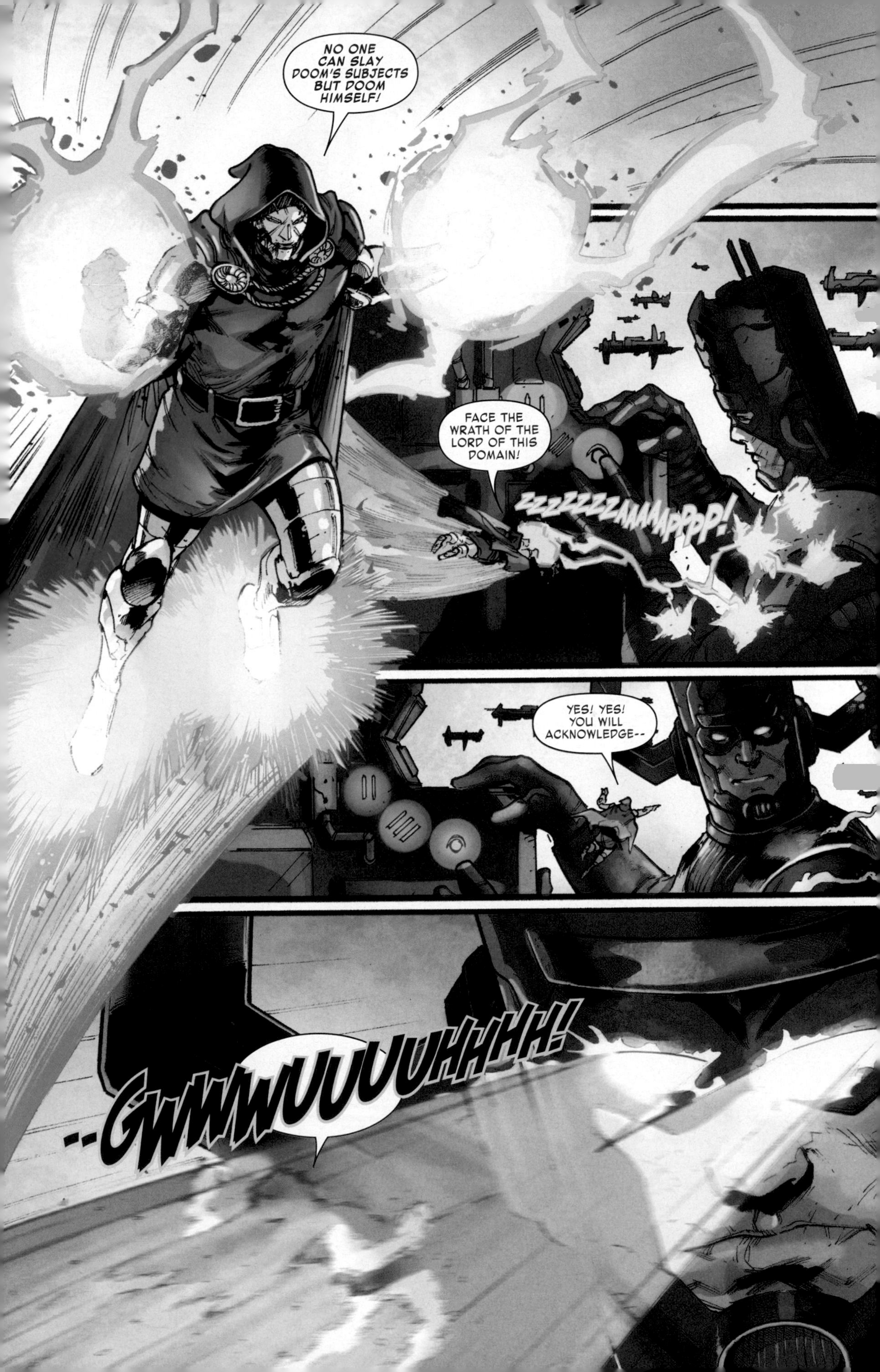
NO ONE CAN SLAY DOOM'S SUBJECTS BUT DOOM HIMSELF!
FACE THE WRATH OF THE LORD OF THIS DOMAIN!
ZZZZZZZAAAAAPPPP!
YES! YES! YOU WILL ACKNOWLEDGE--
--GWWWUUUUUHHHH!

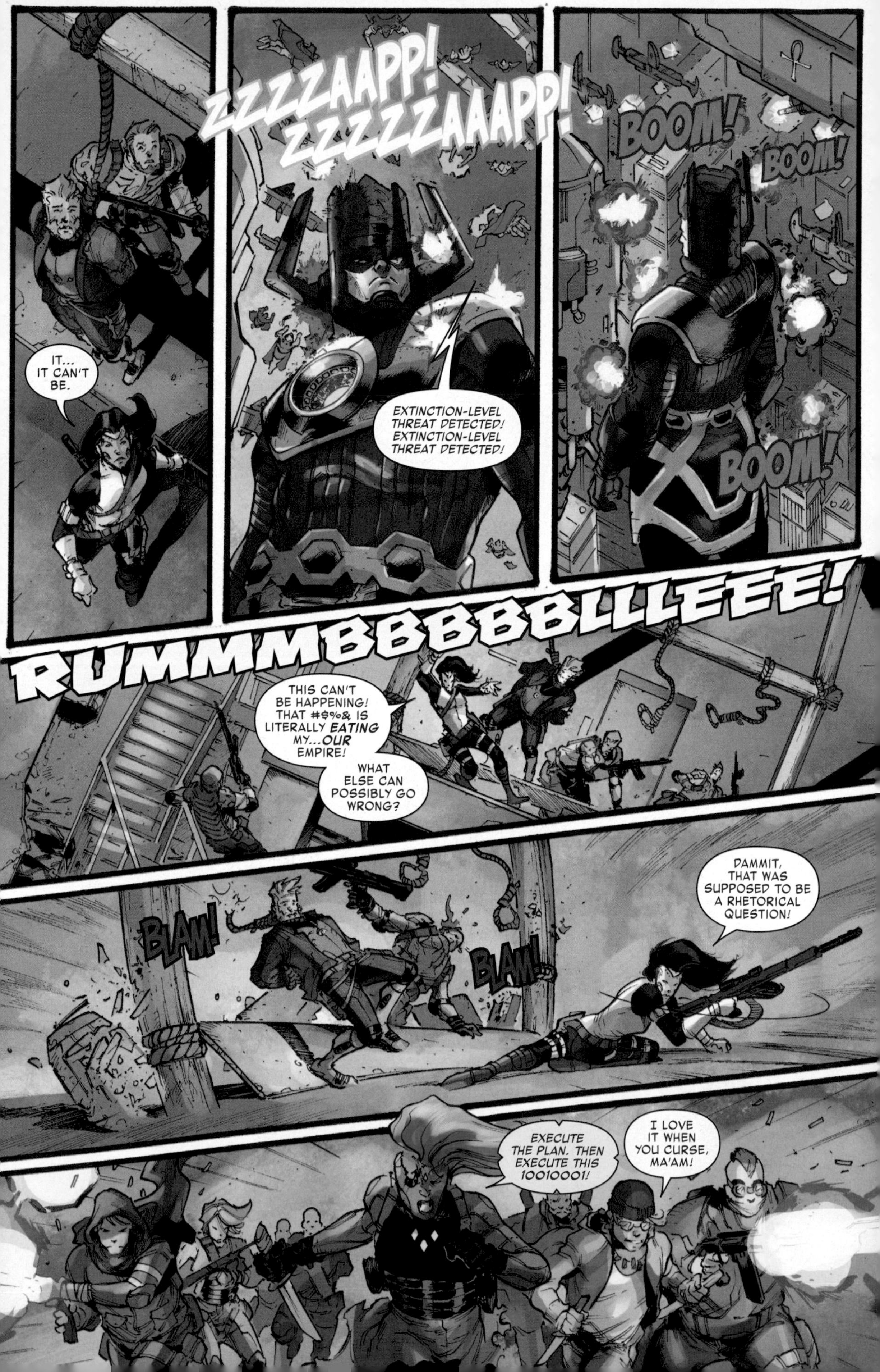

IT... IT CAN'T BE.
ZZZZZAAPP! ZZZZZAAAPP!
EXTINCTION-LEVEL THREAT DETECTED! EXTINCTION-LEVEL THREAT DETECTED!
BOOM!
BOOM!
BOOM!
RUMMMBBBBBLLLEEEE!
THIS CAN'T BE HAPPENING! THAT #$%& IS LITERALLY EATING MY...OUR EMPIRE!
WHAT ELSE CAN POSSIBLY GO WRONG?
DAMMIT, THAT WAS SUPPOSED TO BE A RHETORICAL QUESTION!
BLAM!
BLAM!
EXECUTE THE PLAN. THEN EXECUTE THIS 10010001!
I LOVE IT WHEN YOU CURSE, MA'AM!

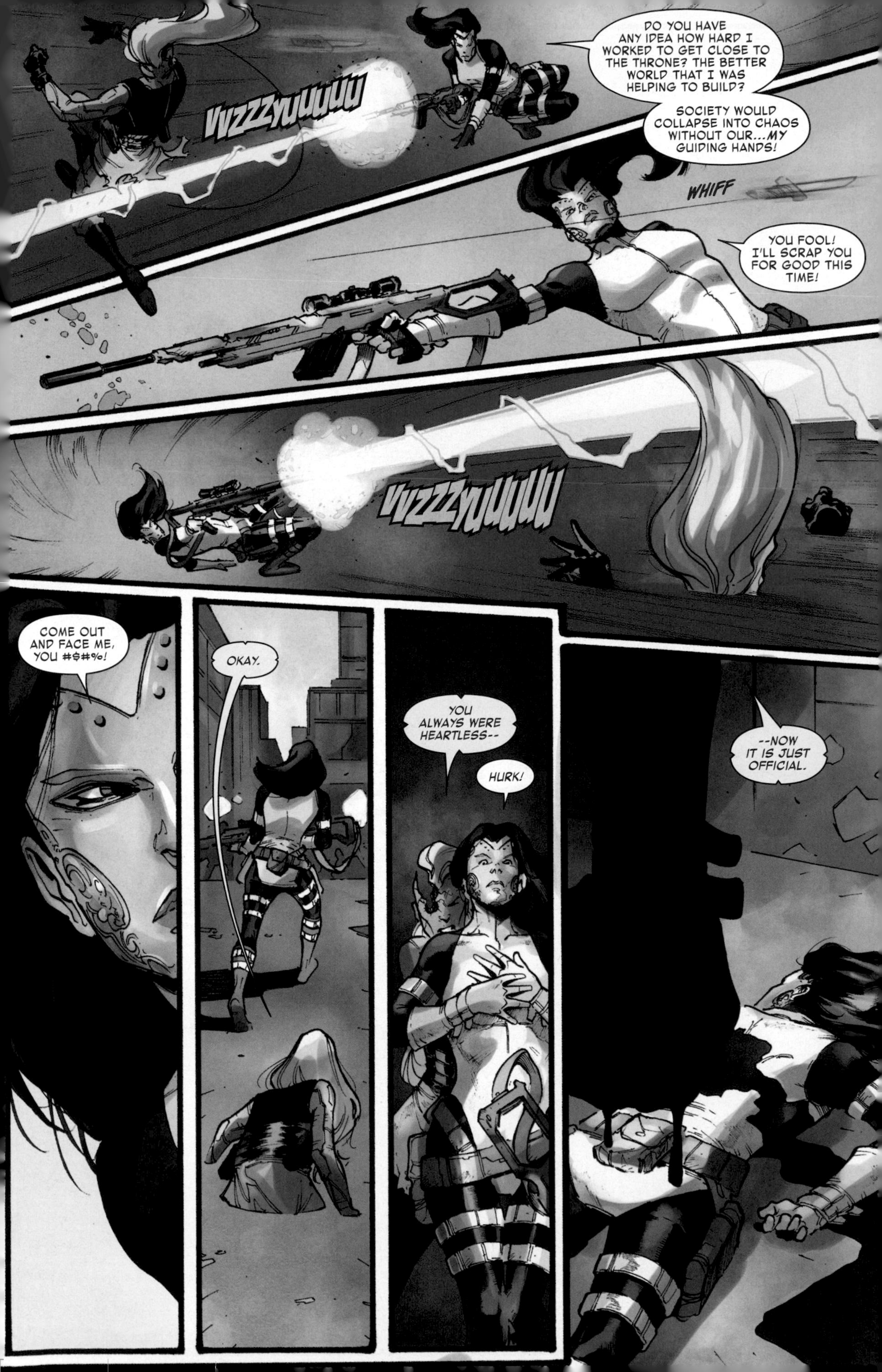
VVZZZYUUUUU
DO YOU HAVE ANY IDEA HOW HARD I WORKED TO GET CLOSE TO THE THRONE? THE BETTER WORLD THAT I WAS HELPING TO BUILD?
SOCIETY WOULD COLLAPSE INTO CHAOS WITHOUT OUR...MY GUIDING HANDS!
WHIFF
YOU FOOL! I'LL SCRAP YOU FOR GOOD THIS TIME!
VVZZZYUUUUU
COME OUT AND FACE ME, YOU #$#%!
OKAY.
YOU ALWAYS WERE HEARTLESS--
HURK!
--NOW IT IS JUST OFFICIAL.

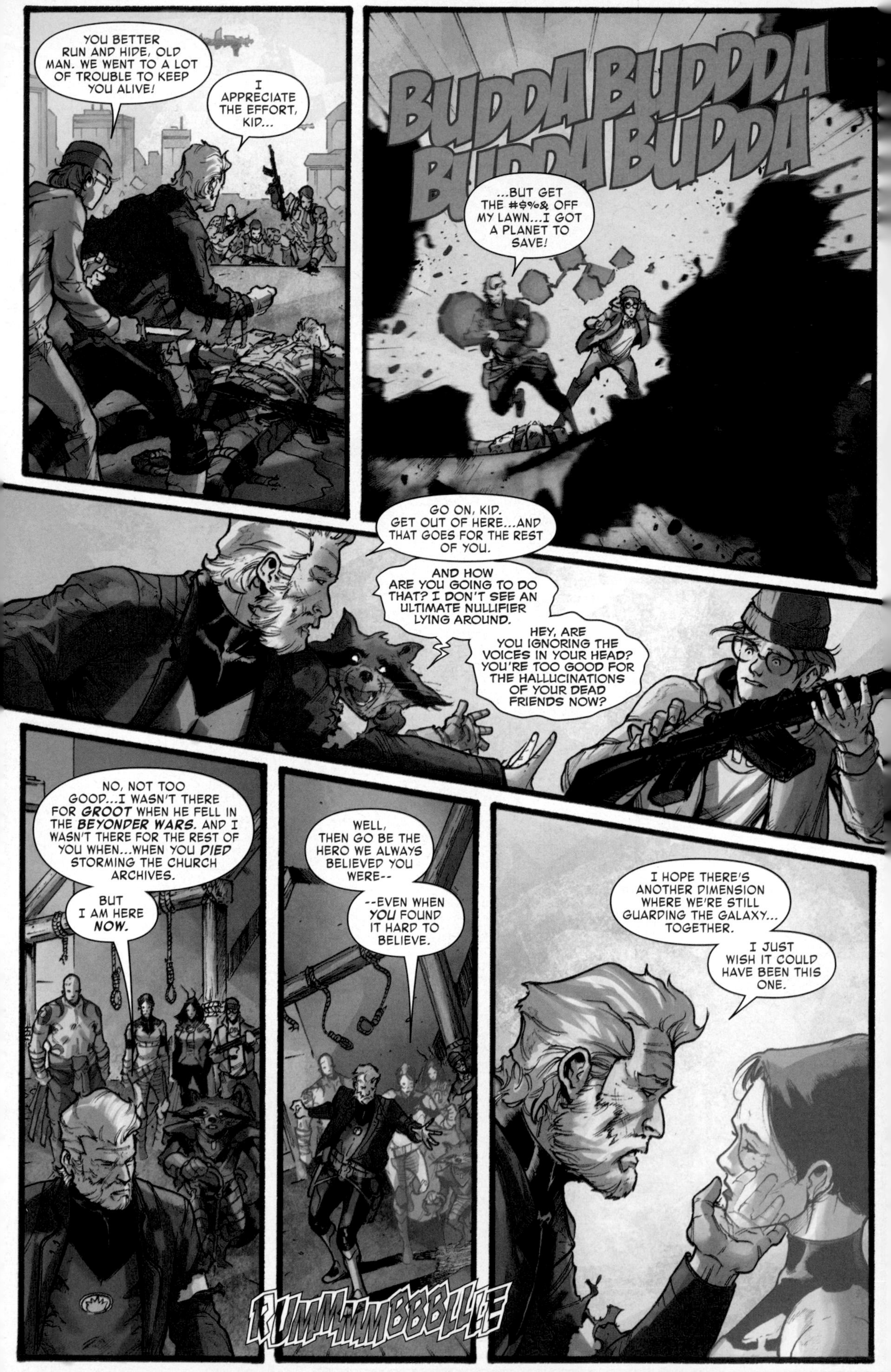
YOU BETTER RUN AND HIDE, OLD MAN. WE WENT TO A LOT OF TROUBLE TO KEEP YOU ALIVE!
I APPRECIATE THE EFFORT, KID...
BUDDA BUDDDA BUDDA BUDDA
...BUT GET THE #$%& OFF MY LAWN...I GOT A PLANET TO SAVE!
GO ON, KID. GET OUT OF HERE...AND THAT GOES FOR THE REST OF YOU.
AND HOW ARE YOU GOING TO DO THAT? I DON'T SEE AN ULTIMATE NULLIFIER LYING AROUND.
HEY, ARE YOU IGNORING THE VOICES IN YOUR HEAD? YOU'RE TOO GOOD FOR THE HALLUCINATIONS OF YOUR DEAD FRIENDS NOW?
NO, NOT TOO GOOD...I WASN'T THERE FOR *GROOT* WHEN HE FELL IN THE *BEYONDER WARS.* AND I WASN'T THERE FOR THE REST OF YOU WHEN...WHEN YOU *DIED* STORMING THE CHURCH ARCHIVES.
BUT I AM HERE *NOW.*
WELL, THEN GO BE THE HERO WE ALWAYS BELIEVED YOU WERE--
--EVEN WHEN *YOU* FOUND IT HARD TO BELIEVE.
I HOPE THERE'S ANOTHER DIMENSION WHERE WE'RE STILL GUARDING THE GALAXY... TOGETHER.
I JUST WISH IT COULD HAVE BEEN THIS ONE.
RUMMMMMBBBLLE

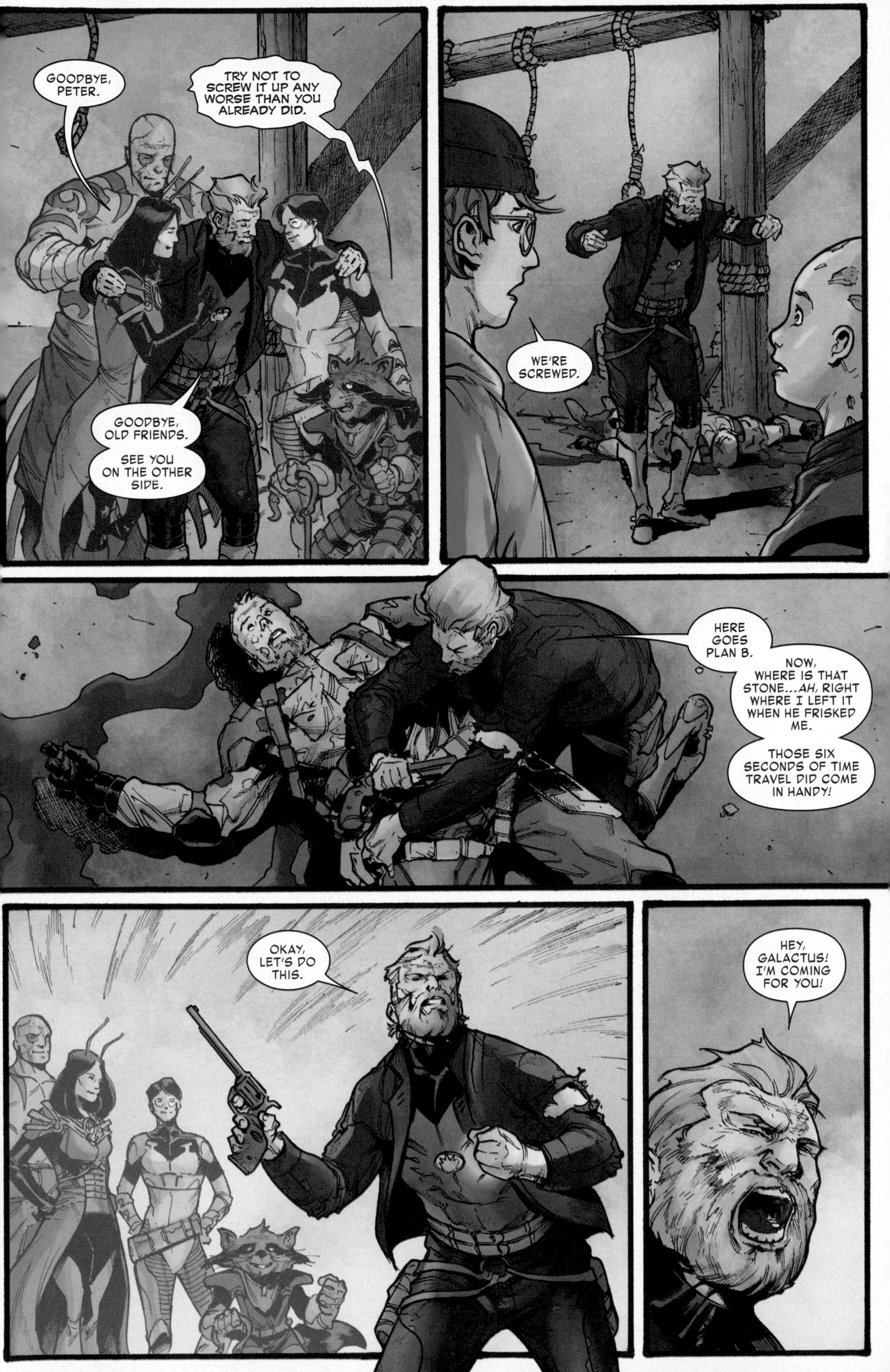
GOODBYE, PETER.
TRY NOT TO SCREW IT UP ANY WORSE THAN YOU ALREADY DID.
GOODBYE, OLD FRIENDS.
SEE YOU ON THE OTHER SIDE.
WE'RE SCREWED.
HERE GOES PLAN B.
NOW, WHERE IS THAT STONE...*AH,* RIGHT WHERE I LEFT IT WHEN HE FRISKED ME.
THOSE SIX SECONDS OF TIME TRAVEL DID COME IN HANDY!
OKAY, LET'S DO THIS.
HEY, GALACTUS! I'M COMING FOR YOU!

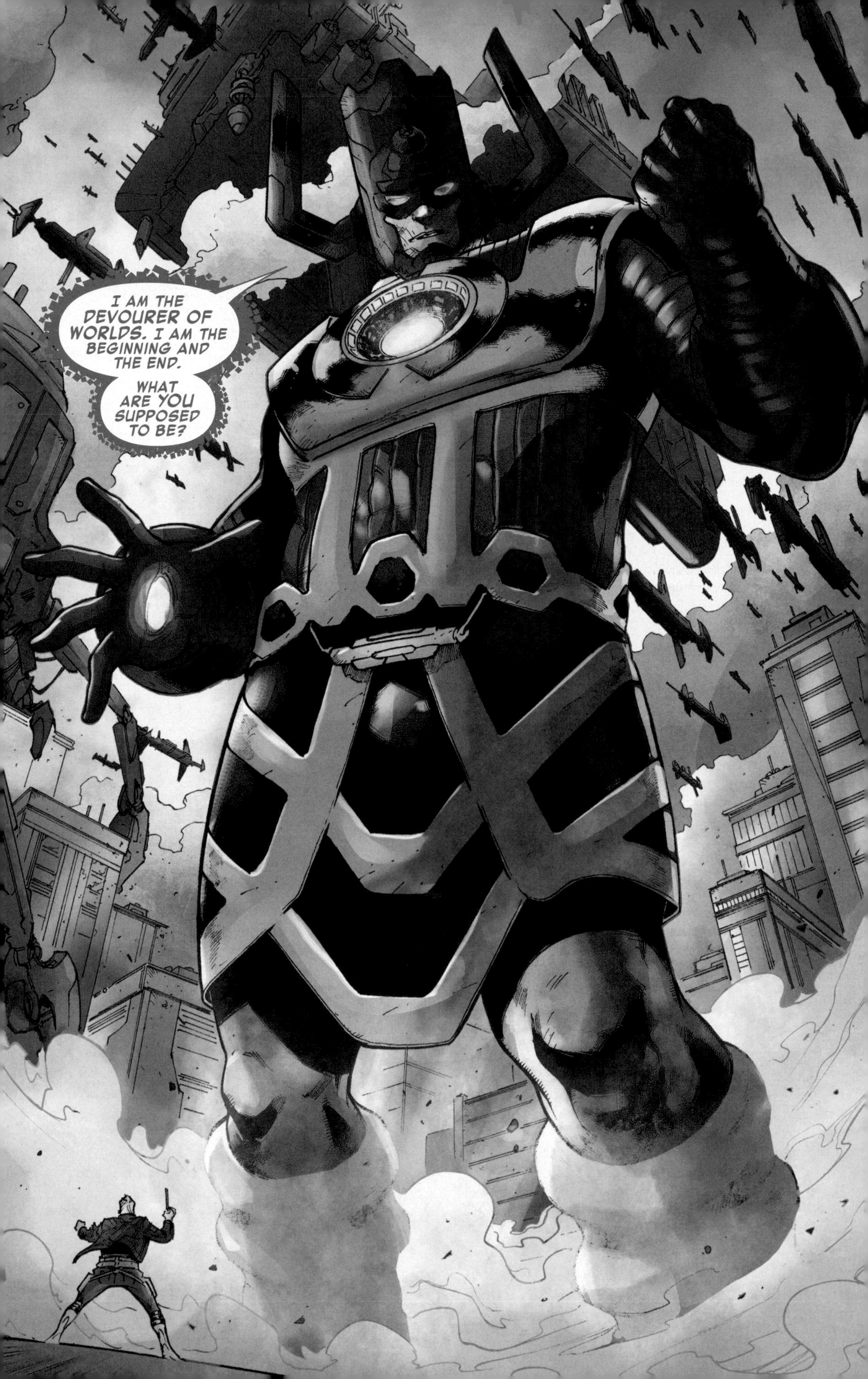
I AM THE DEVOURER OF WORLDS. I AM THE BEGINNING AND THE END.
WHAT ARE YOU SUPPOSED TO BE?

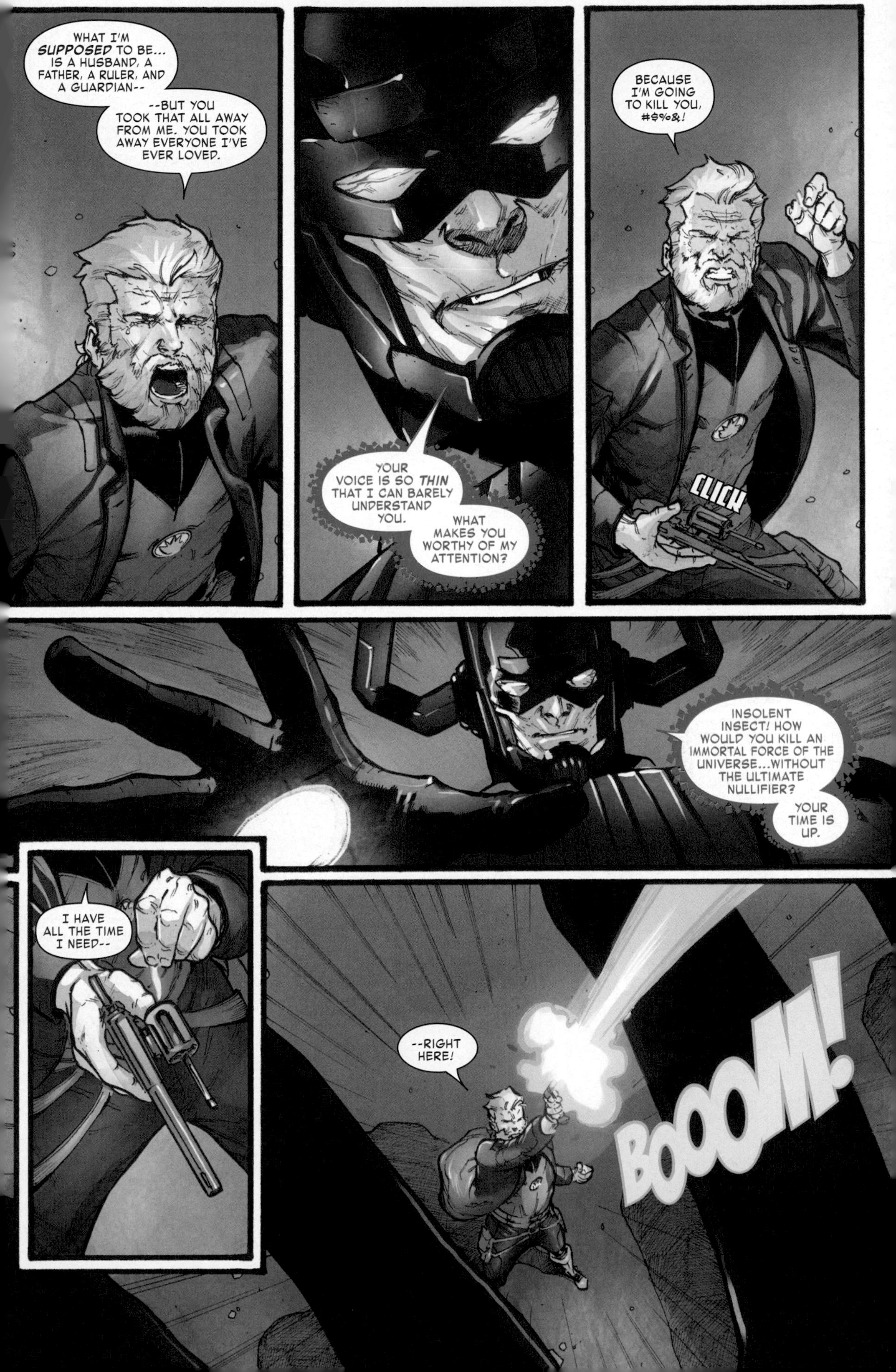
WHAT I'M SUPPOSED TO BE... IS A HUSBAND, A FATHER, A RULER, AND A GUARDIAN--
--BUT YOU TOOK THAT ALL AWAY FROM ME. YOU TOOK AWAY EVERYONE I'VE EVER LOVED.
YOUR VOICE IS SO THIN THAT I CAN BARELY UNDERSTAND YOU.
WHAT MAKES YOU WORTHY OF MY ATTENTION?
BECAUSE I'M GOING TO KILL YOU, #$%&!
CLICK
INSOLENT INSECT! HOW WOULD YOU KILL AN IMMORTAL FORCE OF THE UNIVERSE...WITHOUT THE ULTIMATE NULLIFIER?
YOUR TIME IS UP.
I HAVE ALL THE TIME I NEED--
--RIGHT HERE!
BOOOOM!

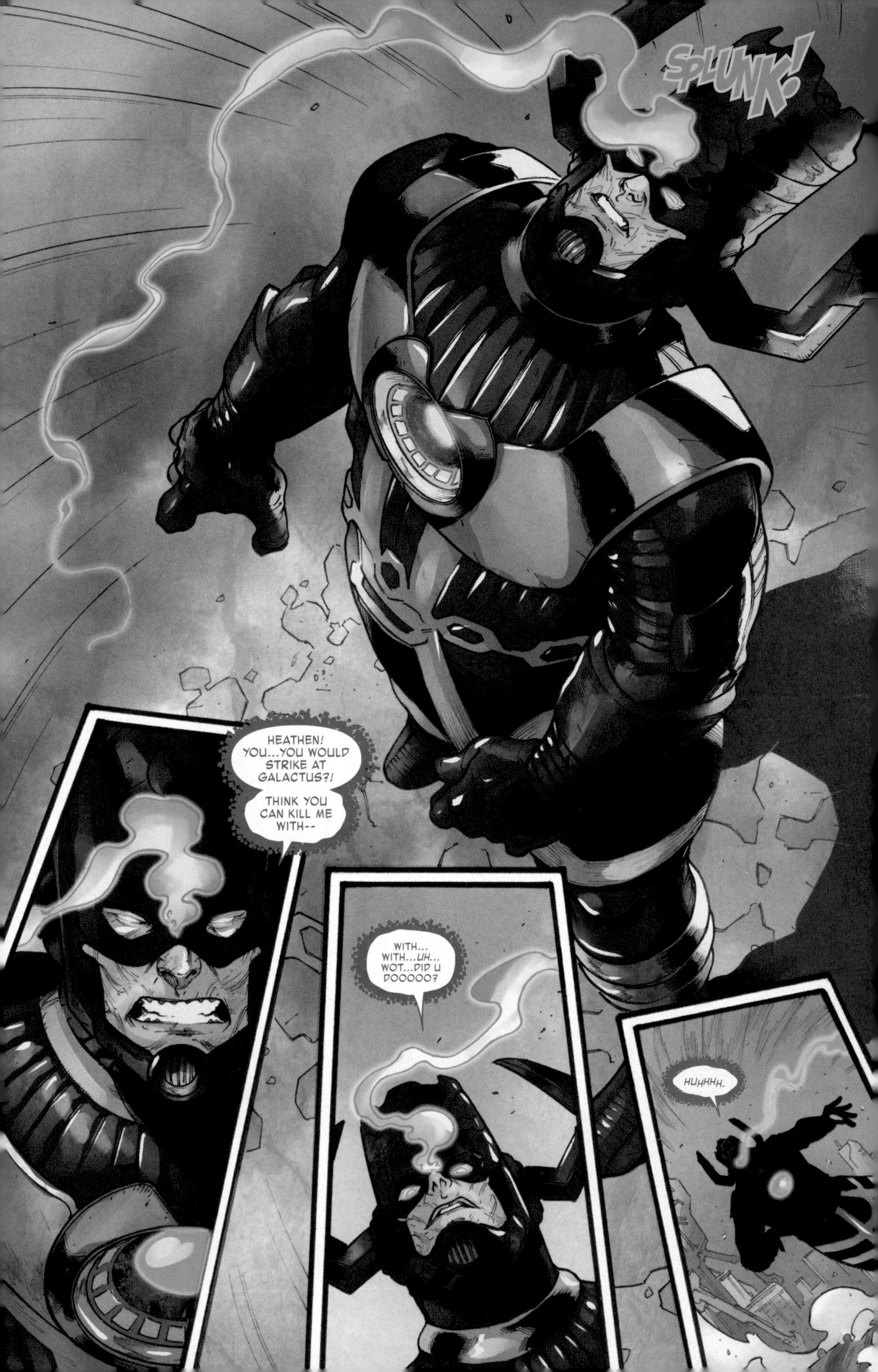
SPLUNK!
HEATHEN! YOU...YOU WOULD STRIKE AT GALACTUS?!
THINK YOU CAN KILL ME WITH--
WITH... WITH...UH... WOT...DID U DOOOOO?
HUHHHH.

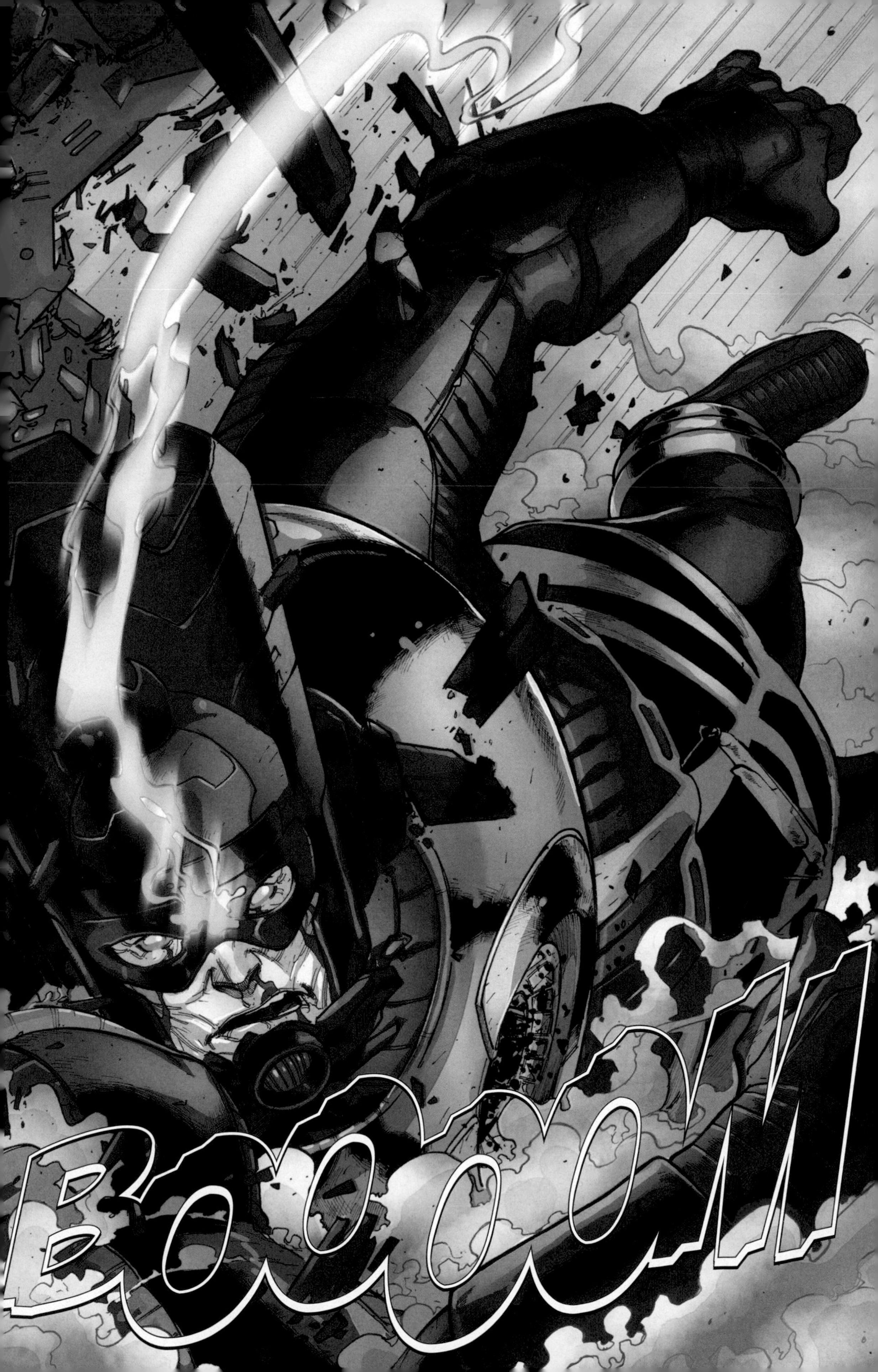
BOOOOOM

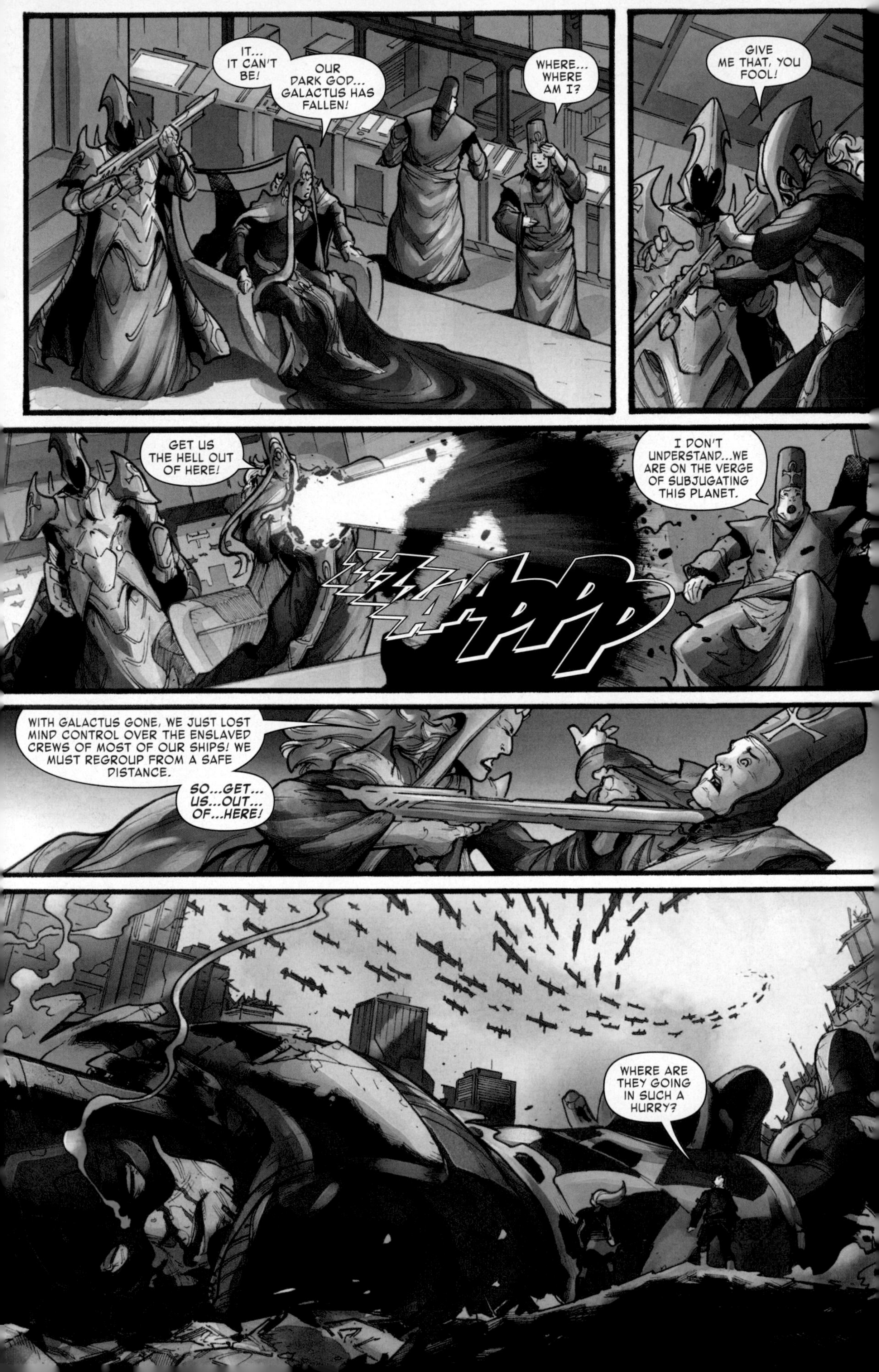
IT... IT CAN'T BE!
OUR DARK GOD... GALACTUS HAS FALLEN!
WHERE... WHERE AM I?
GIVE ME THAT, YOU FOOL!
GET US THE HELL OUT OF HERE!
I DON'T UNDERSTAND...WE ARE ON THE VERGE OF SUBJUGATING THIS PLANET.
ZZAPPP
WITH GALACTUS GONE, WE JUST LOST MIND CONTROL OVER THE ENSLAVED CREWS OF MOST OF OUR SHIPS! WE MUST REGROUP FROM A SAFE DISTANCE.
SO...GET... US...OUT... OF...HERE!
WHERE ARE THEY GOING IN SUCH A HURRY?

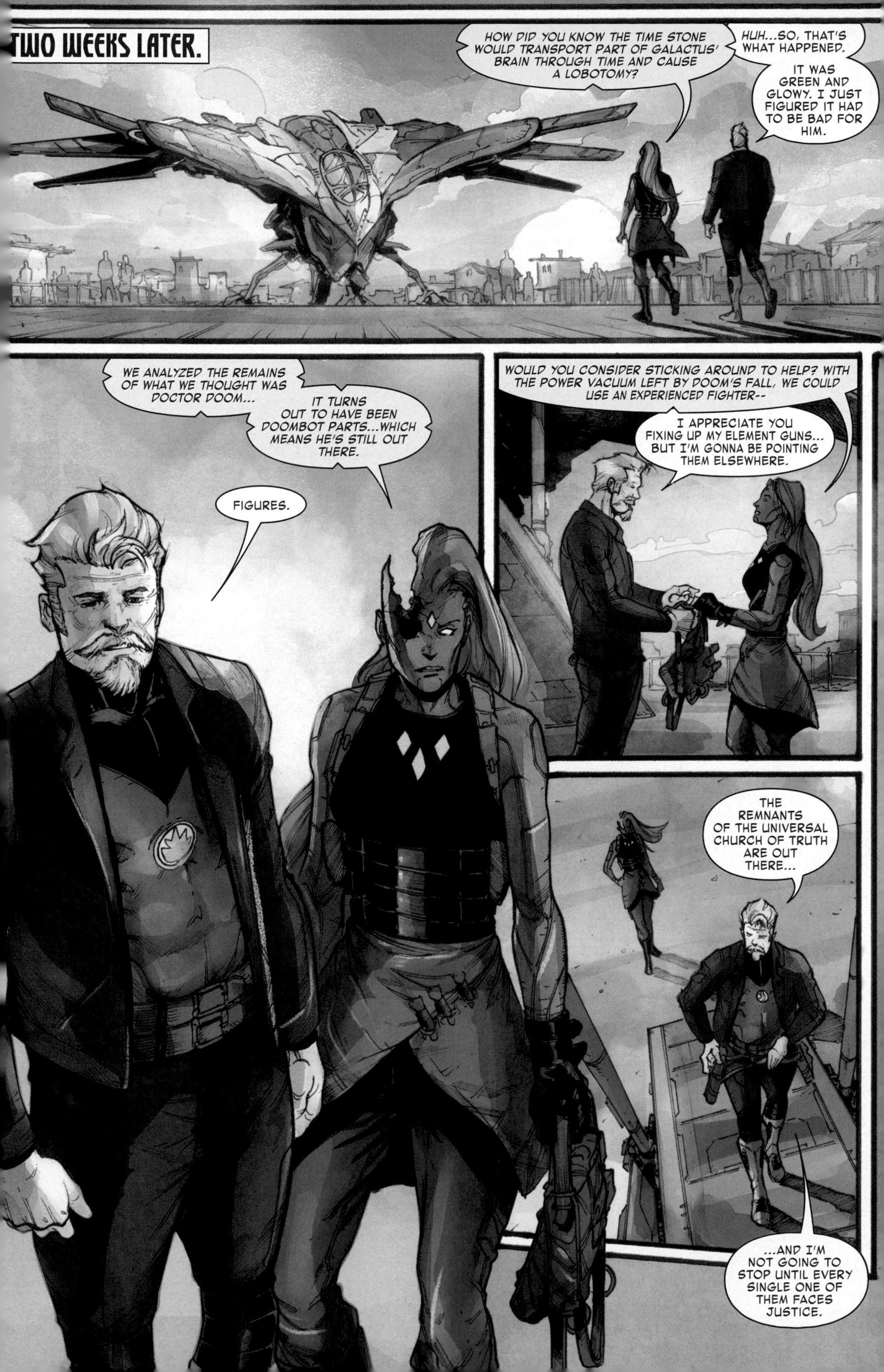
TWO WEEKS LATER.
HOW DID YOU KNOW THE TIME STONE WOULD TRANSPORT PART OF GALACTUS' BRAIN THROUGH TIME AND CAUSE A LOBOTOMY?
HUH...SO, THAT'S WHAT HAPPENED.
IT WAS GREEN AND GLOWY. I JUST FIGURED IT HAD TO BE BAD FOR HIM.
WE ANALYZED THE REMAINS OF WHAT WE THOUGHT WAS DOCTOR DOOM...
IT TURNS OUT TO HAVE BEEN DOOMBOT PARTS...WHICH MEANS HE'S STILL OUT THERE.
FIGURES.
WOULD YOU CONSIDER STICKING AROUND TO HELP? WITH THE POWER VACUUM LEFT BY DOOM'S FALL, WE COULD USE AN EXPERIENCED FIGHTER--
I APPRECIATE YOU FIXING UP MY ELEMENT GUNS... BUT I'M GONNA BE POINTING THEM ELSEWHERE.
THE REMNANTS OF THE UNIVERSAL CHURCH OF TRUTH ARE OUT THERE...
...AND I'M NOT GOING TO STOP UNTIL EVERY SINGLE ONE OF THEM FACES JUSTICE.

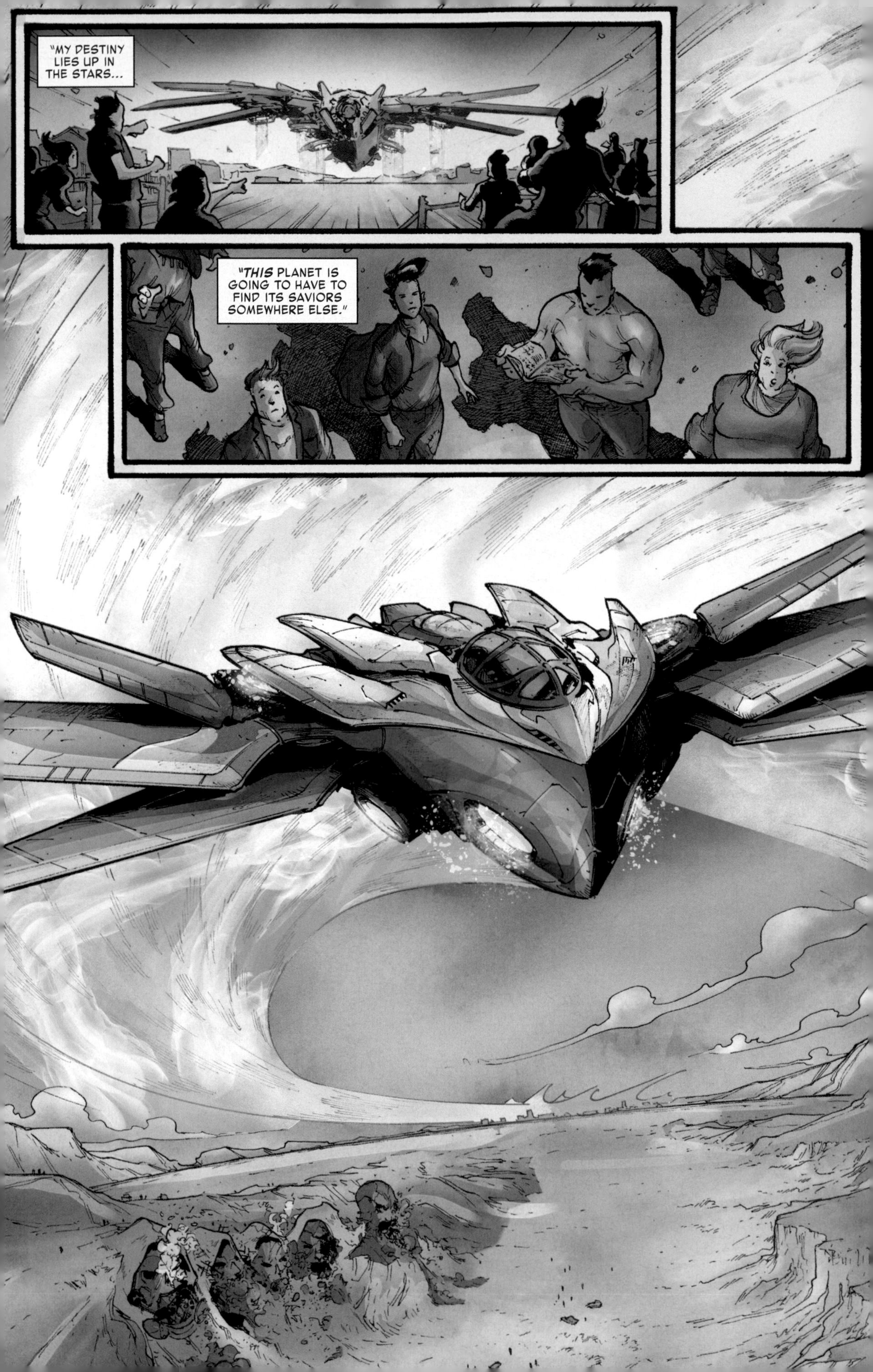
"MY DESTINY LIES UP IN THE STARS...
"THIS PLANET IS GOING TO HAVE TO FIND ITS SAVIORS SOMEWHERE ELSE."

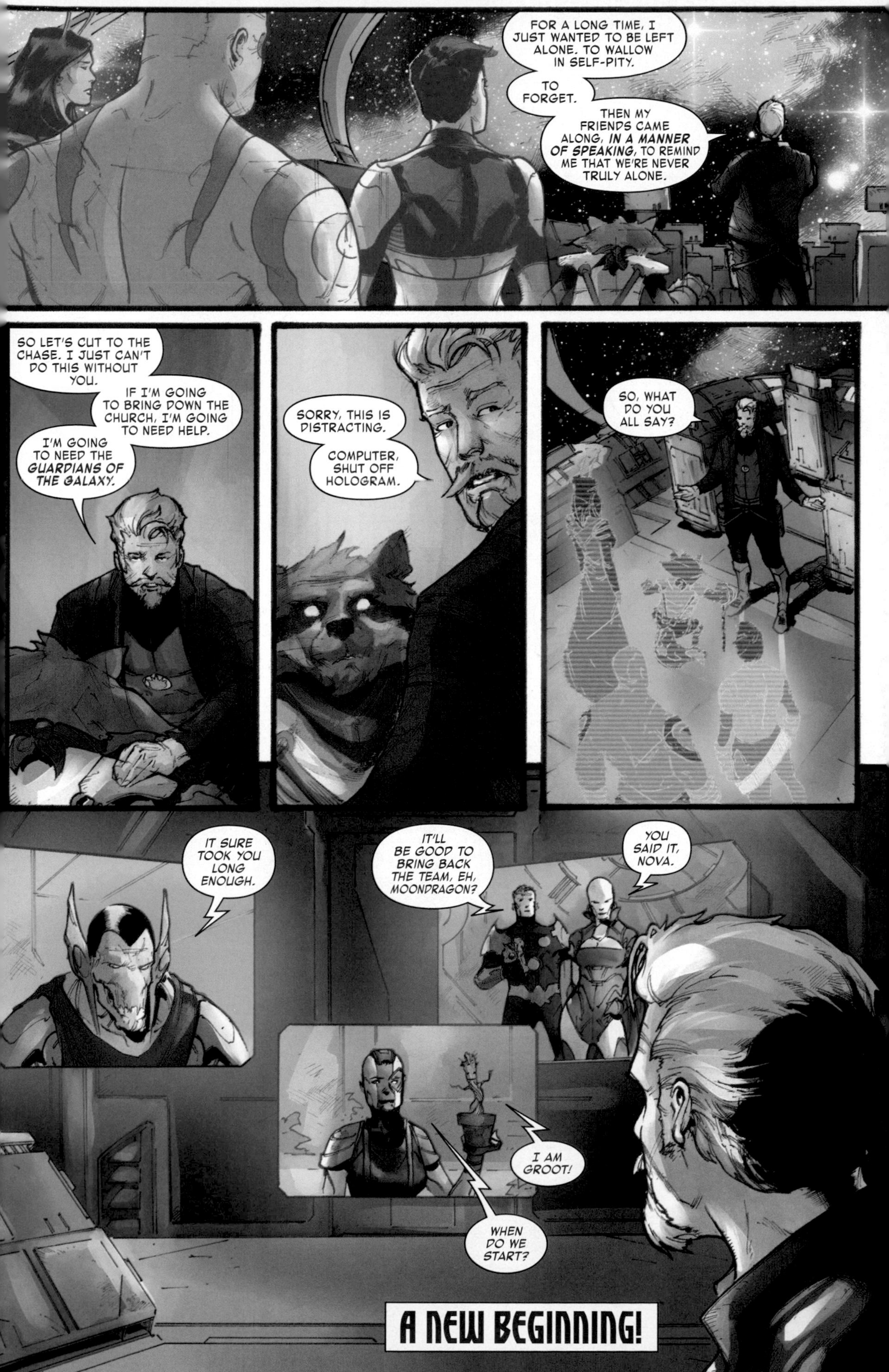
FOR A LONG TIME, I JUST WANTED TO BE LEFT ALONE. TO WALLOW IN SELF-PITY.
TO FORGET.
THEN MY FRIENDS CAME ALONG, *IN A MANNER OF SPEAKING*, TO REMIND ME THAT WE'RE NEVER TRULY ALONE.
SO LET'S CUT TO THE CHASE. I JUST CAN'T DO THIS WITHOUT YOU.
IF I'M GOING TO BRING DOWN THE CHURCH, I'M GOING TO NEED HELP.
I'M GOING TO NEED THE *GUARDIANS OF THE GALAXY.*
SORRY, THIS IS DISTRACTING.
COMPUTER, SHUT OFF HOLOGRAM.
SO, WHAT DO YOU ALL SAY?
IT SURE TOOK YOU LONG ENOUGH.
IT'LL BE GOOD TO BRING BACK THE TEAM, EH, MOONDRAGON?
YOU SAID IT, NOVA.
I AM GROOT!
WHEN DO WE START?
A NEW BEGINNING!

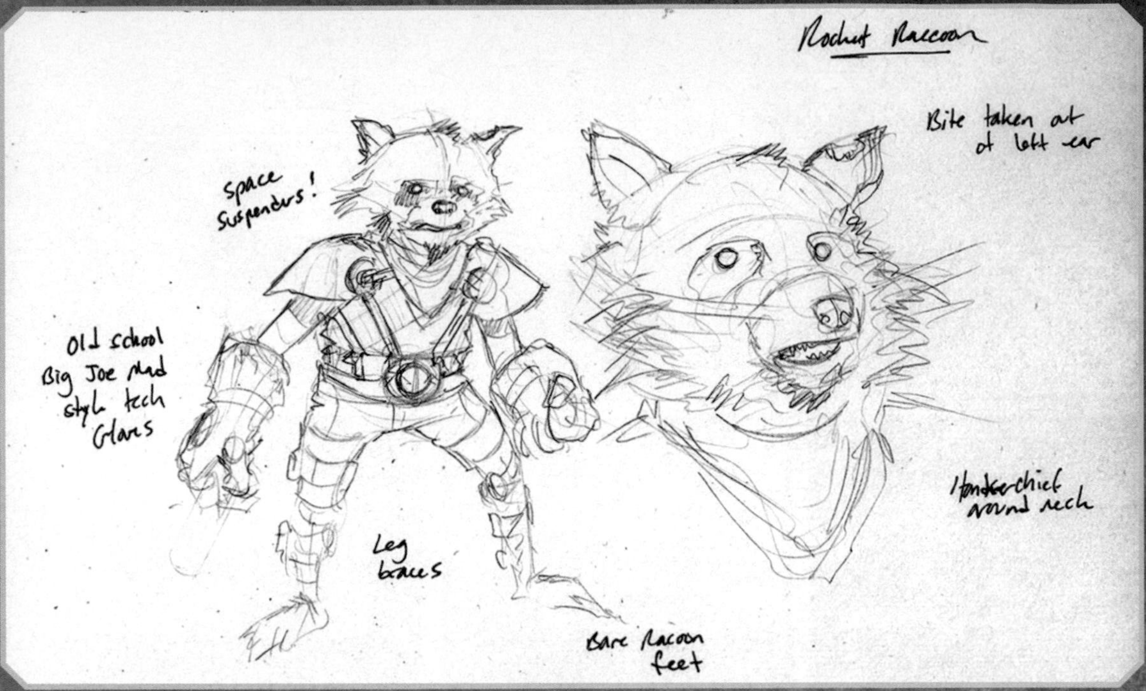
Rocket Raccoon
Bite taken out of left ear
space suspenders!
Old school Big Joe Mad style tech Gloves
Leg braces
Handkerchief around neck
Bare Racoon feet

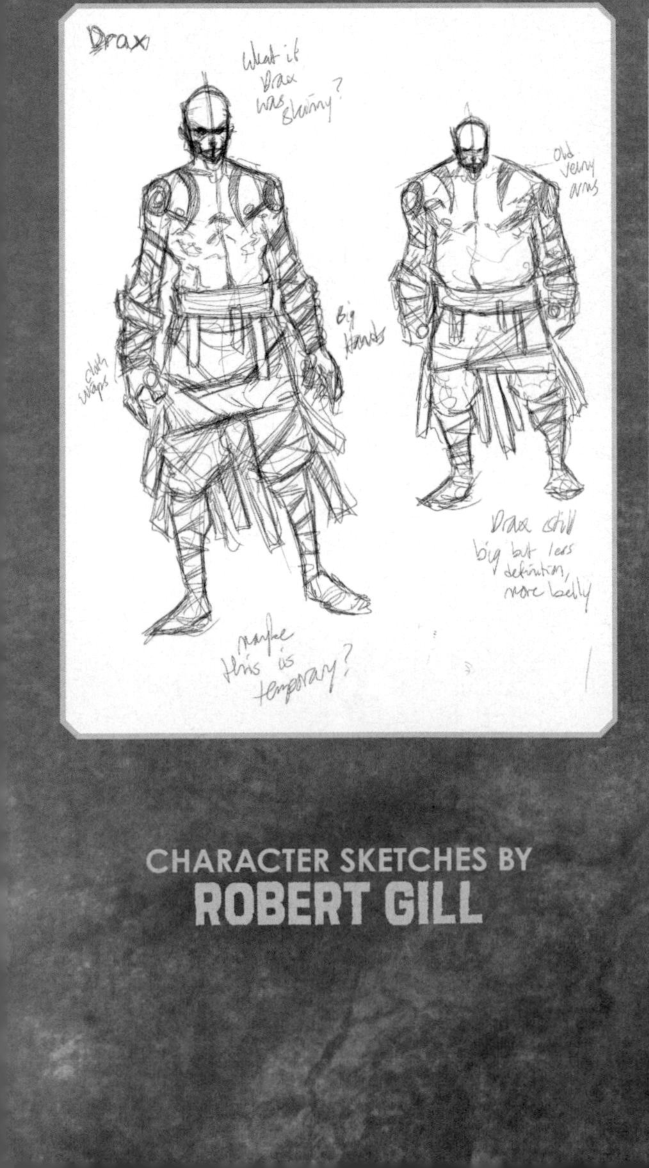
Drax
What if Drax was skinny?
Old veiny arms
Big Hands
cloth wraps
Drax still big but less definition, more belly
maybe this is temporary?

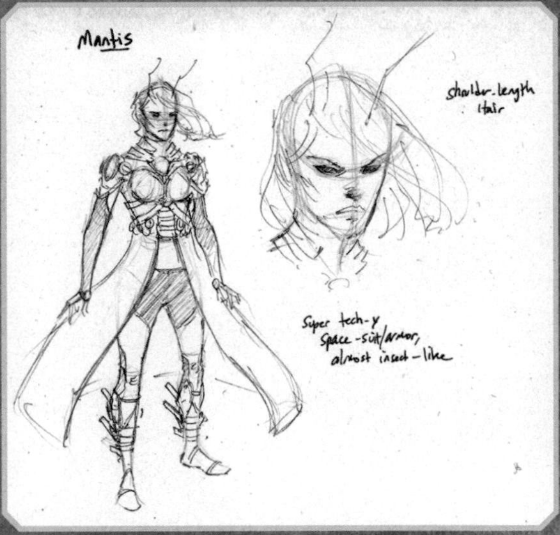
Mantis
shoulder-length Hair
Super tech-y space-suit/armor, almost insect-like

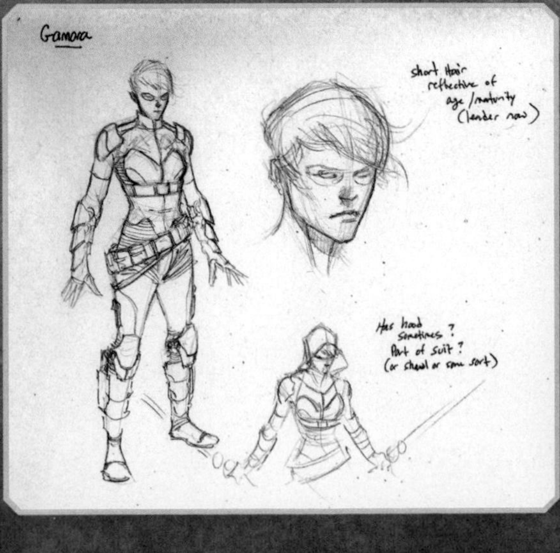
Gamora
short Hair reflective of age/maturity (leader now)
Has hood sometimes? Part of suit? (or shawl or some sort)

CHARACTER SKETCHES BY

ROBERT GILL

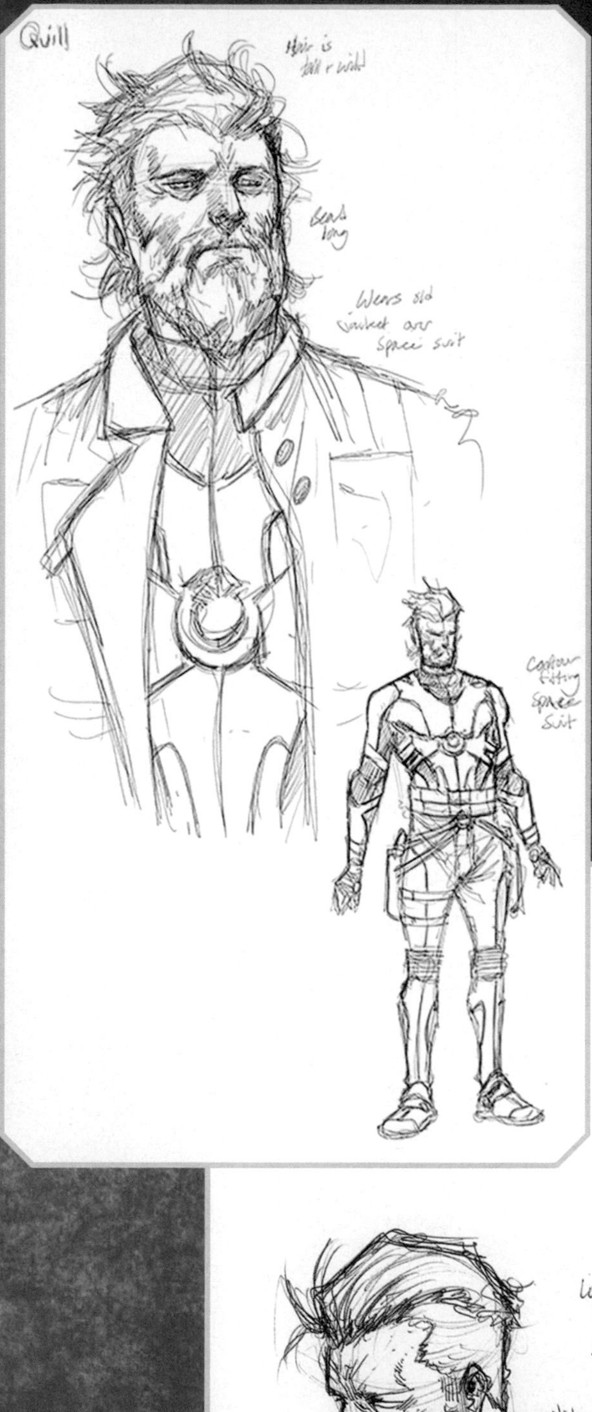
Quill
Hair is tall + wild
Beard long
Wears old jacket over Space suit
Custom fitting Space Suit

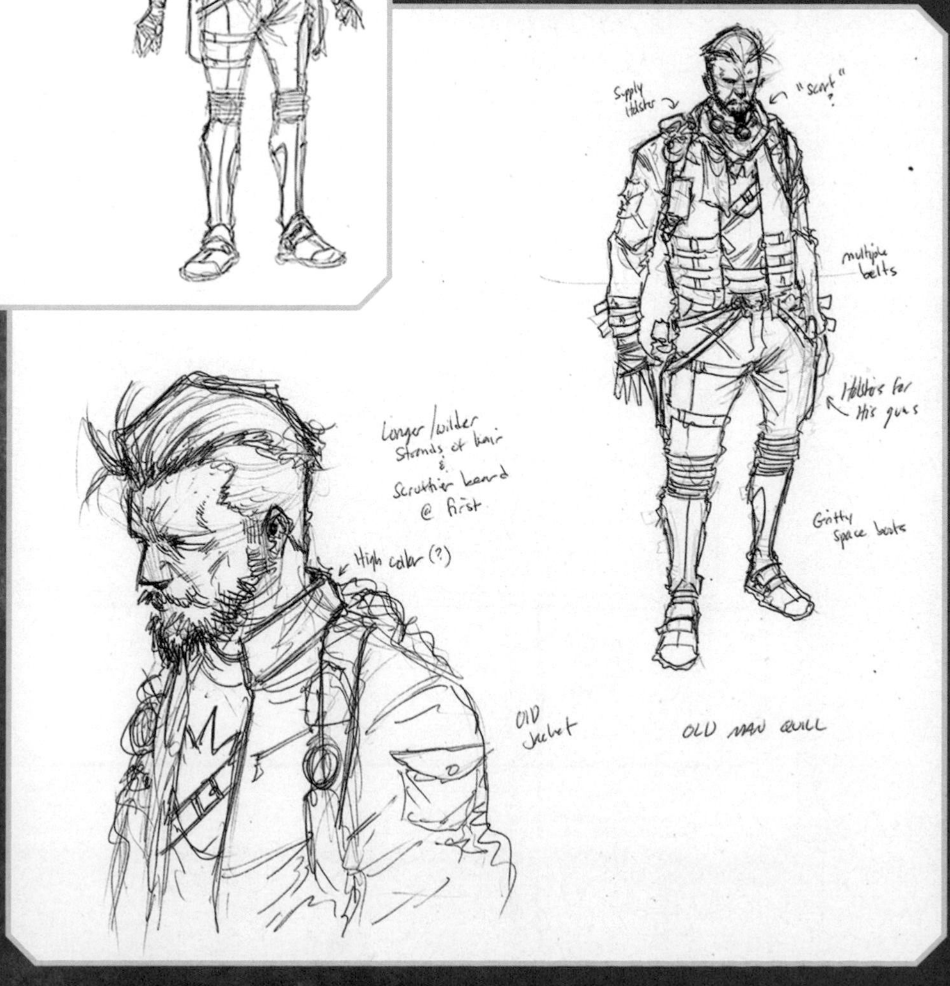
Supply Holster
"Scarf" ?
multiple belts
Holsters for his guns
Gritty Space boots
Longer/wilder Strands of hair & Scruffier beard @ first
High collar (?)
Old Jacket
OLD MAN QUILL

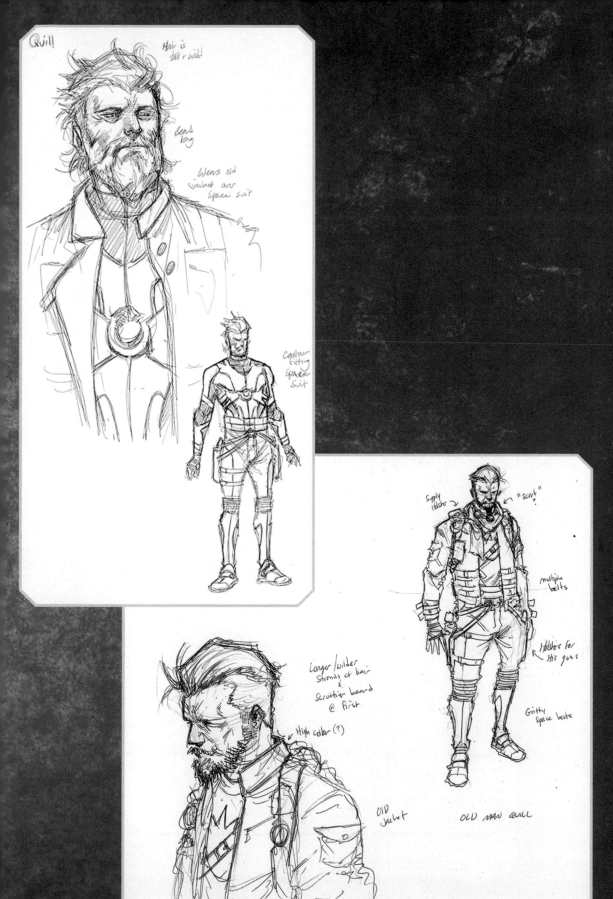

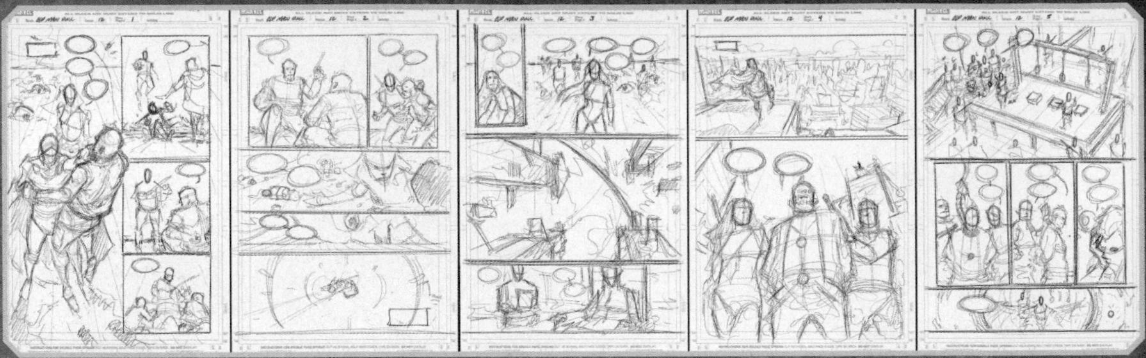

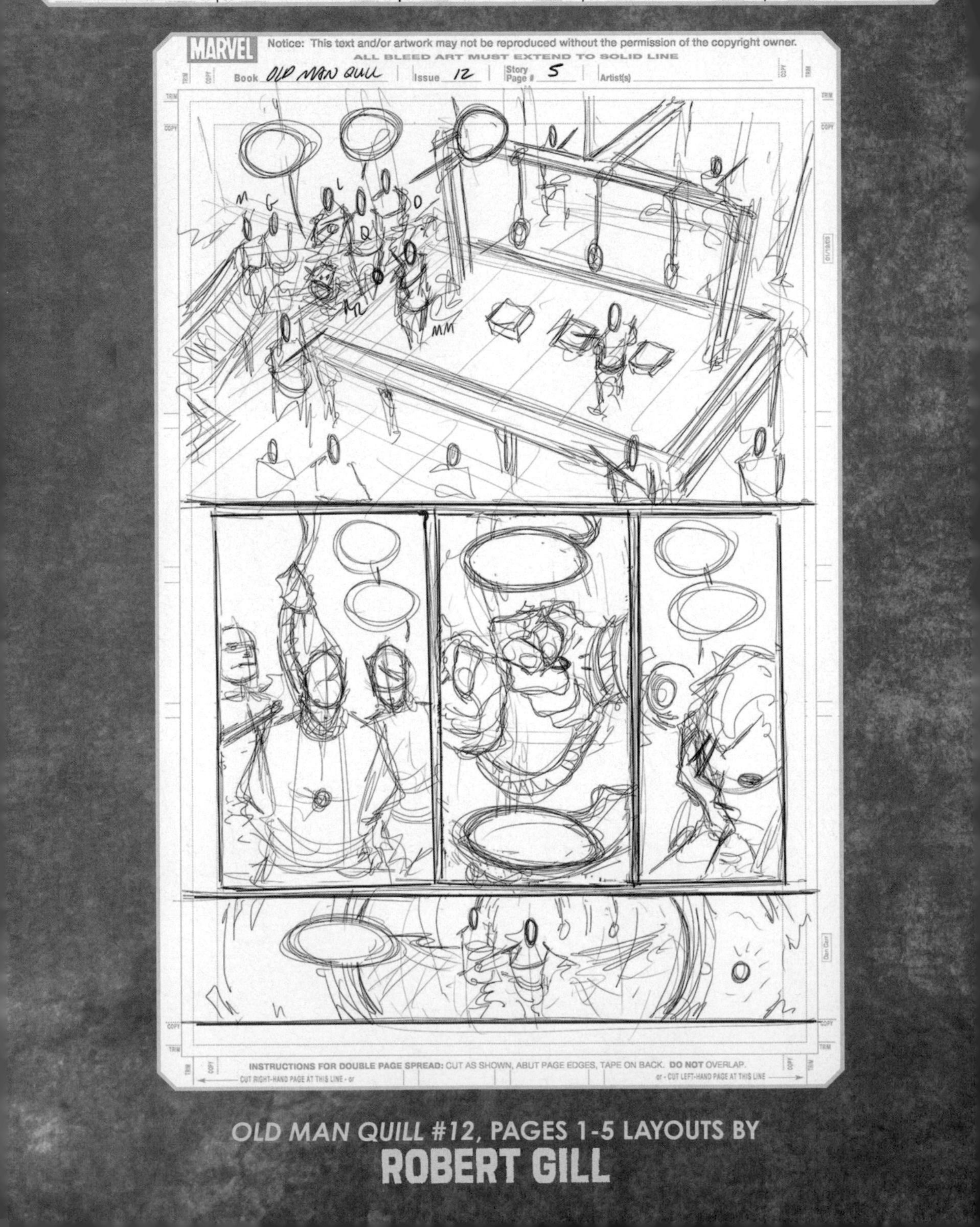
MARVEL
Notice: This text and/or artwork may not be reproduced without the permission of the copyright owner.
ALL BLEED ART MUST EXTEND TO SOLID LINE
Book OLD MAN QUILL Issue 12 Story Page # 5 Artist(s)
INSTRUCTIONS FOR DOUBLE PAGE SPREAD: CUT AS SHOWN, ABUT PAGE EDGES, TAPE ON BACK. DO NOT OVERLAP.
CUT RIGHT-HAND PAGE AT THIS LINE - or
or - CUT LEFT-HAND PAGE AT THIS LINE

OLD MAN QUILL #12, PAGES 1-5 LAYOUTS BY

ROBERT GILL

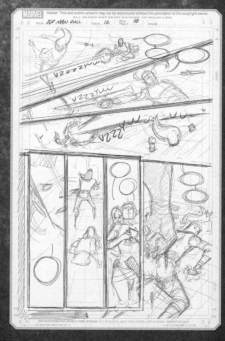

OLD MAN QUILL #12, PAGES 6-10 LAYOUTS BY
ROBERT GILL

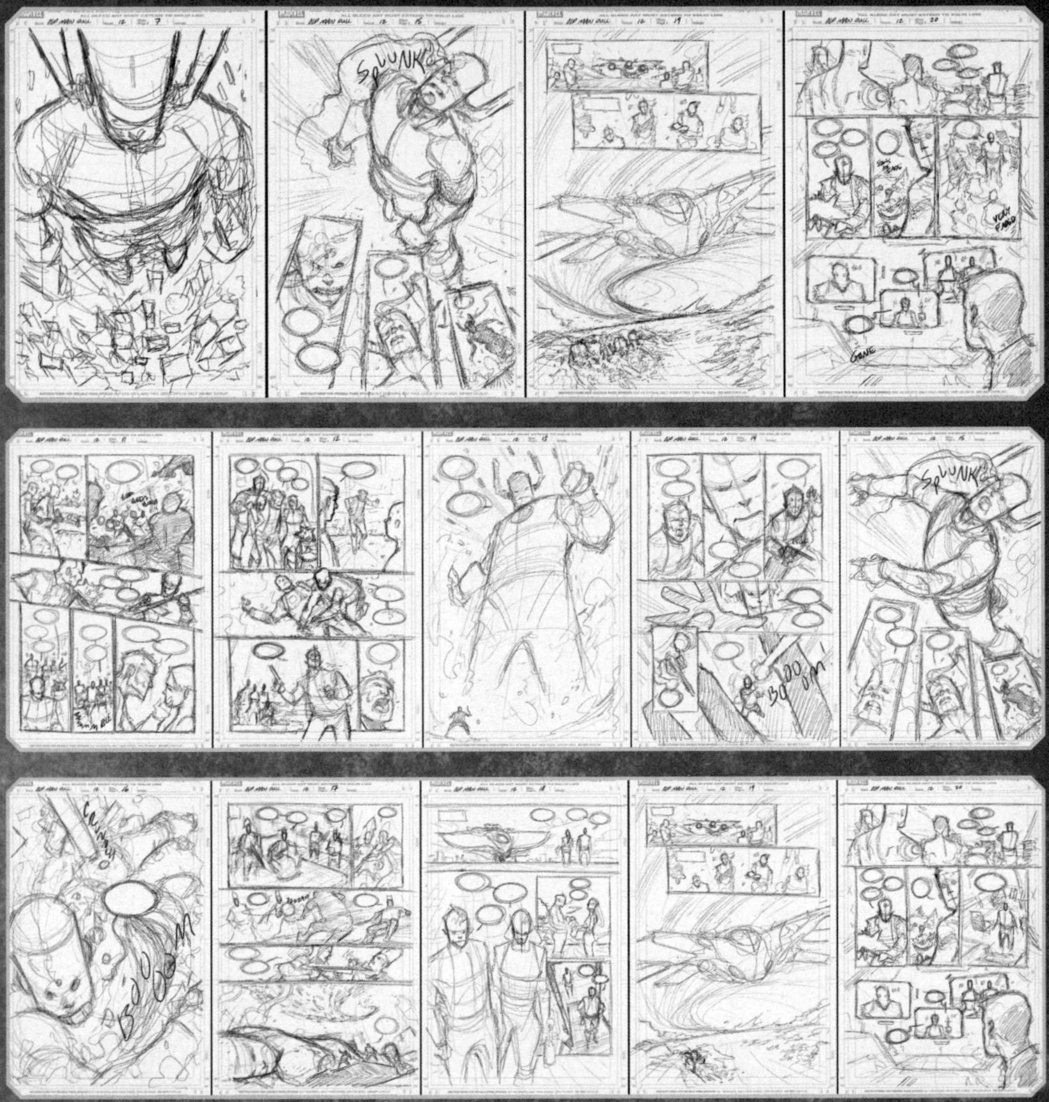

OLD MAN QUILL #12, PAGES 7-20 LAYOUTS BY

ROBERT GILL

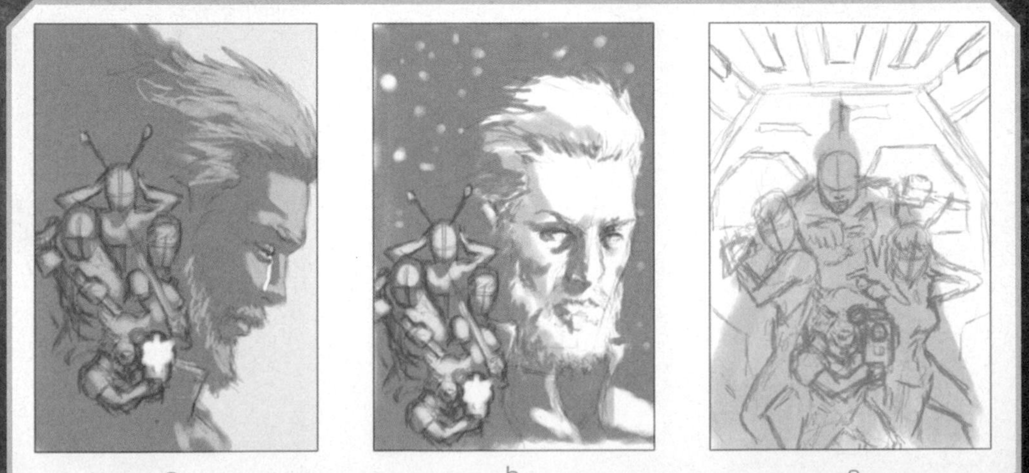

a b c

OLD MAN QUILL #8, COVER SKETCHES BY

JOHN TYLER CHRISTOPHER